D. H. Lawrence and the
Literary Marketplace

To my parents, Clive and Linda Grice

D. H. Lawrence and the Literary Marketplace
The Early Writings

Annalise Grice

EDINBURGH
University Press

Edinburgh University Press is one of the leading university presses in the UK. We publish academic books and journals in our selected subject areas across the humanities and social sciences, combining cutting-edge scholarship with high editorial and production values to produce academic works of lasting importance. For more information visit our website: edinburghuniversitypress.com

© Annalise Grice, 2022, 2023

Edinburgh University Press Ltd
The Tun – Holyrood Road, 12(2f) Jackson's Entry, Edinburgh EH8 8PJ

First published in hardback by Edinburgh University Press 2022

Typeset in 10.5/13 Bembo by
IDSUK (DataConnection) Ltd

A CIP record for this book is available from the British Library

ISBN 978 1 4744 5800 9 (hardback)
ISBN 978 1 4744 5801 6 (paperback)
ISBN 978 1 4744 5802 3 (webready PDF)
ISBN 978 1 4744 5803 0 (epub)

The right of Annalise Grice to be identifie d as the author of this work has been asserted in accordance with the Copyright, Designs and Patents Act 1988, and the Copyright and Related Rights Regulations 2003 (SI No. 2498).

Contents

List of Figures — vi
Acknowledgements — vii
Select Chronology, September 1885–June 1914 — ix
Cue Titles — xiii

    Introduction — 1

Part I: Making a Start (1905–8)

1. 'A collier's son a poet!': Lawrence's First Approaches to the Literary Marketplace — 19
2. Lawrence and Socialism: 'Art and the Individual' (1908) and the *New Age* — 55

Part II: The London Literary Scene: Mentors and Publishing (1909–12)

3. 'I know nothing of the publishing of books': Ford Madox Hueffer, Violet Hunt and William Heinemann — 77
4. 'My dear Garnett . . . why do you take so much trouble for me?': Edward Garnett, 'Friend and Protector' — 104

Part III: Literary Commerce (1910–14)

5. 'A green fresh poet': Self-Fashioning, Networking and Marketing the Contemporary Poet — 151
6. Introducing Mr D. H. Lawrence, Author of *Sons and Lovers*: Transatlantic Connections — 184
    Coda — 209

Bibliography — 213
Index — 231

Figures

All images courtesy of the D. H. Lawrence Collection, Manuscripts and Special Collections, University of Nottingham (UN).

1.1 Letter to D. H. Lawrence from Tom Hewart, Manager, the London and Provincial Press Agency (20 July 1909). University of Nottingham, Manuscripts and Special Collections, La B 186.   35
2.1 D. H. Lawrence's signature in the minute book of the 'Society for the Study of Social Questions', University College Nottingham (1908–9). University of Nottingham, Manuscripts and Special Collections, La Z 7/1   56
3.1 Copy in Lawrence's hand of a letter from Ford Madox Hueffer (15 December 1909). University of Nottingham, Manuscripts and Special Collections, La Z 5/8/8.   88
3.2 Letter from Violet Hunt to D. H. Lawrence (3 February 1911). University of Nottingham, Manuscripts and Special Collections, La B 187/1.   93

Acknowledgements

I gratefully acknowledge the support of Katy Loffman and Lesley Pollinger of Paper Lion as the Trustee and Literary Executor of D. H. Lawrence's work. Extracts from *The Cambridge Edition of the Letters and Works of D. H. Lawrence* © Cambridge University Press 1980–2018 are reproduced by permission of Paper Lion Ltd, The Estate of Frieda Lawrence Ravagli and Cambridge University Press. My thanks are due to Manuscripts and Special Collections, University of Nottingham, for granting permission to reproduce the images contained within this book and for Jayne Amat's patient assistance in acquiring them. I thank Jackie Jones, Ersev Ersoy, Susannah Butler and Edinburgh University Press for their interest in the book and their support and practical advice during the course of the project, Barbara Eastman for her careful copy-editing and Caitlin Murphy for the cover design. Grateful thanks are also due to the anonymous reader for the incisive feedback on my typescript and to another reader of the original book proposal.

This book would never have been written without an AHRC Doctoral Award and the support of the School of English at the University of Nottingham. Andrew Harrison and Josephine Guy proved to be the finest supervisors I could possibly have had the good fortune to meet; they kept me on track, modelled a scholarly approach to research, waded through monstrously long drafts and, best of all, inspired and energised me during every meeting. For all their support and advice I am ever indebted. I am also grateful to Jo Robinson for nominating me for a Dean Moore Scholarship for Research Excellence, awarded by the University of Nottingham in 2016. James Moran and Nathan Waddell have long provided very helpful and sensible guidance. I also acknowledge the kind support of the Funds for Women Graduates charitable organisation, which awarded me a Theodora Bosanquet Bursary in 2015 to undertake archival research at the British Library.

ACKNOWLEDGEMENTS

I thank the international D. H. Lawrence community (especially the D. H. Lawrence Society of Great Britain and the D. H. Lawrence Society of North America) for welcoming me into the special world of D. H. Lawrence Studies and awarding me two Graduate Fellowships to attend International Conferences in 2014 and 2017. There are too many names and acts of kindness to mention, but Howard Booth, David Game, Holly Laird, Christopher Pollnitz, Neil Roberts, Betsy Sargent and Jeff Wallace deserve a special mention; Bruce Steele and John Worthen have also very kindly sent books to me as well as nuggets of information which have enhanced the accuracy of my research. Malcolm Gray has been a good friend and a supporter of my work on Lawrence, and so has Carolyn Melbourne.

I am very fortunate to have many wonderful colleagues at Nottingham Trent University. I thank everyone in English and Creative Writing for welcoming me into the department in 2017 and for the lively research environment and collegiality. Catherine Clay and Rory Waterman have been fantastic mentors from the very beginning and have proven to be excellent role models in both research and teaching. Sharon Ouditt has been a very understanding and supportive Head of Department; Nahem Yousaf, Phil Leonard, Andrew Thacker, Tim Youngs, Sharon Monteith, Anna Ball, Sarah Carter, Sarah Jackson, Jenni Ramone, Stephanie Palmer, Nicole Thiara, Andrew Taylor and Pete Smith have offered practical advice on research and career planning and Rebecca Butler and Rebecca Cullen have been invaluable sources of friendship and encouragement, along with our '208' office mates, Nicky Bowring, Francesca Hardy and Amy Rushton. Elizabeth Stewart-Shaw has been a true friend for many years. Finally, but most importantly, to my parents, Clive and Linda Grice, love and infinite gratitude.

Select Chronology, September 1885–June 1914

11 September 1885	Born in Eastwood, Nottinghamshire.
October 1892–July 1901	Pupil at Beauvale Board School, then at Nottingham High School (from 1898).
Late September–December 1901	Clerk with J. H. Haywood and Sons (leaves due to bout of pneumonia).
October 1902–July 1905	Pupil-teacher at British School, Eastwood.
March 1904	Commences part-time attendance at Pupil-Teacher Centre, Ilkeston.
1905	Begins writing poetry.
August 1905–September 1906	Uncertified Assistant Teacher at British School, Eastwood.
Easter 1906	Begins first draft of novel, 'Laetitia'.
October 1906–June 1908	Student at University College, Nottingham.
7 December 1907	'A Prelude' published in *Nottinghamshire Guardian*.
19 March 1908	'Art and the Individual' read to Eastwood Debating Society.
Spring 1908	Sends a manuscript to G. K. Chesterton.
15 April 1908	First correspondence with Blanche Jennings.
October 1908	Takes up post as Assistant Master at Davidson Road School, Croydon.
c. June 1909	Jessie sends manuscripts of DHL's poetry to Ford Madox Hueffer.
July 1909	Approaches London and Provincial Press Agency.
c.11 September 1909	Meets Hueffer.

November 1909	Five poems published under the title 'A Still Afternoon' in *English Review* ('Dreams Old and Nascent': I. 'Old'; II. 'Nascent', 'Discipline' and 'Baby Movements' I; II).
15 December 1909	Offers 'Nethermere' MS to Heinemann.
19 January 1910	Meets Sydney Pawling at Heinemann's offices.
February 1910	'Goose Fair' published in *English Review* (now edited by Austin Harrison).
April 1910	Five poems published under the title 'Night Songs' in *English Review* ('Yesternight', 'Tomorrow Night', 'Wakened', 'At the Window' and 'Rebuked').
October 1910	'Three Poems' published in *English Review* ('Tired of the Boat', 'Sigh No More' and 'Ah, Muriel').
17 November 1910	Gives paper on 'Rachel Annand Taylor' to the Croydon English Association.
3 December 1910	Engagement to Louie Burrows.
19 January 1911	*The White Peacock* (Duffield).
20 January 1911	*The White Peacock* (Heinemann).
June 1911	'Odour of Chrysanthemums' published in *English Review*.
August 1911	Edward Garnett first contacts DHL.
September 1911	'A Fragment of Stained Glass' published in *English Review*.
October 1911	Meets Edward Garnett.
November 1911	Unsigned review of *Contemporary German Poetry* published in *English Review*. Two poems (sent by Garnett) published in *Nation*, 4 November ('Lightning' and 'Violets'). Falls ill with double pneumonia (19 November).
January 1912	Unsigned review of *The Minnesingers* and *The Oxford Book of German Verse* published in *English Review*.
February 1912	Breaks off engagement to Louie Burrows (4 February). 'Second Best' published in *English Review*. Resigns from post at Davidson Road School (28 February).

SELECT CHRONOLOGY, SEPTEMBER 1885–JUNE 1914   xi

3 March 1912	Meets Frieda Weekley.
16 March 1912	'The Miner at Home' published in *Nation*.
3 May 1912	Travels to Germany with Frieda.
11 May–1 June 1912	Six 'Schoolmaster' poems published in *Saturday Westminster Gazette*.
23 May 1912	*The Trespasser* (Duckworth).
June 1912	One poem ('Snap-Dragon') published in *English Review*.
August 1912	'German Impressions: I. French Sons of Germany' published in *Saturday Westminster Gazette* (3 August).
	'German Impressions: II. Hail in the Rhineland' published in *Saturday Westminster Gazette* (10 August).
c. November 1912	*The Trespasser* (Kennerley).
December 1912	'Snap-Dragon' published in *Georgian Poetry 1911–1912*.
Late February 1913	*Love Poems and Others* (Duckworth).
March 1913	Signed review of *Georgian Poetry 1911–1912* published in *Rhythm*.
	'Christs in the Tirol' published in *Saturday Westminster Gazette* (22 March).
	'The Soiled Rose' published in *Forum*.
29 May 1913	*Sons and Lovers* (Duckworth).
July 1913	Review of Thomas Mann's *Der Tod in Venedig* published in the *Blue Review*.
16 August 1913	'The Fly in the Ointment' published in *New Statesman*.
September 1913	'Strike-Pay I, Her Turn' published in *Westminster Gazette* (6 September).
	'Strike-Pay II, Ephraim's Sovereign' published in *Westminster Gazette* (13 September).
	'A Sick Collier' published in *New Statesman* (13 September).
	Three Italian sketches published in the *English Review* under the title 'Italian Studies: By the Lago di Garda' ('I. The Spinner and the Monks', 'II. The Lemon Gardens of the Signor Di P.' and 'III. The Theatre').
	One poem ('Violets') published in *Smart Set*.

17 September 1913	*Sons and Lovers* (Kennerley).
October 1913	One poem ('Kisses in the Train') published in *Smart Set*.
November 1913	One poem ('Service of all the Dead') published in *New Statesman* (15 November).
	One poem ('The Mowers') published in *Smart Set*.
1913	*Love Poems and Others* (Kennerley).
January 1914	Eight poems published in *Poetry* ('Green', 'All of Roses', 'Fireflies in the Corn', 'A Woman and Her Dead Husband', 'The Wind, the Rascal', 'The Mother of Sons', 'Illicit' and 'Birthday').
February 1914	Two poems published in *English Review* ('Twilight' and 'Meeting among the Mountains').
	Love Poems and Others reprinted (Duckworth).
	'The Christening' published in *Smart Set*.
	Article on DHL by W. L. George published in *Bookman*.
March 1914	'The Shadow in the Rose Garden' published in *Smart Set*.
1 April 1914	*The Widowing of Mrs Holroyd* (Kennerley).
	Five poems published in *Egoist* ('A Winter's Tale', 'Song', 'Early Spring', 'Honeymoon' and 'Fooled').
17 April 1914	*The Widowing of Mrs Holroyd* (Duckworth).
June 1914	'Vin Ordinaire' published in *English Review*.
30 June 1914	Signs Methuen contract for *The Rainbow*; takes J. B. Pinker as agent.

Cue titles

Selected Letters of D. H. Lawrence

L, I *The Letters of D. H. Lawrence Volume I: September 1901–May 1913*, ed. James T. Boulton (Cambridge: Cambridge University Press, 1979).

L, II *The Letters of D. H. Lawrence Volume II: June 1913–October 1916*, ed. George J. Zytaruk and James T. Boulton (Cambridge: Cambridge University Press, 1981).

L, IV *The Letters of D. H. Lawrence, Volume IV: June 1921–March 1924*, ed. Warren Roberts, James T. Boulton and Elizabeth Mansfield (Cambridge: Cambridge University Press, 1978).

L, VI *The Letters of D. H. Lawrence Volume VI: March 1927–November 1928*, ed. James T. Boulton and Margaret H. Boulton with Gerald M. Lacy (Cambridge: Cambridge University Press, 1991).

L, VIII *The Letters of D. H. Lawrence Volume VIII: Previously Uncollected Letters and General Index*, ed. James T. Boulton (Cambridge: Cambridge University Press, 2000).

Selected Works of D. H. Lawrence

IR *Introductions and Reviews*, ed. N. H. Reeve and John Worthen (Cambridge: Cambridge University Press, 2005).

LEA *Late Essays and Articles*, ed. James T. Boulton (Cambridge: Cambridge University Press, 2004).

Plays *The Plays*, ed. Hans-Wilhelm Schwarze and John Worthen (Cambridge: Cambridge University Press, 1999).

PM *Paul Morel*, ed. Helen Baron (Cambridge: Cambridge University Press, 2003).

PO   *The Prussian Officer and Other Stories*, ed. John Worthen
            (Cambridge: Cambridge University Press, 1983).
Poems   *The Poems*, 3 vols, ed. Christopher Pollnitz (Cambridge:
            Cambridge University Press [2013] 2018).
STH   *Study of Thomas Hardy and Other Essays*, ed. Bruce Steele
            (Cambridge: Cambridge University Press, 1985).
T   *The Trespasser*, ed. Elizabeth Mansfield (Cambridge: Cambridge
            University Press, 1981).
WP   *The White Peacock*, ed. Andrew Robertson (Cambridge:
            Cambridge University Press, 1983).

Biographical and Scholarly Sources

Draper   *D. H. Lawrence: The Critical Heritage*, ed. R. P. Draper (London:
            Routledge and Kegan Paul, 1969).
E. T.   E. T. [Jessie Chambers], *D. H. Lawrence: A Personal Record*
            (London: Jonathan Cape, 1935).
EY   John Worthen, *D. H. Lawrence: The Early Years, 1885–1912*
            (Cambridge: Cambridge University Press, 1991).
Nehls   *D. H. Lawrence: A Composite Biography*, 3 vols. Gathered,
            arranged and ed.by Edward Nehls (Madison: University of
            Wisconsin Press, 1957–9).
Roberts   Warren Roberts and Paul Poplawski, *A Bibliography of D. H.
            Lawrence*, 3rd edn (Cambridge: Cambridge University Press,
            2001).
TE   Mark Kinkead-Weekes, *D. H. Lawrence: Triumph to Exile,
            1912–1922* (Cambridge: Cambridge University Press, 1996).

Journals

DHLR   *D. H. Lawrence Review* (1968–).
JDHLS   *Journal of D. H. Lawrence Studies* (2006–), formerly *The Journal of
            the D. H. Lawrence Society* (1976–2005).

Introduction

A week after the publication of his first novel *The White Peacock* by Heinemann in January 1911, D. H. Lawrence wrote to his fiancée Louie Burrows 'I want a measure of success, and the book deserves it.'[1] Eager to see reviews of the novel he wrote to Heinemann's reader and general editor Frederick Atkinson, telling him of his hope that the book 'would break me an entrance into the jungle of literature; that it would give me a small but individual name by which I should be known'.[2] His name, while certainly individual, could never now be classed as 'small'. How did a young man from the working class Midlands break in to the Edwardian literary scene and achieve such an enduring and distinctive name for himself? While Lawrence retrospectively criticised some of his early writings ('I was very young when I wrote the *Peacock* – I began it at twenty. Let that be my apology'), this does not necessarily mean that he held them in low regard at the time when he was writing and publishing them.[3] His early work was generally very well received by its first readers and reviewers: both *The White Peacock* and *The Trespasser* went into a second impression two months after publication, *Sons and Lovers* was considered to be the work in which Lawrence had come to 'full maturity as a writer' and *The Widowing of Mrs Holroyd* (1914) received enthusiastic reviews in both the American and British press, with the *New York Times Book Review* describing Lawrence as a young writer who had 'suddenly sprung before playgoing London as the author of a most terrific bit of realism'.[4] Balancing Lawrence's desire to write differently and to challenge his readership with the demands placed on his writing by publishers and editors who were apprehensive about the reading public's reaction to outspoken work, John Worthen observes that

> even an author like Lawrence, who was often very idealist in his own attitude towards writing, was deeply influenced by the fact of being a man writing for his living; and that being a man dependent upon his writing sometimes dictated what he wrote and when.[5]

Providing a rich insight into Edwardian publishing culture, this book finds Lawrence to be an acutely intelligent young man with a good deal of commercial nous; he had a sustained interest in the business of publishing and a commitment to establishing advantageous literary connections. Lawrence's claims to disinterest in commercial transactions belie his unrelenting concern with the publishing of his works and the state of his reputation, which are evident as continual threads throughout his letters.

As long ago as 1989 Worthen called for critical recognition of 'both the struggles and the professionalism of [Lawrence's] life and work'.[6] Despite the 'materialist turn' in modernist studies from the mid-1990s by scholars such as Mark Osteen, John Whittier-Ferguson and Lawrence Rainey, who have demonstrated the importance of 'external' factors on the production of literary texts and the centrality of economics and publicity to modernism, the extent and depth of Lawrence's engagement with the literary marketplace has still not been fully assessed.[7] Editorial theorists such as George Bornstein and online digitisation projects like the Modernist Journals Project (developed by Brown University and the University of Tulsa, directed by Robert Scholes and Sean Latham) have promoted the study of modernist works in their original sites of publication. Bornstein argues that the transmission of modernism's 'texts as texts' (divorced from their original material forms) has resulted in attitudes 'favoring the anti-historical over the historical, product over process, [and] totalizing rather than interrogative discourse', but modernism has undergone a reassessment to emphasise historical contingency, multiple versions and the material features of the text itself.[8] A line of monographs have since explored modern and modernist print culture in the career of a single author.[9] With these broader developments in mind, due recognition is needed that the labelling of Lawrence as a 'genius' who was destined to succeed has concealed the more practical question of how he became a published writer in the first place.

Lawrence's shifting position in literary-critical discourse has been a key factor. Reacting to hostility to Lawrence in the 1930s (notably from John Middleton Murry and T. S. Eliot), F. R. Leavis writing in the Cambridge journal *Scrutiny* in 1955 established Lawrence's claim to inclusion in the literary canon by placing him in a tradition of moral writing, which effectively redressed claims that Lawrence was an immoral or pornographic writer but created an image of the author as a prophetic figure.[10] Then, following the plethora of memoirs that emerged after Lawrence's death, the 1950s was a decade for Lawrence biography.[11] Harry T. Moore authored *The Life and Works of D. H. Lawrence* (1951) and later edited the *Collected Letters* (1962); Edward Nehls published a three-volume *Composite Biography* (1957–9) that brought together excerpts from memoirists and commissioned new memoir accounts which highlighted the unconventional life Lawrence led and the diverse connections he made as he travelled around the world. Alongside this, studies such as Graham Hough's *The Dark Sun* (1956) foregrounded Lawrence's 'doctrine' and contributed towards establishing him as a philosophic writer – a line of enquiry that has tended to isolate Lawrence as an idiosyncratic thinker. Soon afterwards the 1960 *Regina v. Penguin Books* trial of *Lady Chatterley's Lover* secured Lawrence's reputation as an outspoken writer about sex and a harbinger of the decade's 'sexual liberation'; this anti-institutional image and the damaging criticism of his sexual politics by feminist critics such as Kate Millett have been contributing factors in diverting attention away from his engagements with and acquiescence in the marketplace. Late 1960s and 1970s Lawrence criticism by scholars such as Mark Kinkead-Weekes and Keith Cushman sought refuge in the archives and redressed the Leavisite view of Lawrence as writing from some kind of providential internal compulsion by analysing manuscript evidence to stress his craftsmanship and battle with the censors.[12] Then followed the Cambridge Edition of his Letters (1979–2000) and Works (1980–2018) and authoritative biographies by John Worthen (1991; 2005), Kinkead-Weekes (1996), David Ellis (1998) and Andrew Harrison (2016), each enriched by the new insights into Lawrence's life and creativity that this scholarship unearthed.

The Cambridge Edition has been influential in critically assessing the sociological pressures brought to bear on Lawrence's work, with the introduction and apparatus in each volume revealing the extent of third party interventions in the work's textual history.[13] Editorial principles grounded in a concept of authorial intention have formed the basis of the project, which collates the extant evidence of Lawrence's revision process to establish a single 'best' reading text, selecting as base-text the embodiment that represents the most authoritative version 'to provide texts which are as close as can now be determined to those [Lawrence] would have wished to see printed' (see the General Editor's Preface contained in each volume). The base-text (which can be the manuscripts, typescripts, proofs, magazine versions or first printed editions – British or American – or a combination of several of these witnessing documents) is then emended according to the volume editors' best assessment of the available evidence. The emendations are based on assumptions about what Lawrence would have written if he had been given freedom of choice, so it is recognised that publication involves an element of compromise, but this is implicitly viewed as a negative concession rather than taken as an inevitable feature of the construction of the text as social artefact. It unwittingly implies that Lawrence opposed third-party intervention, which can be countered if, as this book outlines, we consider that the young Lawrence took every opportunity to seek advice on his writing and if we acknowledge that a writer's work is shaped, framed and bounded by the language and forms available in its historical moment.

Within these pages a new image emerges of Lawrence as a young writer who was pragmatic, diligent and anxiously determined to achieve and sustain a career as a professional writer. While I do not wish to dilute the appealing perception of him as a radical or maverick figure who operated at the margins of institutions and challenged fixed perceptions, gaining an understanding of the ways in which he cannily learned the 'rules' of the marketplace in order to enter the literary field in the first place provides a more rounded perspective of a man who was astute enough to perceive when – and how – to toe the line and pursue a distinctive name for himself, shifting from amateur to professional within nine years. From when he started writing his first poems in 1905 he had an idea of creativity as being produced collaboratively and sought assistance from a variety of individuals. In 1909 his first sequence of poetry was published by a prestigious new literary journal, the *English Review*. By 1914 he had attained a reputation as a promising writer on both sides of the Atlantic.

This study examines Lawrence's multifaceted authorial identity as a novelist, essayist, lecturer, poet, journalist, short story writer, dramatist and reviewer. The decision to consider Lawrence's writing across multiple genres is driven by the contingency and diversity of the literary marketplace itself, which forced authors to negotiate between the claims of art and the requirements of literary commerce. Lawrence experimented with a range of forms and genres as he sought to secure a foothold as a professional writer in an increasingly fragmented marketplace.[14] The proliferation of a range of reading matter widely available to a more educated mass reading public, the advancement of printing technologies, the configuration of cultural institutions (including libraries, publishing houses and journalism) and strategies of authorial self-fashioning in an age of advanced advertising practices all had an impact on literary authorship and a better knowledge of these factors and their implications for authors' careers allow us to better understand the modernist project and the approaches and ambitions of different writers. To focus on a single genre would produce a simplistic assessment of Lawrence's early engagement with the marketplace and would underplay his ambition in trying out many types of writing for a variety of publications and readerships. Providing detailed case studies to offer a fresh view of Lawrence's early career, this book contributes to the welcome trend of twenty-first century scholarship on Lawrence by scholars such as Neil Roberts, Jeff Wallace, Judith Ruderman, David Game, Susan Reid and John Turner which has focused on offering fuller and more nuanced accounts of his intellectual and literary contexts.[15] Using extensive new archival research, this book analyses the literary marketplace of the 'long' Edwardian period (following

Anne Fernihough, I take this to be the period from roughly 1901 up to the outbreak of the First World War) to assess the circumstances for becoming an author at this time, examining Lawrence's changing conceptions of what kind of writer he wanted to be and who he wanted to write for.[16] The importance of Lawrence's first advisors, Ford Madox Hueffer (1873–1939) and Edward Garnett (1868–1937) in helping the young writer to get his work published has long been acknowledged.[17] However, simplistic accounts of Hueffer's 'discovery' of Lawrence and Garnett's role in editing *Sons and Lovers* have obscured the complex interactions between mentors and mentee and overlooked the important connections they brought for Lawrence as he entered into their circles. I revise the account by highlighting the significance of other intermediaries' patronage of Lawrence, such as Violet Hunt, Walter de la Mare, Edward Marsh and Ezra Pound, all of whom helped Lawrence to approach a range of publication outlets and to reach a number of different sectors of the market. Lawrence fashioned numerous authorial identities for himself with the encouragement and advice of his mentors, who were more aware than he of contemporary market demands. He appeared in various guises as, for example, a romance writer, an 'erotic' writer, a Georgian poet and a working-class realist. This research evaluates how Lawrence's work was marketed and received by the reading public in both Britain and America, examining publishing houses including Heinemann, Duckworth, T. Fisher Unwin, Elkin Mathews and Mitchell Kennerley as well as literary journals and magazines, such as the *New Age*, the *English Review*, *Madame*, *Rhythm* and *Forum*.

The book ends with a consideration of how Lawrence was marketed in both Britain and America in early 1914 as the author of *Sons and Lovers*, the novel that he proclaimed marked 'the end of [his] youthful period'.[18] It was a time when his pre-war reputation was at its height and before he was found to have transgressed the limits of acceptability with the well-publicised withdrawal from sale of *The Rainbow* in November 1915 under the 1857 Obscene Publications Act. Worthen has calculated that in economic terms, too, 1914 was Lawrence's 'most financially rewarding year before the early 1920s'.[19] In February 1912 Lawrence resigned from his teaching post in Croydon and became a full-time writer. From this time on he had to learn to support himself (and in due course, Frieda) through his writing. Worthen states that, upon his return to England in June 1913, Lawrence was

> known in literary circles primarily as the author of two novels with a small but good reputation, and as the author of some interesting stories and poems in the *English Review*. From the summer of 1913 onwards, however, he would be 'the author of *Sons and Lovers*'.[20]

As Andrew Harrison observes, by November 1913 '[t]he need was obviously there for [Lawrence] to take on an agent to manage his affairs and finances'.[21] On 30 June 1914 he signed a publishing agreement with Methuen for *The Rainbow*, which brought with it J. B. Pinker's professional services as a literary agent. His employment of a literary agent, along with the signing of a prestigious three-book deal with Methuen, may have made it seem that Lawrence had formally achieved the status and relative security of the professional author (with the qualifier that the process of feeling oneself to be a truly 'professional' writer, able to sell literary work as a main occupation, can be lengthy). While Lawrence was officially a professional writer from the moment he resigned from his teaching post at the end of February 1912, in June 1914 he became an independent professional writer, in that he would be paying Pinker 10 per cent commission for the placement of his work. Until this time, he had been intensely aware of – and latterly rather ashamed about – his reliance from August 1911 on Edward Garnett as a mentor who had taken on the role of an unpaid agent. It might be expected that a book exploring Lawrence and the literary marketplace would discuss Lawrence's interactions with Pinker; however, a chapter on this subject has been written by Joyce Wexler, in one of the few studies to focus on Lawrence's relation to the literary marketplace.[22] Although there is still more to be said about Lawrence and Pinker, my research is primarily concerned with exploring how Lawrence came to be a writer and which authorial identities he assimilated as he learned how to negotiate the literary marketplace and pursued beneficial connections that were informal rather than professionally validated. During these formative years, Lawrence began to work out his literary values, consider what kind of author he could be and assess what type of literature readers, editors, publishers and printers would accept; in turn he was positioned as a noteworthy young author by others in the field.

Methodologically this book seeks to understand authorship in sociological terms, drawing on Pierre Bourdieu's theory of the field of cultural production to determine how Lawrence's notions of authorship, publishing, literary movements and debates, the ways in which he could situate himself in relation to other writers and so forth, involved developing a breadth of knowledge about the field. Bourdieu leads us to ask 'how the position or "post" [the author] occupies – that of a writer of a particular type – became constituted'.[23] This book explores the ways in which Lawrence's identity as a writer was fashioned by a combination of internal and external factors (that is, I explore his *habitus* and how this disposition enabled him to negotiate the Edwardian literary *field* and the nature of the field itself as a complex social structure). The habitus is the 'practical sense' (*sens pratique*) or 'second nature' that disposes one to act when placed in particular circumstances in a way that is often intuitive rather than a consciously calculated observance of typical procedure. The habitus is comprised of a 'system of dispositions' that constitute a 'present past'; it is 'accumulated through a long process of acquisition or inculcation which includes the pedagogical action of the family or group members (family education), educated members of the social formation (diffuse education) and social institutions (institutionalized education)'.[24] By exploring what the status of being 'a writer' entails at a particular moment in time, this book considers 'the social conditions of the possibility of this social function [of being a writer], of this social personage'.[25] I avoid inflecting my account with retrospective understandings of the writer that Lawrence later *became* by looking only at the evidence pertaining to the specific historical moment. Lawrence gathered information about the literary field through, for example, his reading and through various modes of discourse (through mentors, everyday communication with potential readers and his education). If it was figures like Hueffer and Hunt who provided beneficial contacts and advice at an early stage in Lawrence's career, facilitating the publication of his first novel at the age of twenty-five, then it was Lawrence's own cultural knowledge, proficiency and disposition that enabled him to take advantage of the opportunities that then opened up before him. Lawrence's intensive literary study was not merely the passing whim of an intellectually curious youth; at some level the works he read were potential models for his own writing practice. Hunt recalled that Lawrence was 'more conversant with decadent poetry than I or [Hueffer], and that is saying a great deal, in fact, I think he had studied it too deeply'.[26]

Bourdieu makes it clear that gaining the requisite knowledge about one's possible position in the field is most often an involuntary (and always a *partial*) process. Reading, for example, can provide a less conscious, more intuitive understanding of the literary marketplace. For Bourdieu, practices such as reading afford one

> a 'nose' and a 'feeling' *without any need for cynical calculation*, for 'what needs to be done', where to do it, how and with whom, in view of all that has been done and is being done, all those who are doing it, and where.[27]

To address the limited understanding of Lawrence's early career, I examine the set of social conditions of the production, circulation and consumption of specific examples of Lawrence's work, considering the ways in which he continuously accrued knowledge about the literary field (both consciously and subconsciously), assessing the extent of his understanding of his readership and how he responded to the feedback he received when revising his writing.

Lawrence's creative strategy is clear in letters he wrote to Frederick Atkinson. Having almost completed a first draft of *The Trespasser* on 15 July 1910, Lawrence told Atkinson: 'During the next six or seven weeks I will lend the book to one or two of my people: then I will overhaul it rigorously: then I will send it to you.' Three weeks previously Lawrence assured him: 'I read newspaper crits, I listen to the advice of my best friends.'[28]

Peter D. McDonald uses Bourdieu's model to structure his study of the publishing careers of Joseph Conrad, Arnold Bennett and Arthur Conan Doyle in the period 1880 to 1914. Conrad is configured as a 'purist' man of letters; Bennett, the 'profiteer', is shown to 'play the field' by writing 'literary' novels, engaging in serialisation and producing journalism. The 'populist' Conan Doyle is said to offer 'light' reading with a dignified approach: 'Neither a purist nor a profiteer, he occupied a more uncertain position between these two extremes as a populist with high aspirations who became increasingly anxious about his own literary standing.'[29] The difficulty in defining the shape of authors' careers is made evident by McDonald's use of the label 'literary' to describe some of Bennett's novels: writing a literary novel is the opposite of profiteering and so McDonald blurs the boundaries between each category to show the complex nature of writers' negotiations of the social structures that determined the attribution of symbolic capital and economic value at the turn of the century. Symbolic capital is defined as 'accumulated prestige, celebrity, consecration or honour and is founded on a dialectic of knowledge ... and recognition'. Economic success, or writing a bestseller, may signal a barrier to the attribution of symbolic capital: it is the 'economic world reversed'.[30] Publishing is an activity that demands a shrewd player with a steady nerve, the eye for an opportunity and (for the literary writer, whose artistry must be seen to supersede financial concerns) the ability to conceal one's strategic tracks. Participants can occupy several different positions within a brief duration of time: within three months in early 1913, for example, Lawrence experimented with a range of forms including 'an historical novel, a first-person narrative by the central character, a dialect play, a symbolic fable, and the first of his philosophical writings'.[31] While Conrad is (like Lawrence) generally understood to be a serious literary writer, his collaboration with Hueffer on popular novels such as *The Inheritors* (1901) and *Romance* (1903) shows that, despite his insistence on his purist credentials, his writing was not 'a strenuous private act of supreme integrity'.[32] The premise is that authors' writings lay claim to this grandiose epithet, but the writing itself can never be wholly immune from market demands. McDonald's conferral of the labels 'purist', 'profiteer' or 'populist' is the combined result of a number of factors, such as the way the author views his art, the way he is positioned alongside all the other participants in the field, the marketing of his work and readers' responses to the work (particularly the commentaries offered by reviewers and critics). Bourdieu's methodological framework offers a fluid and nuanced approach to the position of the individual author in literary culture. We must be alert to the provisional status of the writer's position, because the literary field is a dynamic concept and 'its structure, at any given moment, is determined by the relations between the positions agents occupy'.[33] However, due to the perpetually incomplete and revisionary nature of an author's grasp of the literary field and the expansive and partly unconscious nature of the author's habitus, the literary historian will only ever be able to possess a partial understanding and we are able to reconstruct only a limited account of the contributing sociological factors in the cultural field that had the greatest impact on Lawrence's work. As a newly professional writer working in a variety of genres, it was difficult for Lawrence to establish a coherent authorial identity and at times he thought he had appealed to the principles of a particular journal or readership but was mistaken in his perception and his work was rejected.[34] Bourdieu's theory allows us to see Lawrence's authorial identity as conflicted and unsettled.

While the chapters herein will not return to cite these theories explicitly, my approach combines Bourdieu's sociology of the author with the work of Gérard Genette, Jerome McGann and D. F. McKenzie: theorists of the 'socialization of texts'.[35] Genette's theory emphasises the significance of the materiality of the published artefact and the collaboration between author and publisher in delivering the work to its readers. Genette analyses the threshold between the 'text' (the poem, the story and so forth) and the 'paratext'. The latter is comprised of the internal text (the peritext) and what is external to the text (the epitext). The peritext is constituted by all the framing features that act to mediate the book to the reader, such as the book's title(s), chapter headings, the presence of an authorial pseudonym, foreword, dedication, epigraph, preface, notes, epilogue and afterword. The epitext describes the elements that form the 'public' history of the book, such as the publisher's promotional activity (through, for example, periodical advertisements, blurbs and dust jackets) and the author's self-publicity through interviews, portraits and commentaries on his work. It also refers to the 'private' history of the book, including authorial correspondence and 'pre-text' aspects, such as discarded drafts, notes and chapter plans. Whereas the paratext has a 'lack of internal borders', the epitext has a 'lack of external limits'; it 'gradually disappears into . . . the totality of the authorial discourse', which begs the question of how much paratextual material one should attend to.[36] Since I discuss a number of textual embodiments (and Genette's theory is most conducive to the analysis of *books*) this study often draws more heavily upon the 'epitextual' features of works and so in the case of Lawrence's contributions to magazines I consider factors such as the implied reader of the magazine, its circulation, regular contributors and editor/s and its history (how and when it began and ended) as well as its contents and format, including visual material such as advertisements.

For Genette, the paratext is seen as secondary to the text. McGann, however, stresses the interdependent relationship between the 'main textual event' and material phenomena in his theory of the sociohistorical conditions affecting the (re)production of texts. He uses the terms 'linguistic' and 'bibliographical' to describe the types of textual features that Genette defines as 'text' and 'paratext', respectively; McGann's investigation into the nature of textuality also explores non-linguistic aspects such as ink, typeface and paper.[37] While Genette is primarily concerned with exploring the literary function of features such as the dedication, epigraph and preface, McGann applies his own sociohistorical theory to the work of authors such as William Blake and Ezra Pound in order to discuss issues of textual instability. For McGann, '[t]he universe of literature is socially generated and does not exist in a steady state. Authors themselves do not have, *as authors*, singular identities; an author is a plural identity.'[38] Authors have a variety of artistic intentions and their 'texts change under the pressure of immediate events'.[39] McGann's statements here are the fundamental principles underpinning this book. An author is also a plural identity in the sense that there is more than one author of any work: editors, printers, typesetters and so forth, are also 'authors', to an extent. But while McGann is primarily interested in the work as material artefact, my study places a greater emphasis on the impact of the institutions of publishing on Lawrence. Like McKenzie, whose 'sociology of texts' indicates that 'forms effect meaning', this book is similarly concerned with the social processes of textual transmission and considers the 'physical forms, textual versions' and 'institutional control' of specific examples of Lawrence's early writings.[40] Without the intervention of intermediaries – and if Lawrence had refused to create or revise a text in line with the ethos of a particular publisher or journal – he may not have been able to live by his pen. He both challenged and necessarily acted upon the pressures of the literary marketplace. By foregrounding the sociohistorical conditions of the text and considering Lawrence's evolving conceptions of the field, examining the plural nature of authorship and the paratextual allows us to explore the ways in which the text was, from its inception, already socially generated.

Since it is impossible to present a comprehensive account of all Lawrence's work up to spring 1914, I focus instead on case studies that reveal important aspects of Lawrence's interactions with the marketplace and the development of his early career. Acknowledging the challenge of writing about events that occur simultaneously, the method adopted to describe these intricate exchanges is to juxtapose different episodes to create a multifaceted picture which acknowledges the complexities of my subject, but which is broadly chronological. Chapter 1 sets out to revise the perception that Lawrence took little interest in attaining a professional writing career before Hueffer accepted his poetry for publication in the November 1909 number of the *English Review*, examining how Lawrence understood his position in the literary field at the time when he was making his first approaches to representative readers in preparation for submitting his work to publishers. His initial interests were in sentimental and romantic poetry and short stories with regional settings; in Easter 1906 he also began a melodramatic novel, 'Laetitia' (the earliest extant version of the novel that became *The White Peacock*). I provide evidence that Lawrence saw writing as a social and collaborative activity and draw attention to his creative practice of circulating manuscripts to an increasing circle of (mostly female) friends and acquaintances. Chapter 2 considers Lawrence's early interest in socialism and provides evidence that he was interested in a career in journalism from as early as 1908; it explores how his reading of A. R. Orage's the *New Age* shaped writing such as his paper 'Art and the Individual' (1908), which was revised and given the subtitle 'A Paper for Socialists' before it was sent to his correspondent Blanche Jennings, a socialist and suffragist who represented Lawrence's ideal reader at this time.

Chapter 3 focuses on the support and advice that Lawrence's literary mentors offered him at a crucial early stage in his career. It reconsiders Lawrence's relationship with Hueffer, examining archive evidence such as the letter Hueffer sent to Lawrence in December 1909 in which he offered an appraisal of the manuscript of 'Nethermere' (later revised and entitled *The White Peacock*). The chapter argues that Violet Hunt played a larger role in the launching of Lawrence's career and in his approach to Heinemann than has previously been acknowledged. In the eyes of Hueffer and Hunt, in autumn 1909 Lawrence was a marketable proposition and an author whose works were likely to appeal to the circulating libraries. Drawing on new archival research, this chapter reveals that Lawrence's first novel was enthusiastically reviewed in publications such as the little-known theatrical woman's magazine *Madame*. Arguing that traditional criticism on Lawrence's career has studied certain figures such as the publisher's reader Edward Garnett largely in one-dimensional terms, Chapter 4 focuses on Garnett's vital editorial assistance with the 'Saga of Siegmund', which became Lawrence's second novel *The Trespasser* (1912). Hueffer had warned Lawrence not to publish the book, believing that its 'phallic' content would ruin Lawrence's reputation. The chapter considers the help Garnett gave Lawrence in placing his poems, sketches, plays and short stories in a climate of censorship enforced by influential bodies such as the Circulating Libraries Association.

I outline the extensive experience Garnett had as a publisher's reader and his status as a critic and a writer who had been involved in high-profile censorship disputes. These various experiences enabled him to manage the 'erotic' content of *The Trespasser* and to secure its publication by Duckworth. If Garnett had not intervened at this stage in Lawrence's career then *The Trespasser* and *Sons and Lovers* may never have been published and his career could have been over before it had really begun.

Chapters 5 and 6 explore how Lawrence understood the necessity of self-fashioning and self-advertisement. Chapter 5 concentrates on Lawrence's early connections with esoteric poetry circles in London as he mixed with Ezra Pound, W. B. Yeats, Florence Farr, Ernest and Grace Rhys and Rachel Annand Taylor. He wrote a controversial paper on Taylor for presentation at the Croydon branch of the English Association. While in 1909–10 he was fascinated by Taylor's sensual love poetry, at the invitation of Edward Marsh in 1913 he associated himself with the Georgian Poets and so began his friendship with Katherine Mansfield, John Middleton Murry and other *Rhythm* contributors. Chapter 6 examines transatlantic publishing culture to assess Lawrence's early reputation both in Britain and America. I consider the interest that the New York publisher Mitchell Kennerley took in Lawrence's work and address the significance of Lawrence's name appearing under the Kennerley imprint at this time. Kennerley published Lawrence in his magazine *Forum* and commissioned the Swedish-American literary critic and author Edwin Björkman to write an Introduction to the first American edition of *The Widowing of Mrs Holroyd* (1914). In London, W. L. George wrote an article on Lawrence which was published in the February 1914 number of the *Bookman*. Lawrence supplied biographical notes to both Björkman and George, involving himself in their promotional writings and cooperating (albeit with discomfort) in their construction of his identity as a working-class writer. Providing a multi-dimensional view of Lawrence, illuminating his unseen side as an amateur and then a newly professional author, this study seeks to discover a pattern in the strategies Lawrence developed for approaching the literary marketplace while providing new insights into Edwardian publishing culture and the opportunities on offer to aspiring authors.

Notes

1. *L*, I, 223–4.
2. *L*, I, 222.
3. *L*, I, 233.
4. Anon., Review of *Sons and Lovers* (1913): 5; see Draper, 58; *New York Times Book Review* (4 October 1914): 416.

5. John Worthen, *D. H. Lawrence: A Literary Life* (1989), pp. xx–xxi.
6. Worthen, *D. H. Lawrence: A Literary Life*, p. xxii.
7. Mark Osteen, *The Economy of 'Ulysses': Making Both Ends Meet* (1995); John Whittier-Ferguson, *Framing Pieces: Designs of the Gloss in Joyce, Woolf, and Pound* (1996); Lawrence S. Rainey, *Institutions of Modernism: Literary Elites and Public Culture* (1998). See also Kevin J. H. Dettmar and Stephen Watt (eds), *Marketing Modernisms: Self-Promotion, Canonization, Rereading* (1996). These build on earlier studies such as James Hepburn, *The Author's Empty Purse and the Rise of the Literary Agent* (1968).
8. Available at <http://modjourn.org> (last accessed 19 June 2019). George Bornstein, *Material Modernism: The Politics of the Page* (2001), p. 1.
9. These titles include Jenny McDonnell's *Katherine Mansfield and the Modernist Marketplace: At the Mercy of the Public* (2010); Jeanne Dubino's edited collection *Virginia Woolf and the Literary Marketplace* (2010); *Samuel Beckett in the Literary Marketplace* (2011) by Stephen Dilks; Jonathan Cranfield's *Twentieth-Century Victorian: Arthur Conan Doyle and the* Strand Magazine, *1891–1930* (2016); and Chris Mourant's *Katherine Mansfield and Periodical Culture* (2019).
10. John Middleton Murry, *D. H. Lawrence: Son of Woman* (1931); T. S. Eliot, *After Strange Gods: A Primer of Modern Heresy* (1934); F. R. Leavis, *D. H. Lawrence: Novelist* (1994).
11. Memoirs include E. T. [Jessie Chambers's] *D. H. Lawrence: A Personal Record* (1935); Catherine Carswell's *The Savage Pilgrimage* (1932) is a defensive rejoinder to Murry's unsympathetic *D. H. Lawrence: Son of Woman*. See also Ford Madox Ford, *Portraits from Life* (1937), pp. 70–89 and Richard Aldington's *Portrait of a Genius But . . .* (1950).
12. Mark Kinkead-Weekes, 'The Marble and the Statue: The Exploratory Imagination of D. H. Lawrence' (1968), pp. 371–418; Keith Cushman, *D. H. Lawrence at Work: The Emergence of the* Prussian Officer *Stories* (1978).
13. Paul Eggert assesses the strengths and limitations of 'The Cambridge Edition' (2018), pp. 304–14.
14. Paul Delany discusses the 'segmentation' of the literary marketplace towards the end of the nineteenth century in *Literature, Money and the Market* (2002), pp. 97–124. For an empirical study, see Alexis Weedon, *Victorian Publishing: The Economics of Book Production for a Mass Market, 1836–1916* (2003).
15. Neil Roberts, *D. H. Lawrence, Travel and Cultural Difference* (2004); Jeff Wallace, *D. H. Lawrence, Science and the Posthuman* (2005); Judith Ruderman, *Race and Identity in D. H. Lawrence* (2014); David Game, *D. H. Lawrence's Australia* (2015); Susan Reid, *D. H. Lawrence, Music and Modernism* (2019); John Turner, *D. H. Lawrence and Psychoanalysis* (2020).

16. See Fernihough's reasoning for the time span in *Freewomen and Supermen: Edwardian Radicals and Literary Modernism* (2013), p. 48.
17. Hueffer changed his surname to 'Ford' in 1919; since the focus of my book precedes this date I use his original surname throughout. In the first scholarly biography of Lawrence, Harry T. Moore discussed Hueffer and Garnett's assistance of Lawrence: *The Life and Works of D. H. Lawrence* (1951).
18. *L*, I, 551.
19. Worthen, *D. H. Lawrence: A Literary Life*, p. xxv.
20. Worthen, *D. H. Lawrence: A Literary Life*, p. 30.
21. Andrew Harrison, *The Life of D. H. Lawrence* (2016), p. 114.
22. Joyce Piell Wexler, *Who Paid for Modernism? Art, Money, and the Fiction of Conrad, Joyce, Lawrence* (1997). The other essays on Lawrence and the literary marketplace are Andrew Harrison's 'Dust-Jackets, Blurbs and Forewords: The Marketing of *Sons and Lovers*' (2009), pp. 17–33; and John Worthen's 'D. H. Lawrence and the "expensive edition business"' (1996), pp. 105–23. More recently, see the essays by Wexler ('Book Publishers', 2018, pp. 37–46), Grice ('Journals, Magazines, Newspapers', 2018, pp. 47–56) and Harrison ('Private Publication', 2018, pp. 57–67).
23. Pierre Bourdieu, *The Field of Cultural Production*: *Essays on Art and Literature* (1993), p. 162.
24. The quotation is Randal Johnson quoting and then paraphrasing Bourdieu in his 'Introduction' to Bourdieu, *The Field of Cultural Production*, pp. 6–7.
25. Bourdieu, *The Field of Cultural Production*, p. 163.
26. Nehls, I, 127.
27. Bourdieu, *The Field of Cultural Production*, p. 95.
28. *L*, I, 169–70; 167.
29. Peter D. McDonald, *British Literary Culture and Publishing Practice, 1880–1914* (1997), p. 121.
30. Johnson, 'Introduction' to Bourdieu, *Field of Cultural Production*, p. 7.
31. *TE*, 67.
32. McDonald, *British Literary Culture and Publishing Practice*, p. 66.
33. Johnson, 'Introduction' to *Field of Cultural Production*, p. 6.
34. In April 1912, for example, Lawrence wrote to Garnett: 'The *Daily News* sent me back the article – "The Collier's Wife Scores". Would *The Eyewitness* have it, I wonder' (*L*, I, 379). Hilaire Belloc's radical journal did not take the sketch, which was later entitled 'Strike Pay I, Her Turn' and then 'Her Turn'; it was finally first published in the politically liberal *Westminster Gazette* and the *Saturday Westminster Gazette* on 6 September 1913.

35. This phrase is the title of Jerome McGann's third chapter in his *The Textual Condition* (1991), pp. 69–87.
36. Gérard Genette, *Paratexts: Thresholds of Interpretation* (1997), p. 346.
37. McGann, *The Textual Condition*, p. 13.
38. Ibid., p. 75.
39. Ibid., p. 74.
40. D. F. McKenzie, *Bibliography and the Sociology of Texts* (1994), p. 13.

PART I
MAKING A START (1905–8)

1

'A collier's son a poet!': Lawrence's First Approaches to the Literary Marketplace

Critical accounts of how Lawrence came to be a published writer have tended to take similar narrative lines to those Lawrence provided in his late autobiographical sketches. In a January 1927 essay entitled 'Getting On', he wrote:

> It was Miriam who first sent poems of mine to the English Review: when I was twenty-three. It was she who got back the answer, accepting them. And she was still at home in Underwood, I was in London, far away. Ford Madox Hueffer, who had just begun to edit the English Review – and he did it so well – immediately told me I was a genius: which was a mere phrase to me. Among the working classes, geniuses don't enter. Hueffer was very kind to me, so was Edward Garnett. They were the first literary men I ever met – and the first men *really* outside my own class. They were very kind, very generous. Hueffer read the Manuscript of the *White Peacock*. I had by now finished the novel, having struggled for five years to get it out of the utterly unformed chaos of my consciousness, having written some of it eleven times, and all of it four times. I hewed it out with infinitely more labour than my father hewed out coal. But once it was done, I knew more or less what I had to do.[1]

Lawrence foregrounds Jessie Chambers's involvement in launching his career. By calling her 'Miriam', he makes reference to his characterisation of her in *Sons and Lovers* and gives the reader a context in which to view their relationship; she is the devoted but ultimately spurned lover who, by believing in his ability, unwittingly succeeds in creating an insuperable distance between them as he is drawn towards the city lights. Jessie is placed in the role of provincial secretary, 'still at home in Underwood', while Lawrence is 'in London, far away'. The late autobiographical essays, commissioned by newspaper editors, are simplified romanticisations of Lawrence's early career in which he mimics a particular kind of journalistic discourse which provides its readership with what they want to read: appealing snapshots of a literary 'celebrity' (and a working class one at that). In 'Which Class I Belong To' (April 1927) Lawrence asserts, 'published I was, and always have been, without any effort on my part'. He repeats this sentiment in 'Myself Revealed' of February 1929: 'It all happened by itself without any groans from me . . . The girl had launched me, so easily, on my literary career, like a princess cutting a thread, launching a ship.'[2] These self-mythologising accounts also uphold the notion that Lawrence was indifferent to a literary career until Jessie sent his poems to Hueffer in summer 1909. While Jessie's action is typically seen as the watershed moment in Lawrence's writing life (and Lawrence viewed as fortunate to enter the literary scene just as Hueffer was looking to publish high-calibre new authors from the working class), little critical attention has been paid to the fact that Lawrence had considered a career in journalism as early as 1908 and had looked to short story syndication in the provincial press in June 1909. These early approaches to the marketplace have been overshadowed by the more appealing narrative of Lawrence's entry into literary society through the pages of the prestigious *English Review*. Hueffer and Garnett were instrumental in encouraging Lawrence to cultivate his identity as a working-class writer in the belief that this was a position in the field where he could be a strong competitor, but Lawrence's contemporary opinion about the relative merits of his literary mentors deserves more recognition than it has hitherto received. On 14 November 1912 he wrote to Ernest Collings:

> How queer to think of 'A Still Afternoon in School'. It's the first thing I ever had published. Ford Madox Hueffer discovered I was a genius – don't be alarmed, Hueffer would discover *anything* if he wanted to – published me some verse and a story or two, sent me to Wm Heinemann with the *White Peacock*, and left me to paddle my own canoe. I *very* nearly wrecked it and did for myself. Edward Garnett, like a good angel, fished me out.[3]

This letter shows the difficulties Lawrence had finding his way without assistance, but in the late essays Lawrence implies that getting published was no problem and that a professional career in this line was inevitable. In his 1927 essay Lawrence foregrounds Hueffer's description of him as a 'genius', self-deprecatingly emphasising his prickliness at the description because of its class connotations (in 'Myself Revealed' Lawrence recalls that 'they were always telling me I had got genius, as if to console me for not having their own incomparable advantages').[4] By referring to his class background he reminds the reader that he had not had the usual advantages of a middle-class writer.

This appears to underline Hueffer's point about Lawrence having a great natural talent, but it also leaves Lawrence with the problem of having to explain how he went from being a miner's son to a prominent author. He switches his image from indifferent but patronised urbanite to suffering provincial artist within a single paragraph. As if to hint at the amount of work he had to do to achieve his authorial status, he signposts the effortful composition of *The White Peacock* before maintaining that the writing process represented a key turning-point: 'I hewed it out with infinitely more labour than my father hewed out coal. But once it was done, I knew more or less what I had to do.' Yet as he acknowledges in 1912, his efforts to achieve and then maintain his fledgling career and to shape an identity within the capacious and congested marketplace were painstaking.

There is evidence that Lawrence was exploring opportunities and strategies to conceive of himself as a writer and finding ways of submitting his work to publishers long before he met Hueffer. However imperfectly he understood the social conditions of being a writer, Lawrence instinctively attempted to gain a sense of what the literary field was and he explored and evaluated potential literary models for his own work through his readings and engagements with literary culture. To locate a position for himself Lawrence had to negotiate the tensions that existed in this complex social space and also those within himself, to explore the nature and possibilities of his artistic disposition – and to perceive the limits that might be imposed on him by external forces. We cannot ignore the significance of Lawrence's class status. According to Bourdieu, entering the 'particular social game' of the literary field is to 'participate in domination', but as a '*dominated*' agent'; it is to take on a contradictory position which results in power struggles in the social world. The dynamic nature of the field is such that an initially dominated agent, once 'in' the field, may come to reshape the field on their own terms. An agent is, however, dominated to some extent by their requirement to pay heed to marketplace demands to earn the money needed to begin and sustain a writing career. The ambiguity of their position in the field of power leads writers to

> maintain an ambivalent relationship with the dominant class within the field of power, those whom they call 'bourgeois', as well as with the dominated, the 'people'. In a similar way, they form an ambiguous image of their own position in social space and of their social function.[5]

Richard Salmon discusses the uncertainty concerning the social position and class status of professional authors: 'should authorship be viewed as an ordinary form of wage-labour (either "noble" or "degrading" depending on one's perspective) or as a professional service guaranteeing membership of the respectable middle classes?' If the emphasis of a writer's career lies in an accommodation to the commercial enterprise of literary production, then authorship could appear 'synonymous with the activity of literary hacks, an eighteenth-century model in which writing occupies the status of alienated labour'.[6] If it lies with their sense of detachment from marketplace concerns, then their writing may move closer to acquiring cultural capital. Writers had to seem disinterested in literary commerce for fear of appearing servile, or as grasping for success. The expansion of mass culture in the late nineteenth century placed cultural and economic capital in direct conflict; writers grappled with the consequences this had for their works and the ways in which they could fashion their reputations. In his study of Henry James's relationship to British Aestheticism, Jonathan Freedman explores how artists such as Walter Pater, Oscar Wilde and James Abbott McNeill Whistler saw themselves as 'existing in a marginal elite or, to adopt the aestheticists' own neo-Arnoldian term, as "aliens" within a society that nourishes and rewards alienation with fame, notoriety, and even, at times, tenure'. Pre-Raphaelite artists such as John Everett Millais and William Holman Hunt sought to become 'as bourgeois as possible', while others aimed to 'question the limits of social acceptance, by affirming and reaffirming their own social marginality. Swinburne and Wilde in particular can be seen as devoting their lives to testing the line between tolerance and taboo.'[7] This is a position that Lawrence himself held (especially after the banning of *The Rainbow*), largely to the detriment of his finances.

'Wickedly ambitious socially'

Lawrence had an indistinct and shifting impression of his social position. While living in the close-knit mining community of Eastwood he was known to be an intelligent, artistic youth living in a particularly aspirational household. He attended Beauvale Board School until 1898, when he won a scholarship to a prestigious grammar, Nottingham High School. In June 1905 he passed the London Matriculation examination and from 1906 to 1908 attended University College Nottingham, obtaining a teacher's certificate but choosing not to take a degree. His education had given him the opportunity to enter a lower-middle-class occupation like his brother Ernest, who had been living in London as a shipping clerk before his death in 1901. Lawrence needed to earn a regular wage from full-time teaching, which initially restricted the time he could dedicate to pursuing a writing career. His desired profession was loaded with improbability and the expectation of financial instability; the new opportunities presented by significant changes in the publishing industry were exploited by a great number of writers jostling for position in the field. Authorship was first recognised as a profession in the 1861 census, with 1,673 individuals (including editors, journalists, artists, actors and musicians) classifying themselves as belonging to this category. By the 1880s the number had risen to 6,111. By 1911, 13,786 people officially declared themselves to be professional authors.[8] By this time, the monopoly that the circulating libraries had held over the literary marketplace was still influential but was to an extent loosening its hold; the rise of professionalisation and the establishment of the Society of Authors in 1884 had been part of that process. From the 1890s the literary marketplace had been affected by forces such as changes in international copyright law following the 1891 Chace Act, the demise of the three-decker novel from 1894, the rise of the literary agent, the establishment of new publishing houses and venues for publication, innovative marketing and changes in the format of the press and printing technologies. Memoirs indicate Lawrence's perception of his shifting social position in 1909, after he was introduced to Hueffer's circle. His Croydon landlord John Jones records that '[s]ome London writers had recently taken Lawrence up, and when he came back from a weekend with them he used to speak with a different accent'.[9] Louie Burrows recalled that, around this time, Lawrence was 'wickedly ambitious socially – tho' it was the last thing he would admit or condone in another'.[10] Similarly, during her first visit to London in November 1909 Jessie was surprised to hear Lawrence exclaim, '[w]ith the spectacle of London's opulence' before him, 'I'll make two thousand a year!'; she noted his admiration for 'the kind of "distinction" that titles confer'.[11] Jessie signals her discomfort with her use of the term 'distinction', a word which 'may or may not imply the conscious intention of distinguishing oneself from common people'.[12] That is, Lawrence may not consciously have been intending to break from his social origins, but he recognised that the literary society he was entering into was generally privileged; at some level he may have considered that he would stand more chance of becoming accepted as a writer if he could minimise observable differences between himself and his perception of the London literati. Lawrence would have been aware that he was exposing himself to potential derision by established literary figures as he moved outside the circle of his trusted peers, who had sanctioned his accomplishments. In meeting members of Hueffer's circle he would be competing for the recognition of those with 'titles' that conferred on individuals a degree of cultural nobility, such as 'editor', 'author' and 'publisher'. Jessie's account criticises what she perceived as Lawrence's snobbery about this kind of 'title', although he was likely performing his newly metropolitan self-conception for her benefit.

The evidence we have of the authorial identity Lawrence cultivated from around 1908 and as he encountered the *English Review* set shows him anxiously wavering between the adoption of two marginal positions: boundary-testing aesthete and zealous young autodidact. Hueffer was to prefer the latter; he took pleasure in celebrating Lawrence's intelligence as a self-taught working-class man. Jessie records that during a meal at Violet Hunt's house, '[s]omebody mentioned Carlyle and Ruskin, and Lawrence admitted that he had read them both'. Her choice of the word 'admitted' to describe Lawrence's confession suggests that he considered his intensive reading in these Victorian figures a marker of his self-imposed learning, which signified his difference from the personalities around the dinner table whose habitus had been formed more 'naturally' due to their upbringings in artistic environments. Figures such as Hueffer and Hunt were inheritors of cultural nobility due to their artistic lineages and their own anxieties would be in living up to the expectations that their family names commanded. Hueffer's reported response to Lawrence's revelation underlined their disparity: 'You're the only man I've ever met ... who really has read all those people.'[13] The works of Carlyle and Ruskin need not be actually read by those for whom these writers are familiar voices. Hueffer's memoir recording their first meeting in the *English Review* offices in September 1909 implies that both men were apprehensive about addressing each other and, tellingly, that Lawrence's attitude was restive and aloof.[14]

Peter D. McDonald argues that

> for the culturally and socially privileged, being a purist is like speaking a first language, while, for the more marginalized, it is like learning a second late in life. Biography or sociobiography, that is, affects how 'natural' a writer feels occupying a particular position in the field, and introduces a potential tension between positions and dispositions.[15]

This offers a perspective from which to understand Lawrence's complex position in at once aspiring to achieve the middle-class occupation of a writing career and yet remaining scornful of bourgeois sensibilities. An emphasis on self-improvement implies an assimilation of middle-class cultural ideals, about which Lawrence felt uneasy. Since he was not economically privileged, he took advantage of the intellectual opportunities available to him in order to lessen the gap between feeling like an imposter in the literary field and feeling as 'natural' to the position as those with social and economic advantage. McDonald observes that, in the 1890s, Wilde, James and Conrad 'were all "born" literary intellectuals [who] were relatively comfortable in their position as purists', while Arnold Bennett, H. G. Wells and George Bernard Shaw, 'whose more modest backgrounds made them "born again" members of the intelligentsia, were either aggressively against the purists or at least very ambivalent about the whole idea of art for art's sake'.[16] This helps to illuminate why Lawrence has been labelled a 'genius' ever since his early interactions with Hueffer. As a writer from a working-class background who has been placed squarely in the 'purist' category, Lawrence is something of an anomaly. In 1914 he was judged as one among a new generation of promising novelists (alongside Gilbert Cannan, Compton Mackenzie, E. M. Forster and Hugh Walpole) but with the exception of Forster, these writers have not subsequently been awarded symbolic value and their reputations have not endured.

It is fair to say that Lawrence is the working-class writer whose *oeuvre* has been most strongly consecrated by readers and the academy, but as is clear from the autobiographical accounts documented at length by Jonathan Rose in *The Intellectual Life of the British Working Classes* (2001), Lawrence was not unusual among his class in his authorial ambition. Rose builds a complex picture of the self-taught individual (raised in a working-class society that had experienced a steep increase in levels of literacy following the 1870 Education Act) whose extensive reading and wide-ranging intellectual activities are identifiable in Lawrence's biography. The class that comprised the 'growing army of Edwardian clerks' were men who were 'born into the working classes around 1890, attended Board schools, read cheap editions of the classics, enjoyed 2s. concerts, and took one step up the social ladder into the lower reaches of the middle class'.[17] Particularly significant for these readers was the inauguration in 1906 of J. M. Dent's Everyman's Library. Dent himself had been raised in a working-class household and his editor Ernest Rhys had formerly been a mining engineer apprentice in Durham who had set up a small library and discussion group for the colliers.[18] Lawrence's letters reveal his preference for these relatively inexpensive and scholarly Everyman hardbacks and Worthen has observed that, even up to 1916, Lawrence was influenced in his choice of readings by the titles published in the series.[19] Dent's poetry editor and the author of twenty books published by the firm, Richard Church, was a postman's son who shared Lawrence's study of John Ruskin, Charles Lamb, Thomas Love Peacock, Lessing's *Laokoon* and Arthur Schopenhauer.[20] Neil Bell, the son of a Southwold boatbuilder, entered literary competitions, wrote children's verses and published light verse in the *London Opinion* before getting a sonnet published in the *English Review*; in 1912 he earned £5 per week from writing and teaching and by 1955 he had published eighty books, many of them science-fiction novels.[21]

Although Lawrence was a prolific writer, until the publication of *Lady Chatterley's Lover* (1928) he earned only enough money to get by. He demanded an alert, reflexive, broad-minded and intellectually ambitious reader, intuiting that a work that possesses symbolic value derives its distinction from a cultivated reader like himself. His earliest work, however, was sentimental poetry and fiction shaped by his readings of British and American bestsellers. These readings included Louisa May Alcott's *Little Women* (1868–9); Charles Reade's *The Cloister and the Hearth* (1861); Anthony Hope's *The Prisoner of Zenda* (1894) and *Rupert of Hentzau* (1898); R. L. Stevenson's *Treasure Island* (1883) and *Kidnapped* (1886); James Fenimore Cooper's *Last of the Mohicans* (1826) and *The Pathfinder* (1840); Walter Scott's historical romances and the poetry of Henry Wadsworth Longfellow and Alfred, Lord Tennyson. He moved from these often sentimental, moralistic works with romantic, escapade-riven plots to the tragic realism of George Eliot, Thomas Hardy, the Brontës and several French authors; Lawrence particularly admired Honoré de Balzac. Palgrave's *Golden Treasury of Songs and Lyrics* (which included Percy Bysshe Shelley, William Wordsworth, John Keats, William Cowper, Robert Burns, Thomas De Quincey and William Shakespeare) 'became a kind of Bible' to him; he read essays by Francis Bacon, Ralph Waldo Emerson, Henry Thoreau and Thomas Carlyle.[22] Initially aiming his writing at a young, middle-class, female reader, Lawrence had this readership in mind when he produced writings such as the short story 'A Prelude' and the poem 'Study'. However ambitious it seemed at the time, his decision to write a novel in the hope that he could get it published to earn money and authorial status is suggested by his May 1908 comment to Blanche Jennings about the second draft of 'Laetitia': 'if I were not vain and poor I should like to put it in the fire'.[23] The literary marketplace could not function without relying on consumer demand for goods which are relatively familiar and so Lawrence could only achieve and sustain a full-time writing career by selling work according to already existing tastes.

His solution for combining his literary values with his financial needs was to compromise: he would write for the middle-class female reader (the primary target audience of Mudie's Select Library, which still provided a guaranteed market for publishers), but not without challenging and critiquing this readership.[24] *The White Peacock* illustrates this tension: as a tragic romance novel addressed to middle-class readers, it simultaneously interrogates bourgeois social aspirations and cultural illusions. Lawrence's characters in *The White Peacock* believe that artistic culture offers refinement and upward mobility and their expectations for life and relationships are shaped according to the promises that romantic narratives hold, yet in the real world they experience only disillusionment. In critiquing romantic narratives within a tragic romance novel, Lawrence appears both to reinforce and challenge his own ideas about the effect that aesthetic receptivity can have on the reader; high art can cultivate and humanise, but it can also deflect from the immediate claims of life. The novel's frequent artistic and literary allusions serve as a shorthand reproduction of the literary tastes of the characters: Laetitia's preference for 'stories from Balzac, Théophile Gautier, Daudet, de Maupassant . . . D. G. Rossetti [and] Swinburne' prompts the reader to draw on their cultural knowledge to classify the character and to connect Lettie's pregnancy outside marriage to her affinity for literature that was then considered subversive (first version of 'Laetitia'[25]). The contradictions and shifting positions in the novel reflect the changes in social position and aesthetic sensibility that Lawrence underwent during the process of its composition. Although it now reads as a clever, socially engaged period piece (a perfect example of the 'literary' Edwardian novel), *The White Peacock* was a statement about the kind of writer Lawrence thought himself to be during those years – a cultivated and refined young man who was serious about attaining a writing career of some distinction.

'Look how serious I am'

Jessie recalls that it was during 'the year when he was an uncertified teacher in the British School at Eastwood that Lawrence first spoke to me about writing'.[26] Lawrence was a pupil-teacher at the British School from October 1902 to July 1905; he worked there as an uncertified Assistant Teacher between August 1905 and September 1906. Even then Lawrence was mindful of his social marginality in relation to most published authors and he knew that he would face particular challenges in breaking through with his writing. Jessie recalls a conversation that she had with him in spring 1905, when Lawrence declared his intention to write in the genre that the pair had long held as 'the very greatest thing': 'It will be *poetry*. . . . But what will the others say? That I'm a fool. A collier's son a poet!'[27] His comment betrays a sense of confidence in one day seeing his poems in print, or at least in realising his ambition to be known as a poet. In the May 1928 Foreword to his *Collected Poems*, Lawrence recalled that his first 'effusions' – 'Campions' and 'Guelder Roses'– were written for Jessie's appreciation on a 'slightly self-conscious Sunday afternoon' in 1905, when he was nineteen.[28] Lawrence's self-consciousness may have been the result of his awareness of the attitudes of his peers to such lofty pursuits as the writing of poetry. His closest school friend George Neville recalled:

> We all saw the danger of a literary career for Lawrence. The Little Woman [Lydia] had sniffed, Ada had 'pshawed and rubbished' times without number, 'Injun Topknot' [Emily] had talked of prospective disappointments, 'Beat' [Beatrice Hall] had angered him, as usual . . . Franky and Grit [the

Cooper sisters] had asked him what was the good of bothering, serious Alan [Chambers] had looked upon the prospect with alarm and I, in secret agreement with the 'Little Woman', had adopted an attitude of sheer contempt and often refused even to look at his manuscripts.[29]

The idea of becoming a poet was particularly impractical for someone without a private income since it was hardly the most popular or remunerative form of literature. Due to the rise of mass market fiction it was harder to publish volumes of poetry and although there were plenty of opportunities to publish poetry in magazines, little money could be made from this either. When Elkin Mathews made up the account for Ezra Pound's *Exultations* in March 1910, following its publication the previous September, he was dismayed to note that only 203 copies had been sold, with seventy-four copies having been given away as review or presentation copies. Mathews did not cover his costs and a royalty of just six shillings was due to Pound.[30]

Neville's comment suggests that Lawrence made no secret of his desire for a 'literary career' and that he was determined to carry through his ambition despite others' reservations and pessimism. Neville wrote that 'Lawrence even in those early days knew that he had the capacity for literary greatness and had thoroughly made up his mind to achieve it.'[31] Discussing Lawrence's time at the British School, May Chambers Holbrook recorded that 'it was soon apparent that Bert's thoughts had turned to writing, as well as reading, books'.[32] Jessie suggested that she instilled in Lawrence an awareness of his own ability, which would emerge at times in confident assertions about his future as a 'great man'.[33] Worthen has identified Lawrence's fear of the rejection of his manuscripts: he 'would rather not try than be exposed to his own self-contempt, and what he imagined was the amused reaction of others'.[34] In 1905 Lawrence's sense of the improbability of writing as a career, paired with his fear of humiliation, left him wary of doing anything more with his poetry than furtively passing it to Jessie. In 1905, however, he had only just started writing. By 1908 Lawrence was far more self-assured. He began to develop strategies for approaching the marketplace, which included circulating his manuscripts among carefully selected readers, writing collaboratively with Louie Burrows and advising other literary-minded friends such as Jessie and May Chambers and Blanche Jennings in order to form around him a supportive network with whom he could evaluate literary works and practices. The network reinforced his claim to being recognised as something of an authority on literary matters.

Jessie recollects that 'Lawrence and I had first talked about the publication of his work . . . on a cold evening in the spring of 1908.' Lawrence confessed that 'some weeks or even months' before he had sent 'some of his work to an author, whose weekly article in the *Daily News* we often read and discussed, asking him if he would give his opinion as to its merit'. Jessie had 'not heard of this before'.[35] Worthen suggests that it is

> significant that Lawrence should have approached another writer – in this case, G. K. Chesterton – for his approval, rather than sending his work to a magazine or a publisher. At this stage, he was more anxious about being accepted as a writer than about getting his writing into print.[36]

It is possible to view the approach in another light. Lawrence's direct address to an author – an expert in the field – is arguably a bolder and more strategic action than simply sending his work to a press office, where it might get lost among all the other submissions. If Chesterton was to notice Lawrence's work and mention it to his editor then the writing would be endorsed by Chesterton and Lawrence would stand a better chance of being published. The very act of sending his work shows that Lawrence already thought of himself as a capable writer and one worthy of a fellow writer's attention. If he could obtain Chesterton's written 'opinion as to its merit' then he could use it as a form of reference when approaching publication outlets: this is a strategy he would employ in December 1909 when he copied out and sent on to William Heinemann Hueffer's letter in support of the publication of his first novel.[37] If Lawrence was merely looking for acceptance as a writer then he would likely not have seemed so bitter about his plan being foiled by Chesterton's wife Frances, who returned the manuscript unread. Significantly, Lawrence reportedly commented: 'I've tried, and been turned down, and I shall try no more. And I don't care if I never have a line published.'[38] Evidently the approach to Chesterton was a serious attempt to get published. Chesterton was a shrewd choice on Lawrence's part as he was particularly knowledgeable about publishing; from 1895 to 1902 he had worked as a reader and sub-editor for the London publishing houses Redway and T. Fisher Unwin. From the way Jessie relates the conversation she saw Lawrence's declaration as a face-saving utterance: 'it was futile to argue with him in his present mood. But I began to wonder what would become of him if he should fail to get a hearing.'[39] Telling her of his frustrated plan and stressing his intention never to approach anyone else, but then continuing to bring his writings to her represented an implicit appeal to Jessie for her assistance. Lawrence told her that Chesterton's 'wife acts as his amanuensis', perhaps implying that Jessie might act in the same way on his behalf.[40]

It is significant that Lawrence approached a journalist at the same time as he was considering ways of breaking through into writing. Chesterton first began producing book reviews for the politically liberal *Daily News* in January 1901, aged twenty-six; by then he was the author of two poetry collections, *Greybeards at Play* and *The Wild Knight and Other Poems* (both 1900). In 1903 Chesterton was given a regular Saturday column on the leader page, which became a lengthy weekly column in 1904.[41] Among other literary achievements, he had published a collection of essays, *The Defendant* (1902), a critical study of Charles Dickens (1906), two novels, a number of short stories and he also wrote for *The Speaker*. Chesterton's versatility as a journalist and critic who was also a prolific author may have appealed to Lawrence as a model he could emulate. By 4 May 1908 Lawrence had become confident enough in his abilities to tell Blanche Jennings: 'look how serious I am. I have been writing a long time.' He felt ready to take his literary work further, but stated that he had no choice but to earn money as an elementary schoolteacher: 'a lamentable figure I should cut – unless I can do something with that damned damnation of a Laetitia'.[42] By this date the end of Lawrence's studies at University College Nottingham was in sight and he was earnestly considering his vocation; it was writing that continued to hold his interest. In his next extant letter to Blanche dated 13 May Lawrence expressed interest in pursuing a career in journalism. He stated:

> I could write a good novel, if I thought about it enough. I could do anything in that line. I could write crits. – but who wants me to – who would have 'em? How shall I squeeze my jostled, winded way into journalism? ... Do you know what I shall do when I am out of college? I shall write drivelling short-stories and the like for money.[43]

A career in journalism might have seemed more immediately achievable to Lawrence than getting work published as a literary author. Rose notes that, following the proliferation of inexpensive newspapers from the 1880s, 'journalism had opened an escape hatch for Board School graduates with literary flair'.[44] Lawrence's elder friend Willie Hopkin produced articles for the *Eastwood and Kimberley Advertiser* and he also wrote poetry.[45] All critics and biographers have overlooked the fact that Alfred Inwood (Lawrence's elder cousin on his mother's side) was an established figure in Fleet Street.[46] Lawrence stayed with the Inwood family in Barnet on 26 September 1908 while travelling to Croydon for his interview at Davidson Road Elementary School. He did not imagine that teaching would be his life-long occupation and pointedly asked his cousin about securing a career in journalism. Inwood's son Ewart George was 'about 10 years old' when Lawrence visited but he recalls his father saying:

'[t]he conceited young man seems to think he ought to start straight away on the *Daily Mail*. I told him to go home and try to get a job on his local paper and start from the bottom of the ladder like everyone else.'[47]

This recollection is consistent with accounts by Jessie and Neville which suggest that the young Lawrence strongly believed in his writing abilities and aspired to a position above 'the bottom of the ladder' even in the face of others' cynicism. He was interested in the most prominent newspapers; Hueffer states that A. G. Gardiner, editor of the *Daily News*, was *Daily Mail* founder Lord Northcliffe's 'chief rival in London journalism of the day'.[48] Lawrence's precocity was construed by Inwood as arrogance and it caused offence to a man who had worked hard to earn his position. Hopkin could have helped Lawrence to enquire about openings for young writers in the local press, yet Lawrence had already told him that he was going to be an author. Echoing Inwood's notion of Lawrence's conceitedness, Hopkin recalls: 'I treated it as the pardonable conceit of a clever youth who *knew he was clever*, and told him I wished him the success he hoped for.'[49]

Lawrence's purported desire to start writing for the *Daily Mail* is telling, both in terms of his ambition and his interest in writing for a female readership. The newspaper was founded by Lord Northcliffe (then known as Alfred Harmsworth) in 1896 and during that year it achieved a daily circulation of 200,000. By 1906 it had reached daily sales of one million copies, which was partly aided by Harmsworth's perception that women readers were an underexploited sector of the market for daily newspapers. His various publications 'responded to this vacuum with such innovations as serial fiction, advice columns on domestic economy and childrearing, and coverage of fashion'.[50] Writing articles for women did not daunt Arnold Bennett: within four years of arriving in London he had become assistant editor of *Woman* magazine and penned 'Gwendolen's Column', which discussed women's dress and household management.[51] The prospect of working on a thriving modern newspaper which serialised fiction for women and advised on issues affecting family life would have been attractive for the author of 'Laetitia', 'A Prelude' and 'The White Stocking' and it is not impossible to imagine the Lawrence of these years capably adapting to such a task. Fashioning a journalistic persona would not have been challenging for him since he had already cultivated an auctorial signature. Worthen comments upon the significance of Lawrence adopting the names 'D.H.L.' or 'D. H. Lawrence', which appear consistently in his earliest surviving correspondence: it 'gave him a certain status, a certain refined personality . . . it is as if he were signing his name as an author or as an artist'.[52] Equally, it can be argued that Lawrence had picked up on the conventional use of initials by journalists, reviewers and newspaper editors (such as G. K. Chesterton, A. G. Gardiner, T. P. O'Connor, C. P. Scott, H. W. Massingham, J. A. Spender and H. G. Wells). It afforded a more formal writerly identity than the full name and would therefore have been appropriate for newspaper opinion pages. In a romance context it gave Lawrence an androgynous identity, which would help to disorientate reviewers intent on discovering the sex of an author; it might also have attracted female readers to his work in the expectation that the author could be a woman.[53]

Lawrence needed to make his way as a professional writer by locating an opening in the literary field, but in doing so he realised that he would inevitably become a commodity within the very consumer culture that many of his writings would critique.[54] In the letter to Blanche of 13 May, Lawrence continues: 'I am learning quite diligently to play the fool consistently, so that at last I may hire myself out as a jester, a motley to tap folks on the head fairly smartly with a grotesque stick – like Shaw does.'[55] By sardonically aligning himself with Shaw, Lawrence registers their shared interest in socialist politics: at University College, Nottingham, Lawrence had recently become a founder member of its 'Society for the Study of Social Questions'. He remarks on Shaw's appeal to a popular audience by using comedy to make serious themes more palatable (Lawrence combines comedy with serious moral themes in the first draft of 'Laetitia', in which an inattentive minister errs while baptising Laetitia's illegitimate daughter[56]) and he shows an awareness of Shaw's success in making a profitable living out of his journalistic writing. Shaw could not find a publisher for his novel *Immaturity* (written in 1879 but not published until 1931), but by the late 1880s he had made himself, in the words of Max Beerbohm, 'the most brilliant and remarkable journalist in London'.[57] As Lawrence implies, Shaw was an astute self-publicist and a model from which he could '[learn] quite diligently'. By paying heed in 1908 to the careers of writers such as Chesterton and Shaw, at some level Lawrence may, very ambitiously, have been exploring the possibilities of pitching his career in a similar direction.

Lawrence's idea of writing 'drivelling short-stories' is also an unsurprising first step for the aspiring writer: syndication of serial fiction in the local press had taken off in the 1870s so that, at the turn of the century, print culture had the infrastructure in place to bypass London-based publications and support those produced regionally. The expanding publishing industry created an upsurge in the publication of the 'little magazine', which resulted in a greater demand for short fiction; the Newspaper Press Directory listed 2,531 magazines published in 1903 (four times more than in 1875).[58] Writers such as George Gissing supplemented the writing of novels with short stories, a form which proved to be much more profitable, although he dismissed them as mere 'pot-boilers'. In 1894 he advised his brother Algernon to concentrate on writing short fiction: 'A piece you might write in one morning is vastly more likely to sell than the results of six weeks' toil.'[59] Gissing had learnt this from bitter experience. In 1880, aged twenty-two, he had to pay Remington and Company £125 to bring out his first published novel, *Workers in the Dawn*. The estimated £20 advertising expenses were to be paid out of sales and Gissing was to receive two-thirds of any profits; yet two months after its publication Gissing had earned only sixteen shillings and by Christmas just forty-nine copies of the novel had been sold. He observed in 1892 that Rudyard Kipling, Hall Caine and J. M. Barrie had secured 'enormous reputations' and Mrs Humphry Ward had earned £18,000 from *David Grieve*. With the encouragement of the literary agent A. P. Watt, Gissing turned to writing short stories and in 1895 alone he wrote approximately one third of the total 111 stories he produced during his writing life. Authors' average annual incomes varied greatly: while Gissing earned £290 in 1896, H. G. Wells earned approximately £1,050.[60]

While Lawrence believed that he 'could do anything in that line', it was *how* to make his way that most concerned him and he wondered if there was a place for his work in the field: 'who wants me to – who would have 'em?' He would have to demonstrate his adaptability in order to stand the best chance of locating an opening and in the space of a few lines he considers writing a 'good novel', critical reviews, journalism and popular short stories (his ideal of writing poetry is notably absent from this money-orientated list). By May 1908 Lawrence had written the complete first draft of 'Laetitia', a novel with 'some exquisite passages'.[61] The writing of 'Laetitia' was a serious undertaking from the beginning: it has not previously been noted that in the fifty-eight surviving manuscript pages, drawn from an exercise book, Lawrence wrote on only one side of the page.[62] Due to the rise of authorship as a profession a number of guides were available to support amateur writers. *The Author's Printing and Publishing Assistant* (1839) advises that

> [t]here is another point of which Authors are frequently not aware – the necessity of their Manuscripts being written on one side only ... In the process of Printing, it may, if needful for speed or otherwise, be divided at any given point ... when a Manuscript is therefore about to be written or copied for the Press, it would be desirable to have prepared a Quarto Book, Ruled, with a narrow margin, and lines across, and to have it Paged beforehand, on the right hand page only, on which page only the Manuscript should be written.[63]

Lawrence knew about the conventions of preparing copy when he first began writing the novel in 1906. This practical method of composition allowed him to extract early draft pages and transfer them into later drafts.[64] By 1908 Lawrence had also written a notebook full of poems and out of these he had submitted 'Study' to the University College magazine *The Gong* in 1906, but it was rejected. He had composed four short stories: 'Ruby-Glass', 'The White Stocking', 'A Prelude' and 'The Vicar's Garden'. He had delivered his essay 'Art and the Individual' as a lecture to a group of friends with socialist sympathies at the Eastwood Debating Society at the home of Willie and Sallie Hopkin on 19 March 1908. As I explore in the next chapter, it may have been this piece of writing that he submitted to Chesterton in response to a debate the journalist had sparked in the pages of the *New Age*. It is significant that Lawrence experimented with an array of genres before Jessie submitted his poetry to Hueffer in summer 1909. Lawrence approached Chesterton in spring 1908 entirely independently of Jessie and he told Louie Burrows on 30 June 1909 that he would collaborate with her in writing short stories, which he would send to 'the publisher'.[65] He sent 'Goose Fair' to the London and Provincial Press Agency before 20 July 1909; an extant letter from Tom Hewart, the manager of the Agency, states that 'in our opinion your "Goose Fair" is good & we do not anticipate much difficulty in placing it' and requests from Lawrence a registration fee of five shillings (see Figure 1.1).[66] Conclusively, Lawrence was actively seeking publication opportunities before Jessie received Hueffer's reply to her letter in August 1909.

Collaborative Writing: Louie Burrows

Lawrence made a concerted effort to send short stories to publishers during summer 1909, but the project to get them into print was undertaken collaboratively with Louie. For several years he had considered her to be a competent writer and he fashioned himself as her literary advisor. In September 1906 he told her: 'You are brighter than Jessie, more readable, but you are not so powerful. You will doubtless succeed far better than I who am so wilful.' In December 1907 he told her that he could imagine her in later years 'in your study as you sit writing your newest novel'.[67] In September 1908 Louie was indeed working on a novel: Lawrence told her to 'get those chapters ship-shape . . . I shall look soon for that dainty bit of literature from you.' The following month Lawrence read her 'tale' and offered her a paragraph of advice on writing a short story: 'select the salient details – a few striking details to make a sudden swift impression'. Interestingly, given the addition of Annable to the second draft of 'Laetitia' at Easter 1908, her story includes a

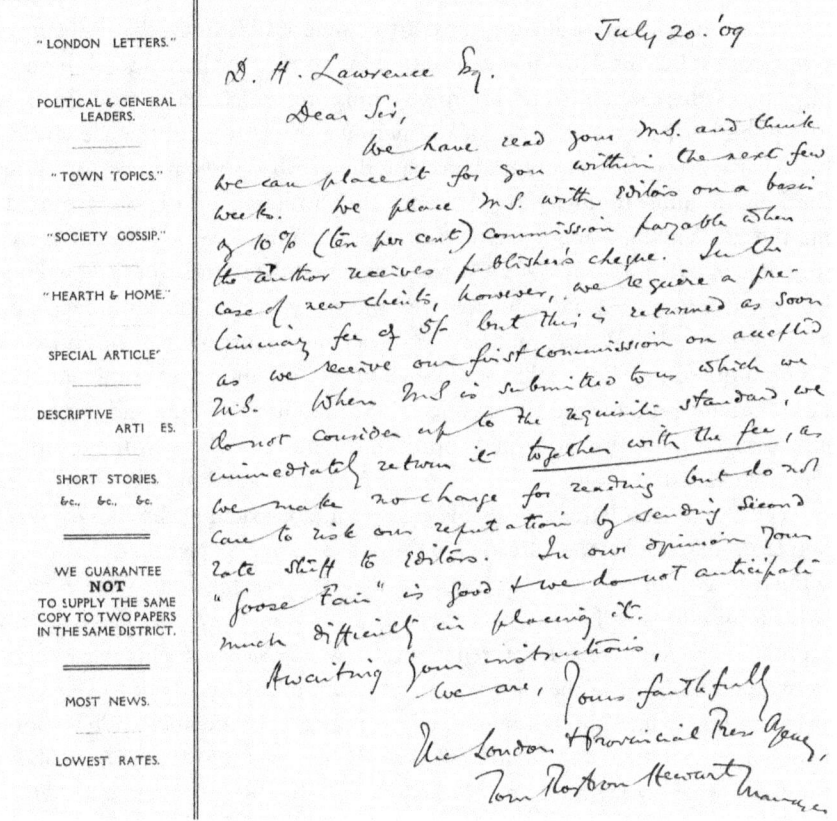

Figure 1.1 Letter to D. H. Lawrence from Tom Hewart, Manager, the London and Provincial Press Agency, dated 20 July 1909. University of Nottingham, Manuscripts and Special Collections, La B 186.

'young keeper'.[68] The following year Louie must have informed Lawrence of her ongoing writing, because on 30 June 1909 he replied to her:

> I am glad you are writing stories. I can't do 'em myself. Send me them, please, and I'll see if I can put a bit of surface on them and publish them for you. We'll collaborate, shall we? – I'm sure we should do well. At any rate send me the tales at once, and I'll send em to the publisher some time or other in your name.[69]

Lawrence initially subordinates himself to Louie by claiming that he cannot write stories, but his deference is qualified by his plea for her to send them to him so that he can add some improving finishing touches and send them to 'the publisher'. Lawrence's use of the definite article implies that he already had a particular publisher in mind: perhaps the pair had spoken in person about the London and Provincial Press Agency, but a reference to Lawrence sending the five shillings agency fee does not appear until their next extant correspondence, dated 26 July 1909. At an unspecified date prior to this Lawrence had written to the Agency and received the reply from them with details on how to proceed.[70] At this point Lawrence becomes more assertive: he answers his own question 'We'll collaborate, shall we?' with an urgent command that Louie should 'send me the tales at once'. The repetition of ''em' and the pointedly casual remark that he would approach the publisher 'some time or other' seem calculated to create an impression of informality and indifference.

Yet Lawrence's letter reveals his anxiety in approaching the literary marketplace: despite having already composed a range of writing, Lawrence wished to collaborate with his friend so that their submission to the Agency was a joint effort. As far back as September 1906 Louie's writing had helpfully represented a test-case for Lawrence which would safeguard his self-esteem; he would rather see Louie take a chance by submitting her work to *The Gong* than risk his own. Although he judged it to be 'a very mediocre publication', his next letter rather impatiently asks Louie: 'Do you know any more about the *Gong* – have you sat down yet to adorn it.'[71] In 1907, Lawrence had given himself the best chance of winning the *Nottinghamshire Guardian* Christmas writing competition by sending in three stories, two of which were entered in the names of Louie and Jessie. Lawrence entered the historical romance inspired 'Ruby-Glass' for the 'legend of some historic building' category. He asked the women to submit the more sentimental stories under female pseudonyms: Louie entered 'The White Stocking' for the 'amusing' category and Jessie entered 'A Prelude' as the tale of an 'enjoyable Christmas'.[72] When 'A Prelude' won the competition, Lawrence's first appearance in print on 7

December was publicly attributed to Jessie. Lawrence did not have a strong sense of ownership of his text and co-authorship was a beneficial strategy for exploring the possibilities of publication and testing out his abilities as a writer without exposing himself to personal rejection. His appropriation and adaptation of someone else's text would be behind the composition of 'The Saga of Siegmund' (later, *The Trespasser*) in April 1910, which was inspired by Helen Corke's tragic relationship with Herbert Macartney; she had recorded these memoirs in 'The Freshwater Diary' which she shared with Lawrence in early 1910. Other significant early collaborative enterprises included Lawrence adapting Jessie's notes on the manuscript of 'Paul Morel' in November 1911 and April 1912 and Frieda writing to Edward Garnett in November 1912 that she had added to it 'little female bits'.[73]

Louie acceded to Lawrence's request that she should share her stories with him, but his deep commitment to writing meant that he did more than 'put a bit of surface on them'. On 27 July 1909 he wrote to her: 'Here is your tale – you will not like it. But tell me what you think of it.' He had sent the money to the Agency and asked Louie to 'go whacks with me in that, if you like, and then we'll go whacks in the profits – when they come'. At the end of the letter he is still concerned about her response to his rewriting of the story: 'Don't let my tone in "Cupid and the Puppy" influence you – you write in your best sentimental vein.'[74] Paul Eggert has identified Lawrence's literary collaboration as first involving the role of:

> tidying up – that is to say, negotiating between the text of the author and that author's potential publisher and audience – he soon found that the negotiation came to involve himself as 'author' as well. He found that the very act of partially rewriting called up aspects of his own deeper interests: it allowed him to extend . . . his imagining into regions of thought and feeling with which he was unfamiliar.[75]

Eggert calls attention to the difficulties of defining the boundaries of authorship for Lawrence, stressing his sensitivity to the demands of the marketplace and his exploratory creativity. On 23 January 1910 Lawrence gave Louie lengthy advice about a third story, 'The Chimney Sweeper'; he likens her writing to the popular short story writer W. W. Jacobs and advises her to offer it to *The Guardian* and *The Strand*. There were at least three stories for which Louie supplied the original ideas but which Lawrence rewrote or gave her extensive advice about; all of these have been lost except 'Goose Fair', which was published under Lawrence's name in the February 1910 number of the *English Review*. We are therefore unable to speculate on the extent of Lawrence's rewriting, but he saw himself as (at least) a co-author of several of Louie's stories. On 16 October 1909 Lawrence writes to Louie: 'I return you the "Goose Fair" – you may as well keep it entirely. If I had it I should write it all out again, and vivify in places.'[76] Lawrence's 'polishing' of 'Goose Fair' gradually erased Louie's writing to the extent that he eventually claimed ownership of the story. Lawrence sent it to Hueffer on 11 December; Louie felt he had done so much work to it that he should publish it as his own. By 27 July 1909 he felt able to write 'I assure you, by the way, that my stories are most freezingly polite.'[77] Lawrence speaks of 'my stories' as if he is an experienced writer: gone is the evasive 'I can't do 'em myself.' By assuming responsibility for the rewriting and making an approach to the publisher, Lawrence makes himself an authority by claiming to know more about the intended readership and procedures of the marketplace than Louie. He had perhaps approached more publication outlets than any of his friends with writing interests and it is possible that Lawrence submitted work to other publishers or agencies at this time that he never told anyone about, or which memoirists forgot or overlooked. The instances we know of were not overwhelmingly successful: his submission to Chesterton was returned unread, *The Gong* rejected 'Study' and he considered 'Ruby-Glass' (which he submitted to the *Nottinghamshire Guardian* competition under the pseudonym 'Herbert Richards') to be a more likely winner than 'A Prelude'.

The approach to the Agency failed because of a dispute over the receipt of Lawrence's postal order covering the agency fee; this caused a delay before Lawrence angrily requested the return of 'Goose Fair'. It is surprising that Lawrence withdrew the story over so small a matter as the agency fee, given the positive tone of their letter to him and their confidence in being able to place the story. Something else was happening in the background. On 19 August 1909 he told Louie: 'I'm going to send my tales direct to the mags now: so let me have the Puppy, and I'll go through it and revise it and send it.'[78] Lawrence was pushing to get short stories into print in summer 1909, before he had contact with Hueffer at a date preceding his twenty-fourth birthday on 11 September. There is a known circumstance that could explain Lawrence's dismissal of the Agency. It was around this time (after Lawrence's return from the Isle of Wight on 14 August) that Jessie remembered giving him the reply from Hueffer stating that he would like to see Lawrence when he returned to London. She writes:

> When we were alone together I said:
> 'Oh, I've got a letter for you'.
> He looked at me quickly, then his eyes narrowed:
> 'From the *English*? About the poems? Show it me'.

I gave him the letter, and his face became tense.

'You are my luck', he murmured. Then he said with suppressed excitement, 'Let me take it to show mother'.[79]

Lawrence was at Haggs Farm on the evening of 17 August: in a letter to Louie dated 18 August Lawrence tells her that he 'went for Alan [Chambers]'s bike' the night before and got drenched 'at the top of Underwood hill'. He finishes the letter in French, telling Louie 'Please send me the Cupid tale. I'll send it to a "Mag".'[80] If Lawrence had seen Hueffer's letter that evening then the news could have prompted Lawrence's confident comment and his following letter declaring that he would send his work straight to the magazines. It may have led him to give up on the Agency more readily, to reserve his writing for more prestigious publication in a journal he revered. Curiously, in his 19 August letter Lawrence demonstrates his knowledge of 'a new Magazine coming out – should be out now – *The Tramp*'. *The Tramp: an Open Air Magazine*, was founded and edited by Douglas Goldring, who was then a twenty-two-year-old part-time assistant sub-editor for Hueffer's *English Review* and an editor of *Country Life* magazine. *The Tramp* (priced at 6d) did not commence publication until March 1910 and it only ran until March 1911. Contributors to its early numbers included Hueffer, Violet Hunt, Arnold Bennett, Edward Thomas, Arthur Ransome and Una Silberrad; it included articles on little-known places in Britain and abroad, articles on all subjects connected with travel, short stories, poetry and reviews. The March and April 1910 numbers of the *English Review* carried advertisements for *The Tramp*, but a specimen issue had been circulated in May 1909.

Lawrence may have seen the specimen issue and/or advance notice advertisements, but it is also possible that Hueffer had written that his friend was bringing out a new magazine which could present Lawrence with publication opportunities. A comment such as this would allow Hueffer to remain encouraging and yet pass Lawrence on to another editor if his work did not prove to be suitable for the *English Review*. Indeed, Jessie's report of the content of the letter makes it sound as if Hueffer was helpful but non-committal:

> It said, as nearly as I can remember, that the poems were very interesting and that the author had undoubted talent, but that nowadays luck played such a large part in a literary career, and continued, 'If you would get him to come and see me some time when he is in London perhaps something might be done.'[81]

Lawrence emphasised to Louie his anger about the failure of the Agency application: 'Are you cross? – well, so I am also. Devil take everything!' His support of Louie intensified, even if his tone became superior: 'For the Lord's sake, send me that draft of a novel, I bet it would amuse me. You know, your forte would be short stories – it will take you at least three years to write a novel – at school.'[82] It had taken Lawrence three years to draft 'Laetitia' and it now seemed to him that he would have more success in getting short stories published. The anger in his letter may be an authentic outburst if he had not yet seen Hueffer's letter; if he *had* seen the letter then it may be an exaggerated response which covers his embarrassment about having found success through a submission of his own work that Louie knew nothing about. Lawrence's next extant letter to her, dated *c*.11 September 1909, follows his first meeting with Hueffer. Firstly, he admits that he has 'never even written for the story from those people' at the Press Agency; he had had more exciting opportunities to pursue. He continues:

> The truth is, I am very much occupied with some work of my own. It is supposed to be a secret, but I guess I shall have to tell you. The editor of the *English Review* has accepted some of my Verses, and wants to put them into the *English Review*, the November issue.... The editor, Ford Madox Hueffer, says he will be glad to read any of the work I like to send him – which is a great relief, is it not? No more thieving agencies for us. Before I do anything with the Puppy tale, I want to write it out again, and I don't know when I shall have time to do that. I never thought of myself blossoming out as a poet – I had planted my beliefs in my prose.[83]

Lawrence felt awkward about his newfound success: he appeals for Louie's confidence so that she might forgive him for neglecting to mention Hueffer's letter and his attempt to get his own work published separately from hers. His repetition of the esteemed name of the *Review*, the mention of its editor and his appreciation of Lawrence's writing, the capitalisation of 'my Verses', the repetition of 'I' and 'my' and the assured comment about 'blossoming out' shows Lawrence's pride in having found such an opening – and with his poetry rather than prose. He implies that his opportunity may present an opening for Louie too ('No more thieving agencies for us'), but he also reminds her that he now has too much to do: 'I am very hard at work, slogging verse into form. I shall be glad when I have finished: then I may get on with the prose work.' Lawrence had finally been rewarded for his efforts and was eagerly writing more; Jessie writes that '[s]oon after the meeting with Hueffer, Lawrence ... had so much to tell me and to show me. He had written a play [*A Collier's Friday Night*], and there were poems.'[84] Hueffer had encouraged Lawrence to continue writing poetry: on 20 November Lawrence wrote that Hueffer 'says I ought to get out a volume of verse, so you see how busy I am'.[85] Over the next three months up to the end of 1909 Lawrence had revised 'Goose Fair' and sent it to Hueffer on 11 December along with a new story, 'Odour of Chrysanthemums'. He revised 'Laetitia', now entitled 'Nethermere' and submitted it to Hueffer before 20 November. Then he approached Heinemann on 15 December about its publication. During December he wrote short observational sketches based on his teaching career ('A Lesson on a Tortoise', 'Lessford's Rabbits' and 'Two Schools') and he may also have begun the short story which became 'A Modern Lover'.[86]

'He knows W B Yeats and all the Swells'

Lawrence's social calendar in these few months is remarkable. After his initial meeting with Hueffer at the *English Review* office around 11 September, Lawrence dined 'with celebrities', then again with 'two R.A.s'; he is then 'kept' by Hueffer and is late meeting his teaching colleague Agnes Holt, whom he was considering marrying.[87] On Sunday 14 November he had lunch with Hueffer and Hunt and then went to tea with Ernest and Grace Rhys, afterwards calling on H. G. Wells at Hampstead. On Tuesday 16 November Lawrence went to Hunt's '"at home" at the Reform Club in Adelphi Terrace, on the Embankment'. He met Elizabeth Martindale (Hueffer's wife, 'Elsie'), Ellaline Terriss (a well-known variety actress) and Mary Cholmondeley, author of the 1899 satirical novel *Red Pottage*. It was there that he also met the twenty-four-year-old Ezra Pound, who took him to supper at Pagnani's restaurant and back to his flat in Kensington. On Saturday 20 November Lawrence had tea with Pound and told Louie that they were 'going out after to some friends . . . He knows W B Yeats and all the Swells.'[88] On 21 November Lawrence began writing to Pound's American friend Grace Crawford; he sent an early version of his poem 'Song' to her on 23 December.[89] At 'the end of November' (probably the weekend of Saturday 27th) Jessie visited Lawrence; they went to the National Gallery and then to see Alfred Sutro's *Making a Gentleman* at the Garrick Theatre. The next day Lawrence took Jessie to meet Hueffer at his flat in Holland Park, then to dinner at Hunt's house in Kensington, where they all dined together with Hunt's mother Margaret Raine Hunt, herself a satirical novelist and the translator of a definitive 1884 edition of *Grimm's Household Tales*. Pound was there and so was Réné Byles, the manager of the publishing firm Alston Rivers which had published Hueffer's *The Fifth Queen* trilogy (1905–7).[90] On Saturday 11 December Lawrence dined with Pound again; they met a crowd of other literary folk and he stayed the night. The following week, possibly on Saturday 18 December, Lawrence had plans to go 'up to Grace Rhys to meet various poetry people. I am to take some of my unpublished verses to read.'[91] Hueffer, Hunt,

Pound and the Rhyses all introduced Lawrence to their literary contacts and these are just the social events that Lawrence documents in his extant letters. At the same time he kept abreast of productions at the London theatres. He visited the Lyceum in early September to see Justin McCarthy's *Proud Prince* (he found it to be 'such rot'), to the Grand Theatre, Croydon on Friday 15 October to watch The Royal Carl Rosa Theatre Company perform Wagner's *Tristan and Isolde* ('I would much rather have seen [John Galsworthy's] *Strife*') and on Saturday 30 October he enjoyed Rudolf Besier's comedy *Don* at the Haymarket.[92] He was holding down his first full-time teaching post and keeping in contact with his friends and family in Eastwood. He continued to advise Louie on her literary efforts, telling her how to arrange for a typist: 'look in any newspaper among the Authors, Agencies list in the adverts'.[93] On 22 December he felt 'as if I had not had a rest for years'.[94]

The young Lawrence, then, was keen to attain a literary career, but he was repeatedly reminded of the difficulties he would face along the way. He was eager to be viewed as the most able writer and as a literary authority among his circle of close friends. He developed a canny awareness of strategies that might help him to get into print (learning the correct preparation of manuscripts, practicing collaborative writing and locating potential authorial models) and he actively sought publication opportunities while writing in a variety of genres in readiness for exploiting different openings in the field. When he was given the opportunity to break into London literary society he took it with open arms. He produced work swiftly and in diverse genres in order to discover his strengths; between September 1909 and the end of the year Lawrence presented Hueffer with sentimental poetry such as the 'Baby Movements' sequence, new prose sketches with a schoolteacher narrator, the draft of a romantic novel and writing with working-class settings such as 'Goose Fair', 'Odour of Chrysanthemums' and *A Collier's Friday Night*. He ensured that he was present at the literary events which he was invited to attend so that he might become recognised as a member of an important literary circle and made use of the patronage bestowed on him by Hueffer and Hunt to find contacts with whom he could talk about his work. In this way he began to build up his knowledge of current trends in the field and sought to discover further publication opportunities.

Constructing an Amateur Literary Network: Manuscript Circulation

Considering in greater detail the early networks and audiences that Lawrence constructed enables us to perceive how he adapted so quickly and capably to his widening circles of readers. By 1908 Lawrence had intuitively begun to lay claim to the identity of 'author' by gathering around him a small group of fellow amateur writers and readers, to whom he offered (and from whom he received) support and mentorship. The circulation of manuscripts to a selected readership created a safe discursive space which anticipated the structure of literary networks and bolstered Lawrence's confidence in approaching the marketplace, where he would have much less control over the reception of his work. His chosen readers and supporters were largely female, although close male friends such as Alan Chambers, George Neville and Arthur McLeod also saw some of Lawrence's writing in its early stages (it was Chambers who had urged Lawrence to enter the *Nottinghamshire Guardian* competition and Lawrence asked McLeod to read a 1909 draft of 'Nethermere').[95] As evidenced in the series of letters from Lawrence to Blanche Jennings, by September 1908 Lawrence had sought opinions on the manuscript of 'Laetitia' from Jessie, Alice Dax, Blanche and Blanche's friend, 'J'; Worthen outlines the evidence that Lydia Lawrence (herself an occasional writer) was also a close reader of early drafts of the novel.[96] Willie Hopkin stated that '[w]hen [Lawrence] was writing *The White Peacock*, he and his mother criticised it together, and he rewrote parts of it until it satisfied them'.[97] Lawrence always wrote with an implied reader – or readers – clearly in view. Helen Corke's recollection of their discussions about writing in her 1933 autobiographical novel *Neutral Ground* (adapted from 'The Cornwall Writing' of 1911–12) includes a passage in which 'Ellis' (the Corke character) states that she 'only write[s] for myself'. The Lawrence figure, 'Derrick Hamilton' refutes this, as he believes that '[o]ne wouldn't write at all if one hadn't, though perhaps subconsciously, the presupposition of a reader. You can despise your public as much as you like, but to deny it is absurd.'[98] Corke's impression of Lawrence suggests that he conceived of writing as connected to a particular readership rather than as a solipsistic activity; she indicates that Lawrence was concerned with the essential requirement for the writer of locating a 'public' and satisfying at least some of its expectations. Yet he first had to find a way of perceiving who his readership might be and what they wanted to read, which is where his friends and acquaintances helpfully came in.

Lawrence's need for a reader to comment on each stage of the composition of his works indicates that he valued openness and sociability in literary practice, but it left him vulnerable to damaging criticism. The participation of others in his creativity was important for the progression of his writing but he retained a strong sense of his own literary values. The frank discussion of aspects of his work with individuals he considered might represent his ideal readership is key to understanding how he confronted the necessity of placing his work in front of critical mentors, editors, publishers and readers, but this challenges Worthen's assessment that Lawrence's writing was

> from the start intensely private, seen at most by one or two other people and never by his family; he was extremely reluctant to send it to magazines and very cautious about subjecting it to anyone else's criticism. The writing was difficult, dangerous and independent: [his practice of] painting was a social activity, involving and needing the approval of others.[99]

Although I agree that Lawrence was cautious about subjecting his work to criticism (often pre-emptively pointing out the flaws in his work before correspondents had read it), he repeatedly sought their responses. Lawrence introduces his novel to Blanche by dashing off a checklist of what he has learnt about the conventions of the middle-class romantic novel: 'all about love – and rhapsodies on spring scattered here and there – heroines galore – no plot – nine-tenths adjectives – every colour in the spectrum descanted upon – a poem or two – scraps of Latin and French – altogether a sloppy, spicy mess', but he is perhaps tired of the necessity to abide by these conventions rather than defeatist about his own writing abilities.[100] Although it is true that he only had a small circle of people with whom to share his work (he had not yet gained the remarkable networking opportunities that Hueffer, Hunt and their contacts in literary London would provide in autumn 1909), for him writing was nonetheless a social activity and one which was more intensive than his practice of painting with family and friends and giving his own copies of paintings as gifts. The sharing of his manuscripts, which involved Lawrence asking readers such as Jessie and Blanche for their opinion of his writing and which then sparked him either to revise or defend his work, is a more seriously collaborative imaginative practice than the sharing of a hobby or the reproduction of others' artworks.[101] Lawrence's school friend Mabel Thurlby recalled that even as a child Lawrence delighted in linguistic play and invited others to join in: 'One day he looked across the field and said, "'Everywhere is blue and gold'. Now you say a line".' Mabel records Lawrence's first poem, 'We sit in a lovely meadow', as being one he wrote for her at the age of around eleven, when he apparently commented: "When I grow up, I will write poetry like Miss Matthews reads to us.'[102] The circulation of manuscripts among Lawrence's circle of friends was a common practice; Jessie and Helen Corke swapped stories from 1910 and Blanche shared her stories with Alice Dax.[103] Arthur McLeod remembers that Lawrence 'soon persuaded' Agnes Mason to 'try her hand at little stories and sketches'.[104] The Head of Davidson Road School, Philip F. T. Smith, recalled that Lawrence 'amplified and edited' a number of his pupils' short articles in order to submit them for publication to one of the numerous 'small periodicals designed to make some appeal to boys . . . Several were accepted.'[105] When his confidence was boosted after he met Hueffer in September 1909 and publication opportunities were imminent, Lawrence involved further women in his creative process, asking them to produce fair copies of his manuscripts to send to publishers. Manuscript evidence shows that Louie copied 'Goose Fair' and 'Odour of Chrysanthemums' in winter 1909 and Agnes Holt copied several poems into Lawrence's poetry notebook, including those that were published in the *English Review* in November 1909.[106] During that month she also copied seventy-six pages of 'Nethermere'. Agnes Mason, Corke and a further unidentified scribe also copied out sections of the manuscript between autumn 1909 and February–April 1910.[107]

Before Lawrence began his college course in 1906 Jessie was the only person he knew who was as well-read as himself; he told her that 'Lots of the things we say, the things you say, would go ever so well into a book.'[108] Jessie states that Lawrence told her: 'Every bit I do is for you . . . Whenever I've done a fresh bit I think to myself: "What will she think to this?"'[109] Jessie's account suggests that Lawrence placed her in a maternal role, a position which is perhaps an extension of the involvement Lydia had in her son's early writing practice. Jessie reports that, on the publication of *The White Peacock*, Lawrence wrote to her that he was 'its creator, you its nurse'.[110] She implies that her role was to 'nurse' his creativity, but her notes on Lawrence's response to William Blake in February 1906 suggest that Lawrence thought of their relationship as reciprocal and mutually nurturing:

> he talked to me in his rapt way about Blake, telling me what a wonderful man he was, quite poor, who taught himself everything he knew . . . He told me that Blake's wife was a poor girl whom he taught to read, and also to print and engrave, and what a marvelous helpmate she was to him.[111]

Jessie indicates that Lawrence saw her as occupying a role akin to Blake's wife, as a female educated by her partner to serve as an industrious 'helpmate'. Lawrence appreciated Blake's humble background and identified with his autodidactic instinct, as well as his compulsion to educate others and urge them into artistic companionship. Authors sharing the weight of creative endeavour was common: June Steffenson Hagen describes Tennyson's pre-publication anxiety about his work and his method of reaching out to carefully selected readers for critical responses and reassurance. For Tennyson, even as an established poet publishing *Poems* in 1842, the usual pattern followed that

> (1) his friends heard him read the poems; (2) his publisher produced a trial edition so the poet could see the poems in print and spend the next year

or so tinkering with them; (3) [his wife] Emily read the poems and called them good; (4) the poems were published.[112]

This augments the ideology of creation, which endows the author with the ultimate say about the value of the work. The initial circulation of manuscripts to a trusted private audience is a way in which writers create the authority by which they feel authorised. Once the text has been privately evaluated by a familiar reader and revised the author feels better prepared to negotiate the complex mechanisms of the marketplace. The text will then circulate among (and be altered by) a publisher's reader, an editor, a publisher, a printer's reader and a printer; its reception (and the author's reputation) will be affected by booksellers, libraries, reviewers and a wider readership.

Lawrence and the 'Woman Reader'

Lawrence placed each of his chosen female readers in various roles according to his requirements, yet this is not to suggest that such an arrangement was consciously designed or systematic. Extant letters to Louie and Blanche and Jessie's descriptions in her memoir suggest that he related to these women in different ways by the invention of personae. Lawrence mocks his carefully fashioned epistolary performances in a letter to Louie dated 29 December 1910:

> I wish you'd tell me which of my epistolary styles you prefer: the gay, the mocking, the ironic, the sad, the despairing, the elevated, the high romantic, the didactic, the emphatic, the bullying, the passionate, the disgraceful or the naïve, so that I can be consistent.[113]

It demonstrates his overwhelming concern with how the style and content of his writing is received by its reader – even in a letter. While Louie was treated as a peer with similar literary aspirations, Jessie was cast in a supportive maternal role and Lawrence tested out his refined narrative voice on Blanche, the ideal reader of 'Laetitia'.

Lawrence's letters to Blanche, the first of which dates from April 1908, show him honing his prose style for the young, middle-class female reader: he performs the role of an affected 'literary' young man through his linguistic playfulness, mischievously provocative comments and wide-ranging cultural references. This is a style appropriate for self-important characters like Cyril Beardsall in 'Laetitia' and *The White Peacock*, Cyril Mersham in 'The Virtuous' (written between late December 1909 and spring 1910 and later revised as 'A Modern Lover') and Bernard Coutts in 'Intimacy' (written *c.* April 1911 and published as 'The Witch à la Mode'). In his first letter to Blanche, Lawrence tells her 'I am not accustomed to writing to women of your class.'[114] Yet Jennings had not enjoyed a comfortable middle-class background: her father had been a master mariner who died in an accident at sea in 1895 when Blanche was fourteen, leaving the family in financial difficulty. After leaving elementary school she worked as a Post Office clerk in Liverpool where she met Alice Dax; both women were socialists and supporters of the suffrage movement.[115] The purpose of his letter is to ask Blanche 'to read and criticise some writing of mine that purports to be a novel' since he believes that she would

> make a really good judge of it on the emotional side . . . I would not ask you to criticise it so much as a work of art – by that, I mean applying to it the tests of artistic principles, and such-like jargon – don't smile too soon, my head is not very swelled, I assure you;– but I would like you to tell me frankly whether it is bright, entertaining, convincing – or the reverse.[116]

By charily asking Blanche to judge the 'emotional side' of his manuscript, Lawrence appears to have assimilated notional stereotypes of the female reader constructed through Victorian medical, physiological, social and educational discourses. Kate Flint has examined the writings of a broad range of social commentators on the subject of the 'Woman Reader' from 1837 to 1914 and observes a general consensus:

> If woman's 'natural', biological function is presumed to be that of childbearing and rearing, of the inculcation of moral beliefs along with physical nurturing, with the ensuing presumption that she is thus especially constructed by nature so as to have a close, intuitive relationship with her offspring, then such instincts as sympathetic imagination, and a ready capacity to identify with the experience of others, are unalterable facts about her mental operations, and hence, by extension, about her processes of reading.[117]

Blanche pressed Lawrence to send 'Laetitia' to a male reader, but Lawrence refused and responded 'I told you most men had only about four strings to their souls; my friends are such. I talk to them about intellectual things, sex matters, and frivolities, never about anything I care deeply for.'[118] In this backhanded compliment Lawrence constructs male/female, intellectual/emotional binary categories: women will suffer emotional 'rot', as he puts it, so Blanche's task is not to critically analyse the manuscript, but to assess its entertainment value and capacity to move the reader.

Although Lawrence's ideas about the young, middle-class female reader were formed by the available discourses prevalent at the time, he was aware of the prescriptive constraints placed upon female readers. Jessie recalls Lawrence's apology after he sent her Maupassant's *Tales* to read in translation, 'telling me to take care my mother didn't see them'. She continues, 'a few days later came a note full of remorse: "What am I doing to you? . . . You mustn't allow yourself to be hurt by Maupassant or by me".'[119] In November 1911 he told Louie of his concern about sending foreign poetry to her family home, fearing her parents' disapproval: 'I really hesitate to send the *Belgian Poetry* into Coteshael.'[120] Significantly, in a letter to Blanche in May 1908 Lawrence offered a strong statement of his views on women's reading matter in response to Blanche having told him about a man's attitude towards her literary tastes:

> Don't let that little fool shove a lot of mental rubbish on you. Systematic reading be damned! You might as well say 'proteids one week, carbohydrates next, then hydrocarbons.' I find that by reading what I feel I want to read, I get the most benefit. Then my soul keeps bonny and healthy. So if you feel like going for something wildly emotional, like *Jane Eyre*, or Balzac, or *Manon Lescaut*, you *have* it, and don't let that pragmatical ass shove shredded wheat down you when you want the red apples of feeling.[121]

Lawrence departs from doctrinaire views that prescribe what women should read to shape their minds as morally upstanding mothers and wives in favour of having them read according to their immediate desires. The health-giving qualities of literature are foregrounded here, alongside the notion of texts as (quite literally) 'consumer' products that are read for leisure. When Lawrence recommended reading matter for his female friends he often encouraged them to read against the grain of convention. In November 1908 he ordered Balzac's *Eugénie Grandet* for Blanche, and a month later advised her to 'get a few more vols of him from Everyman. Begin with *Old Goriot* – then try the *Asses Skin* – then *Atheists Mass* . . . the Walter Scott people publish a fine collection of Balzac's short stories for 1/–'.[122] Lawrence chose to test the boundaries of acceptability in his work as early as 'Laetitia' on the understanding that women's reading matter should not be delimited. As Worthen observes, 'the situation of its heroine Lettie: left pregnant by Leslie, marrying George and giving birth to Leslie's child . . . was an interesting scenario for the first novel by a young man with a strictly religious upbringing'.[123] There is a sense in which, by advising them to read works by contentious writers, Lawrence was preparing women readers to receive his own challenging writing ('[y]ou mustn't allow yourself to be hurt by Maupassant or by me'). Again, this was not a conscious strategy;

Lawrence's writing was shaped by his reading and as a teacher he instinctively shared both with those closest to him. To some extent though, Lawrence may have intuited that his chosen readers were more likely to understand and accept his work if they shared his literary values; by suggesting that they read the books that he considered to be the 'right' ones, he was naturally attempting to shape their ideals.

Lawrence's initial expectations of Blanche's personality (formed by his attitude to her class status) are off key, as she soon prompts him to realise. His switches of code from the precocious, self-aggrandising and assertive to the self-effacing and apologetic reveal how uncertain he was in addressing her and by extension how tentative he was in attempting to adopt the right tone with which to address a middle-class readership. He couches this uncertainty as the effrontery of the aspiring aesthete, whose impudence Blanche is expected to check. While he initially wanted to ward off criticism by presenting himself as young and inexperienced, as the letters progressed Lawrence attempted to goad Blanche into critical response. It is as if he both did, and did not, want to be challenged – or as if he wished to be challenged on his own terms. Lawrence saw Blanche as a free-thinking, wide-reading, socialist and suffragist woman whom he considered the ideal reader of the second version of 'Laetitia', which gradually departed from sentimental melodrama to explore repressed desire and romantic failure. Since he had only met Blanche on one occasion, 'probably after a Nottingham rally in favour of the Woman's Cause', he considered her more likely than Jessie to offer honest and detached criticism of his writing.[124] He sought Blanche's help as an amateur literary advisor in the knowledge that she wrote her own stories (one of which, 'Victorine Cow', was read to him by Alice Dax).[125] Blanche was urged to make notes on 'Laetitia' and encourage him:

> I have pretty well decided to give up study; and to comfort my poor soap-bubble of a soul with writing . . . Now do you play the noble heroine of romance, and send me forth into the mythical fields of literature wearing your badge.[126]

If Jessie was the caregiving 'nurse' of Lawrence and his work and Louie the collaborator, Blanche was the ideal reader, finally fashioned as a romantic 'heroine' who would respond to playful missives with sparring repartee.

In October 1908 he asked Blanche about the new version of 'Art and the Individual: A Paper for Socialists': 'do you think I could do anything with it? Where could I send short stories such as I write? not to any magazine I know of – can you advise me.'[127] Having examined Lawrence's interest in finding an appropriate readership for his work, I next consider how Lawrence tailored 'Art and the Individual' to an Eastwood audience who were readers of the *New Age*. As this chapter has established, Lawrence was keen to enter the literary marketplace in 1908 and there is some evidence that it was the rewritten version of this paper (newly subtitled 'A Paper for Socialists') that Lawrence submitted to G. K. Chesterton in the spring of that year.

Notes

1. D. H. Lawrence, 'Getting On', *LEA*, 25–32; 31. Jessie's memoir *D. H. Lawrence: A Personal Record* (1935) is the primary biographical source for the early years and has been instrumental in forming the narrative of the launching of his career. Harry T. Moore was indebted to it: see *The Intelligent Heart: The Story of D. H. Lawrence* (1955), pp. 86–7 and compare E. T. 159.
2. *LEA*, 33–40 (38); 175–81 (177–8).
3. *L*, II, 471.
4. *LEA*, 179.
5. Bourdieu, *The Field of Cultural Production*, pp. 164–5.
6. Richard Salmon, *The Formation of the Victorian Literary Profession* (2013), p. 213.
7. Jonathan Freedman, *Professions of Taste: Henry James, British Aestheticism and Commodity Culture* (1990), p. 57.
8. Salmon, *The Formation of the Victorian Literary Profession*, p. 6.
9. Nehls, I, 83.
10. Quoted in *EY*, 51.
11. E. T. 168; 176.
12. Bourdieu, *Distinction: A Social Critique of the Judgement of Taste* (1984), p. 31.
13. E. T. 172.
14. Ford, *Portraits from Life*, pp. 70–89.
15. McDonald, *Literary Culture and Publishing Practice*, p. 17.
16. Ibid., p. 17.
17. Jonathan Rose, *The Intellectual Life of the British Working Classes* (2010), p. 404.
18. Ibid., pp. 132–3.
19. John Worthen, *Experiments: Lectures on Lawrence* (2012), pp. 40–63.
20. Rose, *The Intellectual Life of the British Working Classes*, pp. 414–17. Jessie recalls Lawrence reading these authors: E. T. 91–123.
21. Rose, *The Intellectual Life of the British Working Classes*, p. 420.

22. E. T. 91–123.
23. *L*, I, 50.
24. On the dominance of circulating libraries such as Mudie's over the publishing industry, see Guinevere L. Griest, *Mudie's Circulating Library and the Victorian Novel* (1970), pp. 58–86.
25. *WP*, 330.
26. E. T. 56.
27. E. T. 57.
28. D. H. Lawrence, *Collected Poems* (1928) reproduced in *Poems*, I, Appendix 2, 651.
29. G. H. Neville, *A Memoir of D. H. Lawrence: The Betrayal* (1981), p. 188n.
30. A. David Moody, *Ezra Pound: Poet, A Portrait of the Man and his Work, I: The Young Genius 1885–1920* (2007), p. 102.
31. Neville, *A Memoir of D. H. Lawrence*, p. 41.
32. Nehls, III, 600.
33. Lawrence said to Jessie: 'Every great man – every man who achieves anything, I mean – is founded in some woman. Why shouldn't *you* be the woman I am founded in?' E. T. 59.
34. *EY*, 191.
35. E. T. 155.
36. *EY*, 190.
37. *L*, I, 148.
38. E. T. 156.
39. Ibid.
40. Ibid.
41. The newspaper was edited by A. G. Gardiner in 1902 who expanded its literary section. Chesterton left in 1913. See Ian Ker, *G. K. Chesterton: A Biography* (2011), especially Chapter 3. Lawrence approached the *Daily News* in 1911, possibly offering an account of his experience of witnessing 'a riot and a fire' following railway strikes in Lincoln (*L*, I, 297–9). In November 1911 he met the newspaper's literary editor R. A. Scott-James at Garnett's house, telling Louie 'I rather want to get him on my side' (*L*, I, 326).
42. *L*, I, 50.
43. *L*, I, 52–3.
44. Rose, *The Intellectual Life of the British Working Classes*, p. 418.
45. Enid Hopkin Hilton wrote that her father 'always carried in his pocket the *Oxford Book of English Verse*'. *A Nottinghamshire Childhood with D. H. Lawrence* (1993), x. Jessie recalled Lawrence carried Palgrave's *The Golden Treasury of the Best Songs and Lyrical Poems in the English Language* in his pocket: E. T. 99.

46. Inwood's mother was Lydia's sister, Emma. His father was a compositor in London. His obituary details his journalistic achievements: Anon., 'Mr Alfred Inwood' (1951): 7.
47. See article written by 'a correspondent', Ewart George, 'The Day D. H. Lawrence came for Advice' (1963): 14.
48. Ford, *Return to Yesterday* (1931), p. 239.
49. Nehls, I, 71.
50. Patrick Collier, *Modernism on Fleet Street* (2006), p. 18; 13.
51. John Carey, *The Intellectuals and the Masses* (1992), p. 153.
52. *EY*, 135. Lawrence's earliest surviving correspondence is a postcard written to Lettice Berry (step-daughter of his maternal aunt), postmarked 6 August 1903. John Worthen and Andrew Harrison, 'Further Letters of D. H. Lawrence', p. 7.
53. Edwardian female writers who initialised their signatures include C. E. Raimond, D. K. Broster and E. H. Young. Ernest Collings and a reviewer of *The White Peacock* speculated that Lawrence was female: *L*, I, 471; Draper, 36.
54. Such writings include Annable's appearance in the second draft of 'Laetitia'; Annable unsettles middle-class readers and their uncritical consumption of 'culture'. Annable feels manipulated by his aristocratic former wife Lady Crystabel who 'began to get souly. A poet got hold of her, and she began to affect Burne-Jones – or Waterhouse' (*WP*, 150–1).
55. *L*, I, 53.
56. *WP*, 337–8.
57. Michael Holroyd, *Bernard Shaw, Vol. I: 1856–98: The Search for Love* (1988), p. 104.
58. Peter Keating, *The Haunted Study: A Social History of the English Novel, 1875–1914* (1989), p. 34.
59. George Gissing, quoted by John Halperin in *Gissing: A Life in Books* (1982), p. 193; 214.
60. Halperin, *Gissing: A Life in Books*, pp. 38–41; 174; 223; 237.
61. *L*, I, 53.
62. My thanks are due to Dean Smith at the Bancroft Library, University of California, Berkeley for checking the manuscript fragments of 'Laetitia' and confirming that Lawrence's handwriting appears on only one side of the page. There are forty-eight extant pages of the first version of 'Laetitia' and ten pages of the second version; these are published in an appendix to *WP*.
63. Frederic Saunders, *The Author's Printing and Publishing Assistant* (1839), pp. 21–2.

64. A. R. Atkins demonstrates that Lawrence inserted pages from the second version of 'Laetitia' into the final manuscript in 'A Bibliographical Analysis of the Manuscript of D. H. Lawrence's *The White Peacock*' (1991): 352.
65. *L*, I, 131.
66. Ibid.
67. *L*, I, 30; 42.
68. *L*, I, 74; 78.
69. *L*, I, 130–1.
70. *L*, I, 131; 132.
71. *L*, I, 31; 32.
72. *EY*, 190.
73. *L*, I, 479.
74. *L*, I, 132–3.
75. Paul Eggert, 'D. H. Lawrence and Literary Collaboration', (1988): 159.
76. *L*, I, 140.
77. *L*, I, 133.
78. *L*, I, 136.
79. E. T. 158–9.
80. *L*, I, 135.
81. E. T. 158.
82. *L*, I, 136.
83. *L*, I, 138.
84. E. T. 164.
85. *L*, I, 144.
86. See *L*, I, 147; 144; 148 and Paul Poplawski, *The Works of D. H. Lawrence: A Chronological Checklist* (1995), p. 4.
87. *L*, I, 138–9; 140.
88. *L*, I, 144–5.
89. *L*, I, 145; 150.
90. E. T. 165–73.
91. *L*, I, 147.
92. *L*, I, 138; 140; 141.
93. *L*, I, 139.
94. *L*, I, 149.
95. *L*, I, 38; Nehls, I, 91.
96. *EY*, 128–9; 141–3.
97. Nehls, I, 72.
98. Helen Corke, *Neutral Ground* (1933), p. 262.
99. *EY*, 134.

100. *L*, I, 44.
101. See *EY*, 132–4 on Lawrence's presentation of his artwork to friends and family as gifts.
102. Worthen dates this poem to spring 1897 (*EY*, 479); Nehls, I, 29–32.
103. George Zytaruk, 'The Collected Letters of Jessie Chambers' (1979), 10–11; *L*, I, 58.
104. Nehls, I, 90.
105. Nehls, I, 87.
106. *PO*, xlvi.
107. *WP*, xxvi–xxvii.
108. E. T. 57.
109. E. T. 116.
110. E. T. 189.
111. E. T. 62–3.
112. June Steffenson Hagen, *Tennyson and His Publishers* (1979), pp. 124–5.
113. *L*, I, 217.
114. *L*, I, 45.
115. Kenneth and Miriam Allott, 'D. H. Lawrence and Blanche Jennings' (1960): 60.
116. *L*, I, 44.
117. Kate Flint, *The Woman Reader 1837–1914* (1993), p. 57.
118. *L*, I, 71.
119. E. T. 107.
120. *L*, I, 325.
121. *L*, I, 59.
122. *L*, I, 89; 98.
123. *EY*, 136.
124. Allott and Allott, 'D. H. Lawrence and Blanche Jennings', p. 58.
125. *L*, I, 58.
126. *L*, I, 85.
127. *L*, I, 81.

2

Lawrence and Socialism: 'Art and the Individual' (1908) and the *New Age*

I went through the lowest parts of Sneinton to Emily's house to dinner when she lived in Nottingham – it had a profound influence on me. 'It cannot be' – I said to myself 'that a pitiful, *omnipotent* Christ died *nineteen hundred* years ago to save these people from this and yet they are here.' Women, with child – so many are in that condition in the slums – bruised, drunk, with breasts half bare. . . . Men – some – seem to be born and ruthlessly destroyed; the bacteria are created and nurtured on Man, to this horrible suffering. Oh, for a God-idea I must have harmony – unity of design. Such design there may be for the race – but for the individual, the often wretched individual?[1]

Lawrence wrote this passage in a letter to the Reverend Robert Reid on 3 December 1907. It sets out the terms of his recent religious scepticism, which followed from his reading of the work of figures such as Charles Darwin, Herbert Spencer, Ernest Renan, J. M. Robertson, Robert Blatchford and Philip Vivian.[2] According to Jessie Chambers, from 1908 Lawrence began to read materialist philosophy 'in full blast with T. H. Huxley's *Man's Place in Nature*, Darwin's *Origin of Species*, and [Ernst] Haeckel's *Riddle of the Universe*'.[3] An English translation of Haeckel's book had been published in 1901 and it was advertised in the socialist weekly newspaper the *Clarion*, which was founded by the journalist Blatchford in 1891 after he had witnessed the conditions in Manchester slums. The *Clarion* had a wide circulation, selling 75,000 copies in 1903 and a number of clubs and societies were associated with it.[4] As Howard J. Booth observes, Haeckel's book was 'welcomed because it provided a physiological explanation for individuality; no longer was a religious conception of the soul needed'.[5] Lawrence's reading, along with his experience of slum conditions on the outskirts of Nottingham, made him question his religious beliefs and from 1907 he turned to discussion groups to explore topical socialist ideas.

A minute book in the George Lazarus collection at the University of Nottingham provides evidence that Lawrence was a founding member of the University College 'Society for the Study of Social Questions' in 1908. His signature appears on a list of four female and ten male members of the Society (see Figure 2.1).[6]

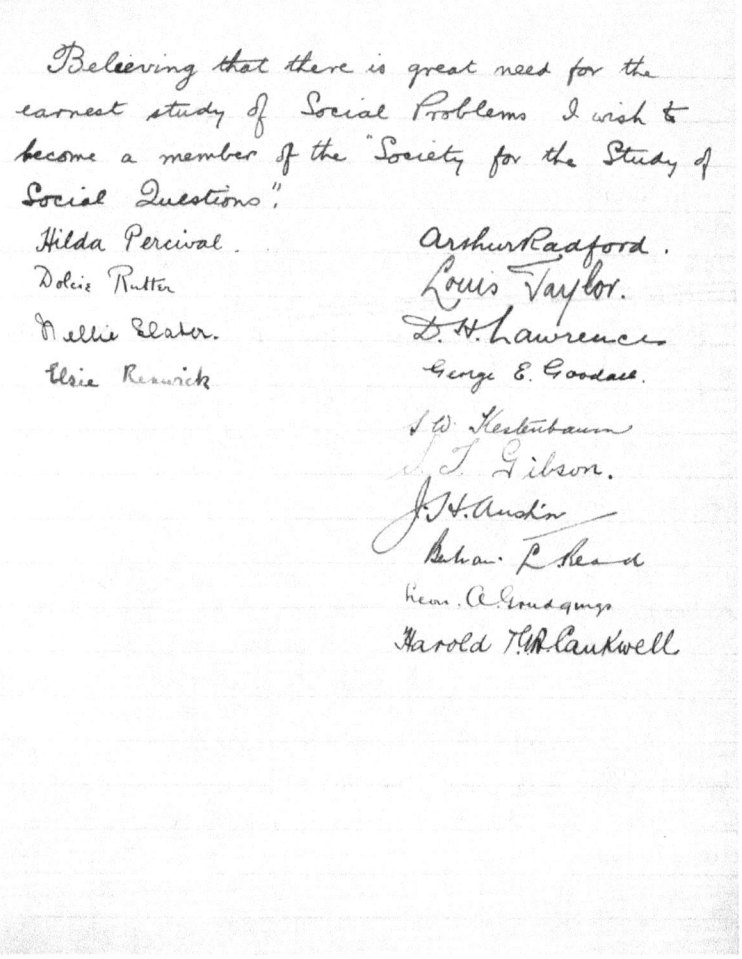

Figure 2.1 Central page of the minute book of the 'Society for the Study of Social Reform', University College, Nottingham, 1908, showing a list of signatories to the Society beneath the declaration 'Believing that there is great need for the earnest study of Social Problems I wish to become a member of the "Society for the Study of Social Questions".' University of Nottingham, Manuscripts and Special Collections, La Z 7/1.

Two of the female Society members (Nellie Slater and Dolcie Rutter) are later mentioned in Lawrence's letters, suggesting that Lawrence knew them well.[7] The handwritten minute book records the Committee's decision that meetings should be held 'on Tuesdays at 5pm' and that there should be 'a minimum of three meetings a term'; papers were to be given, 'limited to half an hour's duration, and succeeding speeches to five minutes'. In addition, members were invited to 'help in forming a catalogue of good books on social questions in the Central Library'.[8] The president of the Society was Ernest Alfred Smith, the lecturer popularly known as 'Botany' Smith and the staff member with whom Lawrence had a close relationship. Lawrence wrote to Smith on 5 December 1909: 'I owe you a debt. You were my first live teacher of philosophy.'[9] It could have been the activity surrounding the meetings that nurtured Lawrence's respect for Smith, whose inaugural lecture for the Society on 12 May 1908 'dealt with "University students and Social Reform", pointing out that University training was good training for the Study of Social Problems'.[10]

Worthen argues persuasively that the minute book 'stands as evidence for a predictable kind of behaviour in Lawrence during 1908. Socialism was an important intellectual staging post for him.'[11] The glimpses we are afforded into Lawrence's reading and social activity during his time at College enable us to contextualise the form and very topical content of 'Art and the Individual', the paper he delivered to a meeting of the Eastwood Debating Society held at the home of Willie and Sallie Hopkin on Thursday 19 March 1908. The minute book has entries for five meetings from February to June 1908, which would have been the University's spring term for the academic year 1907–8, so meetings occurred most frequently during the time that Lawrence was writing and revising 'Art and the Individual' (only two meetings are recorded for the autumn term of the next academic year, when Lawrence had finished his course). Little has been made about the fact that Lawrence was a founding member of an active College Society at a time when he was writing about socialism and when he was telling Blanche Jennings about the possibilities of undertaking a career in journalism and his need to write 'like Shaw'. Alongside the Eastwood Debating Society, the College Society would have played a significant role in developing Lawrence's general interest in socialism, and there is evidence that further organised discussions about issues related to philosophy and religion were held among friends and fellow students just prior to 1908. On 23 December 1907 Lawrence invited Louie to 'a discussion among ourselves on the ultimate questions of philosophy raised in the education class – a discussion of a "Universal Consciousness" for instance – the matter with which we left off last Wednesday'.[12] Emily Lawrence recalled that during 1908 Lawrence was involved with 'a psychological set at the University, who ridiculed religion'.[13]

Jessie's 17 April 1934 letter to Emile Delavenay records that the attendees at the meeting at which Lawrence delivered 'Art and the Individual' were the Hopkins, Alice and Willie Dax, Jessie and her brother and another couple 'whose names I don't remember'.[14] Blanche Jennings was not present at the meeting, but they became acquainted soon afterwards through Alice Dax. It was Blanche to whom Lawrence sent the second, heavily revised version of 'Art and the Individual', newly subtitled 'A Paper for Socialists', on 1 September 1908. He was anxious to receive her 'acknowledgement' of the new version, while vehemently defending himself against the attack on his political views waged by 'J', the friend of Blanche whom Lawrence had suggested might also read his paper.[15] Apart from the letters, 'Art and the Individual' is the first extant text we have in which Lawrence sets out his assessment of the role of the artist and the value of art and literature to society; it is the earliest record of Lawrence offering his work directly to an live audience. Since his audience was known to him, Lawrence knew that they, like he, were the type of audience that read A. R. Orage's left-wing weekly the *New Age*. Recalling the meetings of the Society, Jessie wrote that 'a Socialist and a Suffragette' (probably Willie and Sallie Hopkin, or Willie and Alice Dax) had initially introduced her and Lawrence to the publication.[16] It therefore makes sense that Lawrence paid close attention to the content and tone of the *New Age* while writing a paper to deliver to this audience. Questions about socialism and individualism were particularly topical in the periodical press at that time, as writers assimilated the legacies that a line of influential Victorian figures including Spencer, John Ruskin, Walter Pater, William Morris and Oscar Wilde had left on early twentieth-century thought. Lawrence's engagement with his audience and other writers was part of his self-fashioning as a young writer who was considering ways of breaking into journalism. When he revised the paper into 'Art and the Individual: A Paper for Socialists', he turned it into an essay for potential print publication.

Given this context we can legitimately speculate that Lawrence may have intended 'Art and the Individual: A Paper for Socialists' for publication in the *New Age*. It is clear from several of his editorials during 1907 and 1908 that Orage considered art to play an important role in the cultivation of the individual. G. K. Chesterton's articles on socialism sparked ongoing debate in the *New Age* in early 1908: his initial article, 'Why I Am Not a Socialist', was published in the 4 January 1908 number.[17] It has not previously been considered that 'Art and the Individual: A Paper for Socialists' could have been the essay that Lawrence sent to Chesterton for consideration in spring 1908. Examining the two 1908 versions of 'Art and the Individual', questioning why there are two versions and reconstructing the context of their production, allows us to gain an insight into the very beginning of Lawrence's self-fashioning as a writer long before he had any professional guidance.

'Art and the Individual' and 'Art and the Individual: A Paper for Socialists': Manuscript Versions

Not all the material aspects of Lawrence's manuscripts are reproducible in the Cambridge Edition, so reading from the manuscript provides revealing details about the nature of Lawrence's composition and revision and the manner of his delivery. The eight-page holograph manuscript of 'Art and the Individual' from which it is believed Lawrence gave his paper is extant.[18] In the absence of any evidence to the contrary, I accept Bruce Steele's conclusion that this is the manuscript from which Lawrence read at the Hopkins' house.[19] However, it is written fluently with only light revision, suggesting that he may have completed a prior version or a set of preparatory notes that were subsequently discarded: Lawrence's layers of revision to his work are well known, so it is unusual that this manuscript has so few alterations. He writes in black ink with a few pencil additions, on two bifolios of wide ruled, blue-lined University examination paper. The few pencil additions appear to be cues for the expansion of individual points upon oral delivery (e.g. 'Tolstoi + his simple art – his tales', '*suggestion', 'Emotion tends to issue in action – drawing etc'). Two examples of additions to the essay are made in pen ('& examples' and '<u>Introd. the idea of the fop</u>'); they are possibly later additions because the ink has bled onto the facing page, suggesting that Lawrence jotted them down before quickly turning the page. He may have worked on the essay in two intervals, as the manuscript from 'Flowers + insects have evolved side by side' onward is written in a lighter ink. The writing also becomes more cramped, with the final two pages being written on the verso of folios three and four, suggesting that Lawrence was running out of paper. The script was first published in Ada Lawrence and G. Stuart Gelder's *Young Lorenzo: Early Life of D. H. Lawrence* (1932).

The manuscript of the second version of 'Art and the Individual' (subtitled 'A Paper for Socialists'), which Lawrence sent to Blanche on 1 September 1908, had been revised and expanded between May and September to the extent that it constitutes a work very different from the first version. The manuscript itself,[20] along with six pages of a further holograph manuscript, described as 'comments for the expansion' of the second version,[21] are both now unlocated; they were formerly in the collection of John E. Baker, who must have purchased the manuscripts when they were auctioned at Sotheby's in December 1971. A photocopy of the second 'Art' manuscript survives in the archives of the Harry Ransom Humanities Research Centre, but the 'comments for expansion' remain elusive.[22] The photocopied manuscript consists of eight unlined foolscap pages. The first page bears the title 'Art and the Individual / A Paper for Socialists / D. H. Lawrence', and this title (unsigned) is repeated at the head of the second page. The writing is on rectos only, with the exception of a note reading 'Pardon me if I am a schoolteacher' on the verso of page three opposite the words 'Example number 2' on page four, and an appended note of seven lines on the verso of page six.[23] The pages show a neat and carefully written fair copy, which supports my argument that Lawrence wrote with publication in mind. On 9 October Lawrence wrote to Blanche: 'As for the paper, keep it as long as you like, give it to whom you like, and do you think I could do anything with it?'[24] 'Give it to whom you like' is an appeal for assistance very similar to the one he made to Jessie in June of the following year, which prompted her to take responsibility for the submission of his poems to Hueffer at the *English Review*. The whereabouts of the manuscript between Blanche's receipt of it and the 1971 Sotheby's auction is unknown. Lawrence sometimes left his manuscripts in the care of others who might keep them safe, such as his sister Ada, who preserved the first version of 'Art and the Individual'. The University of Liverpool purchased twenty autograph letters from Lawrence to Blanche from Miss Ellaline Jennings in 1960 and the manuscript of the second version of 'Art' was not with them, suggesting that Blanche may indeed have passed it on.[25] To clearly distinguish between the two different versions of 'Art', I refer to the first version, 'Art and the Individual'[26] as a 'lecture text' or 'paper' in order to emphasise the oral nature of its delivery, whereas 'Art and the Individual: A Paper for Socialists'[27] will be referred to as an 'essay', since it was sent to Blanche as a fair reading copy.

The Lecture in Literary Culture

From his youth Lawrence had been surrounded by venues that facilitated the exchange of ideas, such as the Eastwood branch of the Mechanics' Institution and the Women's Co-operative Guild (for which his mother was a secretary).[28] There was also the Congregational Chapel and its Literary Society, which was founded in 1899 by the Reverend Robert Reid; Willie Hopkin was for a time a leading contributor, and Lawrence was a member.[29] Lawrence would therefore have been familiar with the practice of giving papers and with the kind of local audience that might be in attendance. The papers delivered to the Literary Society ranged widely across disciplines, but the literary subjects included papers on Burns, Browning, early English drama, Tennyson and Longfellow; annual membership cost 1s, and there were 300–400 members.[30] This is a much larger membership than that of the Debating Society, which Hopkin organised in opposition to the Literary Society, but if Enid Hilton's account of her parents' connections is reliable then Lawrence could have met at their house significant political figures such as Ramsay MacDonald and Margaret Bondfield, theosophists such as Charlotte Despard, and reformers such as Edward Carpenter and Sylvia Pankhurst.[31] Pankhurst certainly travelled to the area: she was due to give a talk to University College students in the college theatre in late November 1907, but 'J. A. H. Green from the Nottingham University College Committee protested against the decision' and Pankhurst was forced to address the Nottingham Mechanics' Institution instead. According to numerous press reports there were 'WILD SCENES' when her platform was stormed.[32] Hopkin may have corresponded with Carpenter: he certainly knew Carpenter well enough by September 1915 for Lawrence to ask Hopkin to send on a subscription leaflet for the *Signature*, the journal Lawrence co-founded with Katherine Mansfield and John Middleton Murry.[33] Delavenay notes that Hopkin's name and address appear in Carpenter's address book at Sheffield Central Library (now in the Edward Carpenter Collection at Sheffield City Archives).[34]

The lecture is a significant aspect of nineteenth- and early twentieth-century literary culture that has been neglected by literary historians, who have tended to focus almost exclusively on the printed text (with the exception of Irish studies, which has addressed aspects of oral culture such as storytelling, folklore and dialect). In *Performing Authorship in the Nineteenth-Century Transatlantic Lecture Tour* (2014) Amanda Adams observes that there has been little critical attention paid to the British lecture as a distinctive genre in comparison to the American lecture system, and yet the lecture was an important cultural practice affording writers the opportunity to face their audiences and attain immediate feedback on their work while extending their public profile. There were of course many different types of 'lecture': the Literary Society and the Debating Society were institutions founded so that local voices could be heard and ideas discussed among the community, with perhaps the occasional visiting speaker. The lecture tour for the established writer, on the other hand, was promotional and offered an important source of income in lieu of published work. For the reader, seeing the author in person was a way of becoming more intimate with the individual behind the printed page, and it contributed to the view of the author as a celebrity. For the writer, image (particularly attire and voice) became of great importance in defining a persona and developing an oratorical style. Wilde and Matthew Arnold, for example, 'found themselves represented, reproduced, and impersonated far beyond their lecture tours'.[35] Geoff Dibb, who suggests that the exposure Wilde gained from his lectures led to his first journalistic commission for the *Pall Mall Gazette* in 1885, has explored the extent of Wilde's regional lecture tours throughout Britain and

Ireland at the beginning of his career.³⁶ Wilde's lectures took place in provincial halls and theatres, which was an indication that he hoped to appeal to a wide audience; for example, Wilde's evening lecture on his 'Personal Impressions of America' in the Nottingham Mechanics' Institution on Monday 17 December 1883 was recorded in the *Nottinghamshire Guardian* as having been 'crowded . . . in every part, platform included, with a good humoured and attentive audience'. Wilde appears to have put in a characterful performance; the reporter found him to be 'decidedly and emphatically a wag'.³⁷ The Nottingham Mechanics' Institute was a lively cultural centre; Dickens lectured there on 27 January 1852 and gave a reading on 4 February 1869, Wagner's *Tannhäuser* was performed on 27 January 1898, Ernest Shackleton lectured in November 1909 on his visit to the South Pole and Marie Corelli gave a lecture on 5 February 1915.³⁸ Announcements of forthcoming lectures and reviews and conversation among attendees following the event raised the author's profile and – as Wilde found – increased his column inches. As well as charging an entrance fee, the author could find an increase in sales of his/her published books and spark interest in future output.

Lawrence's contemporary Ezra Pound identified the opportunity to lecture in London early in 1909 at the Regent Street Polytechnic. Beginning on 21 January, Pound delivered a course of six weekly late afternoon lectures there on 'Developments of Literature in Southern Europe' and (from 11 October of the same year) a further course of twenty-one evening lectures on 'Medieval Literature'. The announcement of the first lecture series advertised Pound as an 'M.A. (sometime fellow in the University of Pennsylvania) author of "A Lume Spento", "A Quinzaine for this Yule", etc'; the fee for a single lecture was 1s 6d for the earlier course and 2s for the second, so lecturing served to bolster Pound's very meagre earnings from the publication of his poetry.³⁹ The announcement foregrounds Pound's academic background (with the implication that he is a visiting speaker) and his status as a published poet, in order to establish the young writer's claim to authority as a lecturer on literature. Lawrence used similar terms to describe his new friend to Louie on 20 November 1909: 'He is a well-known American poet – a good one . . . He is an American Master of Arts and a professor of the Provençal group of languages, and he lectures once a week on the minstrels [at] the London polytechnic.'⁴⁰ Reports about the size of the audience vary: while Pound claimed that there were fifty-five people at the first lecture, Noel Stock suggests that the audience numbered just twenty people, among whom was Dorothy Shakespear (who would marry Pound in 1914); she commented in 1965 that the lecture series was 'dismal' because Pound had a habit of overestimating his audience's intelligence.⁴¹ The lecture series was adapted for publication in book form and *The Spirit of Romance* was published by J. M. Dent in 1910, with the assistance of Ernest Rhys.⁴² Pound was advised of the potential financial and career-building opportunities that lecturing offered by his experienced elder patrons at the beginning of his career: he told his parents in October 1909 that 'Hueffer & Miss Hunt are trying to stir up the <u>very very</u> gilded to have me lecture privately'.⁴³ By early December, arrangements had been made for Pound to be a guest of the Poets' Club: on 20 December Pound gave a paper on the twelfth-century troubadour Arnaut Daniel, whom he would laud in *The Spirit of Romance*. More than sixty Club members attended and Joseph Campbell read Pound's 'Ballad of the Goodly Fere', which had been printed in the October 1909 number of the *English Review*. Pound had been elected an honorary member of the Poets' Club before the lecture and had four poems published in the Club's anthology for Christmas 1909, including 'Parcelsus in Excelsis', later published in his *Canzoni* (1911).

Lectures were popular cultural and social events, but they could also be strongly educational: by the 1860s, 'lecturing' had become a profession beyond University lecturing, and it was no longer only an activity carried out alongside one's full-time occupation. University teaching did, however, interest Lawrence. On 23 February 1912 he wrote to Arthur McLeod that he was intending to resign from his teaching post 'to go to Germany in early May . . . [for] perhaps a year or two'; supported by his Uncle Fritz Krenkow, he was (very ambitiously) considering the possibility of pursuing a 'Lektorship' in a German University.⁴⁴ The post of lektor did not necessarily mean a lectureship; a much more likely post for Lawrence would have been that of a foreign language assistant, but these posts were usually occupied by native speakers so the chance of securing such a post was very slim. Nevertheless Lawrence contacted Professor Ernest Weekley at the end of February 1912 and was invited to lunch on 3 March; Weekley had studied in Berne, Cambridge, Paris and Freiburg before taking up his post at University College Nottingham in 1898 and that same month he published an etymological work, *Romance of Words*.⁴⁵ As a trained teacher Lawrence would not have been daunted by the possibility of lecturing and such an opportunity might have offered him the chance to combine his teaching skills with his newly acquired experience of publishing.

Later in his career Lawrence considered lecturing as a way of reaching a potential audience and readership. In June 1915, he wrote to Lady Ottoline Morrell about a plan he and Bertrand Russell had envisaged to 'have a lecture hall in London in the autumn, and give lectures . . . also to have meetings, to establish a little society or body around a *religious belief that leads to action*'.⁴⁶ In September of that year, Lawrence had the idea of setting up the *Signature* to publish his essay 'The Crown'. Following the publication date of each number, there were to be meetings held at 12 Fisher Street, between Holborn and Bloomsbury, where subscribers would discuss ideas in relation to the crisis of the war; the Prospectus for the *Signature* announced that there would be 'a series of six papers on social and personal freedom'.[47] Although only three numbers made it into print before the journal ceased production, for a short time it was for Lawrence a serious endeavour: he wrote to Lady Cynthia Asquith 'we can unite in a bigger effort, a bigger paper, and Russell give his lectures, and we have good club meetings'.[48] Willie and Sallie Hopkin subscribed and Lawrence asked them to send a subscription leaflet to Jessie; he also asked Sallie to contact Alice Dax and he asked Dax to write to Blanche Jennings, to persuade them all to subscribe to the *Signature*.[49] His early experience of political and literary discussion groups may have set a precedent for these 1915 ventures. The examples of Wilde and Pound show how writers at the very beginning of their careers used the lecture for pragmatic, commercial and reputational purposes. More formal and 'educational' lectures enabled writers to distinguish themselves as authorities on literary or artistic matters: Wilde's very first lecture, entitled 'Modern Art Training', was to a specialist audience of Royal Academy students at their club on Golden Square, Westminster on 30 June 1883. William Morris was a frequent lecturer; he delivered his paper 'Art and Socialism', for example, to the Leicester Secular Society on 23 January 1884; the essay was first published as a 3d pamphlet later that year. Lawrence's 'Art and the Individual' covered similar themes; like Morris's and Wilde's lectures it was influenced by writers such as Ruskin and Pater on art and morality and the subjectivity of art.

The extent to which small, local discussion groups had the potential to inspire their members to expand ideas into writing projects is demonstrated by the case of the *New Age* (1907–22). This publication was edited by both A. R. Orage and Holbrook Jackson until January 1908 and originated as an artistic discussion group in Leeds. Orage (a schoolteacher) and Jackson (a clerk in the lace trade) first met at the Walker's Bookshop. Jackson wrote in 1907 that they 'turned quiet corners of local cafes into temporary forums, often extending the lunch-hour in a way quite heretical in Yorkshire'.[50] These meetings led to the founding of the Leeds Platonists in 1902 and the Leeds Art Club a year later, which was permeated by socialist ideas influenced by Carpenter and Shaw and by Nietzschean philosophy. Orage (followed later by Jackson) left Leeds for London in 1906 to establish the Fabian Arts Group. They received the considerable financial backing of £500 from Shaw, which was matched by merchant banker Lewis Wallace; Orage and Jackson were able to purchase the *New Age* in 1907. Shaw and Wallace (the latter under the pseudonym 'M. B. Oxon') contributed to the publication, with Shaw briefly taking over the editorship while Orage considered how to proceed in spring 1908 when Jackson stepped down from their joint editorship.[51] The case demonstrates how small-scale, local fora could escalate to become more widely publicised and how provincial energies reached the metropolis. At the peak of its circulation in 1908 when it was priced at 1d, the *New Age* had a readership of 22,000, although its circulation in other years more typically averaged 3–4,000.[52] The prominence of lecturing within literary culture is seen within the pages of the *New Age*, which printed advertisements for lectures by figures such as Shaw on 'Socialism and the Middle Classes' at the Westbourne Park 'Social Progress Society' on 25 February 1908; tickets cost up to 2s.[53] As Lawrence's plans for the *Signature* demonstrate, the process of giving a lecture, attending a club or organised meeting and writing for publication are seen as interrelated activities and he had identified this pattern as early as 1908.

'Art and the Individual' (Version I)

According to Jessie's account Lawrence delivered his paper to the Eastwood Debating Society in the self-conscious and stylised pose of the dandy: she recalls that he 'lay full length on the hearth rug to read to us, because he was shy'.[54] The casual posture seems deliberately performative (to offset his shyness), with a languorous stance being more fitting for a talk about aestheticism than the authoritatively upright stance of a teacher or politician. The note reminding himself to '*introd. the idea of the fop*' while arguing that art springs 'from sexual desire and propensity to play (Darwin, Schiller, Spencer)' seems to complement this pose; perhaps Lawrence had picked up on the *New Age*'s 'pervasive ... borrowings from Wilde', whose libertarian socialist essay 'The Soul of Man under Socialism' (1891) had greatly influenced Orage.[55] There is a mismatch between Lawrence's apparently casual style of delivery and the paper's lecture-style formality, in which he makes use of his pedagogic training and College textbooks and schematically tabulates German philosopher Johan Friedrich Herbart's 'classification of interests'. The clash of styles continues throughout the paper. Lawrence begins by invoking the purpose of the meetings: they are 'for discussing social problems with a view to advancing a more perfect social state and to our fitting ourselves to be perfect citizens – communists – what not. Is that it?' Lawrence appears unconcerned about seeking a coherent definition for the politics he discusses. By casually offering a provisional description of the group's political affiliations he attempts to provoke debate. Lawrence operates within the formal constraints of the lecture, of his educational materials and of the socialist ideas interesting to his small audience. He suggests that the 'immediate goal of education is to gain a wide sympathy . . . a *many sided interest*.[56] Man must be 'more refined, to understand the hosts of particular qualities which go to make up the human character, and are influences in the progress of things'. Such a statement would have appealed to individuals at the meeting such as the Hopkins, the Daxes and Jessie and Alan, all hard-working, aspirational members of the local community who valued education and were relatively well read. He also makes repeated reference to topical texts and a writer such as Tolstoy, whose book *What is Art?* (1897) he had read in Aylmer Maude's 1898 translation. Tolstoy's discussion covers issues such as what we mean when we talk about art and beauty and what constitutes art; for Tolstoy, art can be anything that communicates emotion and feelings between people, including jokes, home decoration and church services.[57] Tolstoy was a figure of great cultural significance at this time: H. W. Nevinson, a writer for the progressive Liberal weekly newspaper the *Nation*, began organising a 'Tolstoy Celebration' in March 1908, to be held in one of London's public meeting halls and advertised widely in the newspaper. By 19 March Nevinson had secured Shaw's participation in the Celebration, which was finally held in late September 1908; on 12 September Nevinson's article 'The Teaching of Tolstoy' appeared as a 'middle' in the newspaper, which immediately followed the political pages.[58] By discussing Tolstoy Lawrence was participating in a particular kind of topical, intellectual, middle-class and liberal cultural debate.

Since 'Aesthetisicm embraces all Art', Lawrence's definition of what art is encompasses 'socialistic essays . . . poet[ry], a painting, or a novel, or a play'.[59] Art has the capacity to 'convey the emotions of one man to his fellows', which is a 'form of sympathy'; sympathy in turn promotes 'harmony and unity' in which there is 'the idea of consistent purpose'. Art, for Lawrence, is socially beneficial, as well as developing the individual's emotional intelligence. He discusses the concept of 'Beauty' in 'Art', and questions why 'Beauty in Nature' is taken as a given when some of the more naturalistic 'human productions of Art' (such as the 'works of Poe, of Zola, de Maupassant, Maxim Gorky, Hood's "Song of the Shirt"') do not 'excite "pleasurable feeling" . . . Yet they are Art. Why? Somebody would say "They are so true".' Lawrence's answer is that these artistic productions express 'the real feelings of the artist. Something more, then, must be added to our idea of Art – it is the medium through which men express their deep, real feelings'.[60] Lawrence defends works that were commonly deemed ugly or indecent and he makes the case for artistic fidelity. He values medieval depictions of the Madonna for what they can teach us about extending our vision and sympathy: 'only a few can recognise the ideal, the noble emotion which many Mediaeval artists expressed so perfectly in their Madonnas . . . But with a little thought and study you might feel a sympathy grow up for those

Madonnas, and understand.' Lawrence considers that, while artistic production is a subjective expression of the individual, it should extend human experience and help those willing to learn to develop feelings in common; this promotes harmony and unity which are more broadly socially beneficial.

As well as being produced in relation to an inherited tradition of centuries of influential thought (he refers to writers including Dante, Burns and Carlyle), for Lawrence art provides the opportunity for self-expression and productive dialogue with others, which is what discussion groups such as the Debating Society meetings offered him at this time. Lawrence's wide range of reference shows that he conceived of his audience as peers and as having the ability to recognise these writers and their work, or that he wanted to impress them with his own breadth of knowledge (or both). On 30 July he commented to Jennings that '[w]e are not conventional. Our set is a bit astonishing. Mr Dax is quite shocked when he goes out with us – Mrs Dax also.'[61] Lawrence appears to have considered the elder Daxes slightly more conservative in thought than others in his advanced 'set'. The paper shows him inhabiting forms and ideas and addressing an audience with a mixture of authority and assertiveness in his argument but also uncertainty, as is seen in his deliberately poised, but rather formal and stiff delivery. He takes on the hybrid, non-specialist roles of the student of education and the aspiring intellectual with a social conscience.

'Art and the Individual: A Paper for Socialists'

The second version of 'Art and the Individual' is no longer a paper written for delivery at a local meeting but a more controlled and direct essay that immediately makes clear its topical source material. Lawrence opens the essay with the comment that

> This paragraph from a Socialist Member of Parliament is fairly well known: 'The present aim of socialists is to find work for the unemployed, food for the hungry, and clothes for the naked. After that it will make the conquest of the intellectual and artistic world.'[62]

Bruce Steele suggests that Lawrence may have been influenced in his comments by a three-part article series entitled 'The Restoration of Beauty to Life' by A. J. Penty, which was printed in the first three numbers of the *New Age* in May 1907.[63] Indeed, Lawrence directly invokes his own and his intended readerships' familiarity with the publication: 'We who are readers of the "New Age," also remember the critic's comment: "Men, women and children want food and raiment now; we also need our Beauty – in our streets, in our crafts, in our paintings".'.⁶⁴ Lawrence took this quotation from an unsigned review (possibly by Orage) of *Fifty Years of Modern Painting: Corot to Sargent* by J. E. Phythian, which appeared in the 8 August 1908 number of the *New Age*.⁶⁵ By referring to specific articles in the publication as if his readers would have intimate knowledge of them, Lawrence evidently writes with a *New Age* readership in mind. As his use throughout the article of the pronoun 'we' indicates, he affiliated himself with the publication and its readers and the content and argument of his essay is driven by what he understood to be the principles of the *New Age*.

Lawrence takes the position that the purpose of socialism is not merely to offer pragmatic material support to the poor, but principally to expose those willing to learn to art and culture, which was an idea that Orage himself proposed in the *New Age*. The 2 May 1907 unsigned editorial 'The Future of THE NEW AGE' defines socialism in Nietzschean terms as 'the will of Society to perfect itself', which recalls Lawrence in the first version of 'Art and the Individual' discussing 'social problems with a view to advancing a more perfect social state and to our fitting ourselves to be perfect citizens'.⁶⁶ The editorial discusses two versions of socialism, in which 'Socialism as a means to the intensification of man' is 'even more necessary than Socialism as a means to the abolition of economic poverty'.⁶⁷ As Anne Fernihough emphasises, however, 'Orage's distinction between the two socialisms was already a well-established one and would have been familiar to many of his readers': Robert Blatchford's socialist manifesto *Merrie England* (1895) had discussed the difference between 'ideal socialism' (securing liberty and spiritual growth) and 'practical socialism' (governmental reform focusing on economics and dealing with poverty).⁶⁸ Despite his 1907 letter to the Reverend Robert Reid with which this chapter opens, Lawrence's position in 'Art and the Individual' aligns with Orage's 'ideal socialism'; he had, after all, been a grammar school boy raised by an aspirational mother. Like William Morris, Orage was 'a romantic, arty socialist rather than a social engineer'.⁶⁹

Lawrence's discussion of education and Herbart is retained in the second version of 'Art and the Individual', perhaps because this sort of content was appropriate for the *New Age*. He declares that 'we' are not just readers of the *New Age*, but 'we are teachers'.⁷⁰ The main readership of the *New Age* shared Lawrence's class position – as had its editor. Before Orage became a journalist he qualified as a teacher and in 1893, aged twenty, he worked for the Leeds School Board at Chapel Allerton Elementary School on an annual salary of £80.⁷¹ The readership of the *New Age* comprised not just leading literary and political figures, but 'socialist autodidacts and left-leaning graduates of Mechanics Institutes, working men's colleges, teacher-training colleges, extension lecture programs, and provincial universities'.[72] As it had with audience members of the Eastwood Debating Society, the *New Age* 'chimed with the aspirations of thousands of individuals and small groups throughout the country who were uncommitted, progressive and for the most part young'; it extended the 'stimulus of an apparently classic weekly [such as the conservative *Spectator* and the literary *Athenaeum*] to a new, literate, but relatively unprivileged public'.[73] According to John Carswell, there were over 100,000 teachers in training by 1900, in contrast to less than 3,000 in 1870. The increase in educated young minds provided 'a public for progressive journalism on a scale never known before'.[74] Lawrence made a further addition to his essay with reference to an article from the *New Age*. In this instance, he took approximate quotations from F. S. Flint's review of a volume of prose poems entitled *The Great Companions* (1908) by Henry Bryan Binns, which had been printed in the 15 August 1908 number.[75] As well as making use of the materials he had to hand in order to support his writing, Lawrence may have been considering his essay to be appropriate for publication in the *New Age*, which accepted submissions from the general public as well as from well-known writers; its 'Letters to the Editor' columns were extensive. By referencing articles that had been printed in the *New Age* in August 1908, Lawrence was responding to the contemporary journalism and topical issues of the day and it is notable that the new additions he made to the text to transform it into an essay drew specifically and repeatedly on the *New Age* rather than any other publication. Lawrence appears to have been particularly interested in taking part in the sort of national discussion about socialism that was staged in *New Age*, which acted as a space for open dialogue on social questions.

The circulation figures for the *New Age* were so high during 1908 partly because of the debate about the purpose and aims of socialism following the 'Chesterbelloc controversy'. The similar political stances of Chesterton and Hillaire Belloc were humorously discussed by Shaw in the 15 February 1908 number of the *New Age* and in 1934 Chesterton reminisced that '[i]n the very first days of the *New Age*, Orage very generously allowed that monster, the Chester-Belloc, to roll . . . all over his paper in warfare with . . . Bernard Shaw and H. G. Wells'.[76] Lawrence is likely to have followed the debate sparked by Chesterton's article 'Why I Am Not a Socialist', published in the 4 January 1908 number, which was a response to an article by Arnold Bennett of November 1907 entitled 'Why I Am a Socialist'. Bennett had argued that the real intellectual thinkers belong to the party of 'progress', which is 'the left-wing of the Liberal party . . . For me, the political fighting of the immediate future will be a struggle to wrest England from the grasp of the "governing classes"'.[77] Chesterton, on the other hand, complained that, while he believed in democracy and certainly did not identify as a Tory, he considered socialists to be comprised of an idealistic 'handful of decorative artists, Oxford dons, journalists, and Countesses on the spree' who imposed themselves on 'the mass of the common people'.[78] Orage (and Lawrence, given the overarching message of 'Art and the Individual') would have been part of this group of idealists that Chesterton opposed. Articles in response to Chesterton by figures including Wells, Shaw and Filson Young appeared in the publication in subsequent months, in addition to regular correspondence by literary figures such as Florence Farr and many general readers including 'A Pedlar's Son'.[79]

Given the prominence of this ongoing 'controversy' it may be no coincidence that Lawrence contacted Chesterton at an unknown date during that spring. Jessie's memoir is the only record we have of his approach and she does not give Chesterton's name but refers to him as 'an author, whose weekly article in the *Daily News* we often read and discussed'.[80] A plausible speculation would be that the manuscript Lawrence sent was in relation to the *New Age* debate rather than in response to an article Chesterton had written for the *Daily News*. Given Lawrence's interest in socialism at this time and the evidence that he rewrote 'Art and the Individual', it could have been a version of the second 'Art' essay that he submitted. Newly subtitling the essay 'A Paper for Socialists' was perhaps a gesture that highlighted its appropriateness for the *New Age*. Although he first read it to a small audience, if the submission to Chesterton had been successful and if I am right in my speculation that he sent a manuscript in reaction to the *New Age* debate, then Lawrence's ideas could have been part of a much wider dialogue and the submission an even bolder move than an approach to the *Daily News*. Lawrence engaged deeply with the ethos and specific content of the *New Age* to address an audience who read and discussed the publication. He was feeling his way towards getting his writing into print. This early negotiation of the print marketplace, undertaken long before he received any guidance from 'professional' literary mentors such as Hueffer and Garnett, suggests that Lawrence had a canny aptitude for identifying strategies that would help him to achieve a literary career.

Notes

1. *L*, I, 40–1. Lawrence's sister Emily moved to Sneinton after marrying Sam King in 1904.
2. *L*, I, 36–7.
3. E. T. 112.
4. Raphael Samuel, 'British Marxist Historians, 1880–1980: Part I': 57; Martin Wright, 'Robert Blatchford, the Clarion Movement and the Crucial Years of British Socialism, 1891–1900', 74–99.

5. Howard J. Booth, '*The Rainbow*, British Marxist Criticism of the 1930s and colonialism' (2009), p. 36.
6. MS UN La Z 7/1. Prior to 14 February 1908 the society was entitled 'Society for the Study of Social Reform'. The notebook contains minutes for meetings held in 1908 on 11, 14, 18 February, 12 May (sixteen members present), 13 June (eighteen members present to hear Miss Stewart lecture on 'Women + Economics'), 13 October (Principal Symes lectured on 'courses of study and methods' for the Society) and 17 October (to 'study Rowntree's "Poverty" and Symes' "Political Economy"'). In 1909 meetings were held on 30 January (Mr B. L. Read discussed 'Co-operation'), 6 February (Miss Crooks gave a paper on 'Housing') and 13 February (on 'Political Economy').
7. Lawrence enquires about 'Nell Slater' in September 1911 and Louie tells him that 'Miss Rutter' is thinking of becoming a writer (*L*, I, 301; 306).
8. Minute book entry for 14 February 1908.
9. *L*, I, 147.
10. On Smith, see E. T. 76. See also Minute book entry for 12 May 1908.
11. John Worthen, 'D. H. Lawrence and the Society for the Study of Social Questions' (1994): 365.
12. *L*, I, 42.
13. *EY*, 178.
14. However, the *Eastwood and Kimberley Advertiser* reported that 'A highly interesting paper on "Art and the Individual" was read before the members of the society on March 19, when the attendance reached its maximum since the formation of the society' (27 March 1908, p. 2). Either the society had a small membership or Jessie's recollection is inaccurate (she was incorrect about the year in which Lawrence read his paper, insisting that it was 1909). 'The Collected Letters of Jessie Chambers': 82.
15. *L*, I, 80.
16. E. T. 120.
17. G. K. Chesterton, 'Why I Am Not a Socialist' (1908): 189–90.
18. Roberts E24.3c.
19. *STH*, xlii and 222.
20. Roberts E24.3a.
21. Roberts E24.3b.
22. Steele used a photocopy of the autograph manuscript as base-text for the Cambridge Edition, but never had sight of E24.3b (personal correspondence, 5 March 2015). See also 'Note on the texts', *STH*, 130.
23. *cf.* Lawrence's letter to Blanche, which accompanied the manuscript: 'I send you the long promised paper on Art. Don't let the tone offend you; I confess I am a schoolteacher' (*L*, I, 72).

24. *L*, I, 81.
25. 'The D. H. Lawrence Letter Collection', MS University of Liverpool Library Special Collections and Archives, GB 141 MS.2.88 (1-20).
26. Roberts E24.3c.
27. Roberts E24.3a.
28. Nehls, I, 13.
29. E. T. 92–3.
30. *L*, I, 3–4.
31. See Emile Delavenay's 'Foreword' to Enid Hopkin Hilton, *A Nottinghamshire Childhood with D. H. Lawrence*.
32. Anon., 'The University College Difference' (1907): 6; Anon., 'SUFFRAGISTS HOWLED DOWN' (1907): 3.
33. *L*, II, 401.
34. Emile Delavenay, *D. H. Lawrence and Edward Carpenter: A Study in Edwardian Transition* (1971), p. 22.
35. Amanda Adams, *Performing Authorship in the Nineteenth-Century Transatlantic Lecture Tour* (2014), p. 11.
36. Geoff Dibb, *Oscar Wilde: A Vagabond with a Mission. The Story of Oscar Wilde's Lecture Tours of Britain and Ireland* (2013), p. 175.
37. *Nottinghamshire Guardian* (Friday 21 December 1883): 3.
38. Available at <http://www.nottinghammechanics.com/before-the-fire-of-1867.htm> (last accessed 23 February 2019).
39. Charles Norman, *Ezra Pound* (1969), p. 31.
40. *L*, I, 145.
41. Moody, *Ezra Pound: Poet, A Portrait of the Man and His Work*, I, p. 73. Shakespear quoted in Noel Stock, *The Life of Ezra Pound* (1970), p. 73.
42. Stock, *The Life of Ezra Pound*, p. 70.
43. Pound, quoted by Moody in *Ezra Pound: Poet, A Portrait of the Man and His Work*, I, p. 116.
44. *L*, I, 368.
45. *L*, I, 374.
46. *L*, II, 359.
47. Prospectus for the *Signature*, cited in Katherine Mansfield, *Letters of Katherine Mansfield*, I (1928), p. 198.
48. *L*, II, 398.
49. *L*, II, 401; 391. There were 122 subscribers to the *Signature* but numbers attending the meetings never exceeded twelve. TE, 275–7; 812 fn. 96.
50. Holbrook Jackson, Preface to *George Bernard Shaw* (1907), p. 12.

51. See T. Steele, *Alfred Orage and the Leeds Arts Club, 1893–1923* (1990), p. 137 and Andrew Thacker, '"that trouble": Regional Modernism and "little magazines"' (2013).
52. Ann L. Ardis, 'Democracy and Modernism: *The New Age* under A. R. Orage (1907–22)' (2009–12), p. 206.
53. Advertisement for Shaw's lecture, *New Age*, ii (22 February 1908): 337.
54. Letter from Jessie to Emile Delavenay, 17 April 1934: George Zytaruk (ed.), 'The Collected Letters of Jessie Chambers' (1979), 82.
55. Ann L. Ardis, *Modernism and Cultural Conflict, 1880–1922* (2002), p. 160.
56. *STH*, 223.
57. 'Art begins when a man, with the purpose of communicating to other people a feeling he once experienced, calls it up again within himself and expresses it by certain external signs'. Leo Tolstoy, What is Art? (1995), p. 38.
58. Christopher E. Mauriello, 'The Strange Death of the Public Intellectual: Liberal Intellectual Identity and the "Field of Cultural Production" in England, 1880–1920' (2001): 9–11.
59. *STH*, 225; 229.
60. *STH*, 226.
61. *L*, I, 69.
62. *STH*, 135.
63. *STH*, 271 note 135:2. *New Age*, i (2, 9, 16 May 1907): 5; 21; 37.
64. *STH*, 135.
65. *STH*, 271 note 135:6. Anon., 'Fifty Years of Modern Painting: Corot to Sargent' (1908): 295–6.
66. *STH*, 223.
67. Anon., 'The Future of THE NEW AGE' (1907): 8.
68. Fernihough, *Freewomen and Supermen*, p. 4.
69. John Carswell, *Lives and Letters* (1978), p. 25.
70. *STH*, 135.
71. Ibid., p. 18.
72. Ardis, 'Democracy and Modernism', p. 210.
73. Carswell, *Lives and Letters*, p. 35.
74. Ibid., p. 16.
75. *STH*, 274 note 140:25. *New Age*, iii (15 August 1908): 312–13.
76. See Shaw's contribution in the *New Age*, ii (15 February 1908): 309–11; G. K. Chesterton, 'A. R. Orage: An Obituary' originally published in *G. K.'s Weekly* in 1934. Reprinted in the *Chesterton Review*, 20:1 (February 1994): 16.

77. Arnold Bennett, 'Why I Am a Socialist' (1907): 90.
78. Chesterton, 'Why I Am Not a Socialist': 190.
79. Wells's article, 'About Chesterton and Belloc' appears in *New Age*, ii (11 January 1908), 209–10; Shaw's article 'Belloc and Chesterton' in ii (15 February 1908): 309–11; Filson Young, 'On Shaw, Wells, Chesterton and Belloc' in ii (7 March 1908): 370. Correspondence entering into dialogue with these writers appears in each intervening number.
80. E. T. 155.

PART II

THE LONDON LITERARY SCENE:
MENTORS AND PUBLISHING (1909–12)

3

'I know nothing of the publishing of books': Ford Madox Hueffer, Violet Hunt and William Heinemann

It is remarkably fortunate that Lawrence came into contact with Ford Madox Hueffer in September 1909 and that Jessie had the foresight to write to him in the first place, enclosing for his consideration a carefully selected batch of Lawrence's poems. But another important figure in Lawrence's early career has traditionally been sidelined. In an interview Lawrence gave to the American journalist Kyle Crichton in 1925, Lawrence reportedly 'launched into a long defence of Violet Hunt as a novelist, saying that she wasn't at all appreciated properly'.[1] He is not usually so full of praise for a fellow writer so Hunt must have made a considerable impression on him. By that date Hunt's star had waned, but when Lawrence was invited into her home and social circles in autumn 1909 she was a well-regarded and prolific bestselling writer with stellar literary connections. In the same interview, Lawrence declared Hueffer to be 'a born romanticist'. It was within the context of romance that Hueffer spoke about 'Nethermere', the draft of *The White Peacock* that he read in December 1909. This chapter examines Lawrence's interactions with Hueffer and Hunt and his negotiation of the advice they offered him when he approached William Heinemann about publishing his first novel. As well as providing evidence for Hunt's significance in helping to facilitate Lawrence's breakthrough into metropolitan literary society, it explores hitherto unseen archive materials which allow insights into the marketing and implied readership of *The White Peacock*. Lawrence's engagements with literary London first began with his appearance within the pages of Hueffer's prestigious journal the *English Review* in November 1909.

The *English Review*

Lawrence introduced the first number of the *English Review* to the Chambers family on his return to Eastwood from Croydon in December 1908; they subsequently subscribed to it and felt it to be 'an event, one of the few really first-rate things that happen now and again in a lifetime'.² In her 1935 memoir Jessie claims that she had to persuade Lawrence to submit his work to this important new publication in summer 1909 and his reputed obstinacy is balanced with an interest in Jessie's suggestion:

> I'm not anxious to get into print. I shan't send anything. Besides they'd never take it . . . *You* send something. Send some of the poems, if you like . . . Send whatever you like. Do what you like with them . . . Give me a *nom de plume*, though; I don't want folk in Croydon to know I write poetry.³

Jessie remembers Lawrence first coolly denying his desire to have his work published, yet the first sentence and the use of the word 'anxious' suggests that she remembers that he was looking to get into print at some point. Jessie's version of the conversation suggests that Lawrence was fearful of rejection and public exposure. He is seen to refuse to act on Jessie's advice, before deferring the responsibility for his success to her and positioning her as an intermediary between himself and the editor: if the endeavour failed then he could blame Jessie for her ill-judged selection of examples of his work. Yet if he really felt that he would *not* get into print then he would not have been so insistent on concealing his real name. The comment about hiding his poetic side from the Croydon 'folk' is perhaps part of the stubborn persona that Jessie felt Lawrence presented to her in this period, since in the first half of 1909 Lawrence had begun to make new friends among schoolteacher circles in Croydon; at various points in the year Arthur McLeod, Agnes Holt, Agnes Mason and Helen Corke all knew about his literary aspirations.⁴

In her 1926 memoir *The Flurried Years*, Violet Hunt (1862–1942) reports that Jessie introduced Lawrence in her cover letter to Hueffer as 'the son of a miner, and not very strong'.⁵ Jessie recalls her letter stating that

> the author of the poems was a young man who had been writing for a number of years . . . I gave his name, of course, but said that if any of the poems were printed they should appear under the *nom de plume* of Richard Greasley.⁶

Jessie would have read in Hueffer's first *English Review* editorial in December 1908 that he was looking for writers with working-class backgrounds; this, paired with her recognition that 'the Editor was prepared to welcome new talent', spurred her to write strategically on Lawrence's behalf by emphasising his youth and (if Hunt's recollection is accurate) his social status.⁷ Hueffer had written it is astonishing how little literature has to show of the life of the poor . . . of the thousands of books that pour upon us day by day and year by year, the percentage which gives us any insight into the inner workings of the poor man's mind is either infinitesimal or non-existent.[8]

Jessie gave careful thought to the selection of poems she sent to Hueffer in summer 1909, placing 'Discipline' first in the hope that 'the unusual title might attract the Editor's attention'. 'Discipline' stresses Lawrence's work as a teacher and foregrounds his economic status as lower middle class. The other poems Jessie sent were personal choices: 'In "Dreams Old and Nascent" I knew he was trying to explain himself to me; and "Baby Movements" I sent because I loved it.' Jessie also sent 'several other poems', the titles of which she could not recall in 1935.[9] Whatever the exact content of Jessie's cover letter, Hueffer noticed that his correspondent's handwriting was 'as if drawn with sepia rather than written in ink, on grey-blue notepaper' and the address was a 'Haggs Farm' in the Midlands; he would have been able to guess at the nature of Jessie's own social class.[10]

The possibility of gaining the attention of the editor of a journal that Lawrence would later advertise to his friends as 'the best possible way to get into touch with the new young school of realism' played on his mind and the next time he saw Jessie he asked: '"Did you send those poems to the *English*?", adding immediately "They'll never print them".'[11] Hueffer replied to Jessie in August 1909 to say that 'the poems were very interesting and that the author had undoubted talent, but that nowadays luck played such a large part in a literary career'. Hueffer was careful not to raise his correspondent's hopes too soon. Casually, he continued: 'If you would get him to come and see me some time when he is in London perhaps something might be done.'[12] Approximately three weeks later Lawrence visited Hueffer on his return to Croydon for the start of the new school term; the publication of his poems was arranged by 11 September. In November 1909, 'Dreams Old and Nascent', 'Discipline' and 'Baby-Movements' (published in two parts, comprising 'Running Barefoot' and 'Trailing Clouds') were printed under the general title 'A Still Afternoon'. They appeared alongside fictional work by authors including John Galsworthy, R. B. Cunninghame Graham, Ella D'Arcy and Hueffer himself, as well as articles discussing 'Literature of To-day' (Hueffer's editorial), 'The Extension of Liberalism', 'Women's Vote and Men', 'The Constitutional Crisis' and 'Divorce Law Reform'.[13] The poems were published under the name 'D. H. Lawrence', not 'Richard Greasley'; Lawrence's self-confidence had been raised by Hueffer's acceptance of his work and he was proud to be 'launched' as a writer under his own signature in the estimable *English Review*.

The five poems that Hueffer printed were consciously literary and did not directly deal with Lawrence's working-class Eastwood background, but Hueffer identified an opportunity to advise a young writer with the potential to fill what he called a 'lacuna' in the marketplace for fiction dealing realistically with daily life in a working-class community. It can be no coincidence that during autumn 1909 Lawrence increased his output of writing with working-class settings; he worked on his play *A Collier's Friday Night* and in December he wrote several short sketches about the poverty-stricken children he taught in Croydon (such as 'A Lesson on a Tortoise' and 'Lessford's Rabbits'), together with the first iteration of the short story 'Odour of Chrysanthemums'.

Hueffer founded and edited the journal from December 1908 until it ran into significant financial difficulties; it could not maintain its original print run of 5,000 copies and circulation rarely exceeded 1,000 copies per month. Violet Hunt persuaded Alfred Mond to buy the journal in December 1909 (hoping that Hueffer would be kept on as editor) but instead he employed Austin Harrison, who retained the editorship until 1923.[14] Hueffer had envisaged the *English Review* to be a politically disinterested monthly publication 'which sets boldly upon its front the words "no party bias"', but despite this claim Hueffer took a decisive line in supporting female suffrage campaigns and his publication was broadly left-leaning and keenly concerned with social questions in relation to the working class.[15] Hueffer's publication was neither coterie, like the quarterly literary periodical *The Yellow Book* (which ran from 1894 to 1897 and was published by Elkin Matthews and John Lane), nor mass market like *Tit-Bits* or the *Strand*. The *English Review* aimed to treat its readers with the respect due to 'grown-up minds whose leisure can be interested by something else than the crispness and glitter of popular statement'.[16] Its status as an Edwardian cultural review, with roots in impressive nineteenth-century journals such as *The Quarterly Review* and *The Edinburgh Review*, distinguishes it from later, more avant-garde but short-lived modernist 'little' magazines such as *Rhythm* (founded in 1911) and Wyndham Lewis's combative *BLAST* (which ran for two issues in 1914–15). Hueffer intended for the publication to achieve a large readership; he hoped that it would educate the wider English public to appreciate serious literature and engage intellectually with a range of political opinion. He greatly valued French literature and culture and Mark Morrisson has argued that Hueffer looked to Alfred Vallette's *Mercure de France* as the model of a publication that was both 'venerable and commercially successful'.[17] Hueffer emulated the structure of the *Mercure*, beginning each number with the weighty literature of writers such as Hardy, James and Conrad, while including more popular writers like Vernon Lee and Maurice Hewlett. He ended the issue with his own version of the 'Revue de Mois': 'The Month' began with an editorial, followed by articles and reviews of wider interest.[18] The nearest English equivalent on the market was the *Fortnightly Review*, which had been founded by G. H. Lewes and Anthony Trollope in 1865; they in turn had taken inspiration from the Parisian *Revue des deux Mondes* (1829). However, Morrisson's assessment that the *Fortnightly* 'maintained its enviable position of authority and respectability through the Edwardian period' is questionable.[19] The popularity of the *Fortnightly* declined in the 1880s; when the young Frank Harris took over as editor in 1886 he had to revive what was then seen as an ailing publication. Harris achieved this by making the *Fortnightly* less political and more populist.[20] The *Fortnightly* was in competition with reviews such as the *Contemporary* (1866) – which fashioned itself as more of a 'family' entertainment publication – and the *Nineteenth Century* (1877). Despite proclaiming their willingness to explore issues affecting a range of social classes, the *Fortnightly*, the *Contemporary*, the *Nineteenth Century and After* and the *English Review* sold for a costly 2s 6d per issue in 1908, which would have been out of the price range of most working-class households. The buoyancy of the *English Review* under Austin Harrison was in part due to its reduction in price to 1s, but Lawrence considered its quality to have reduced accordingly – in June 1913 he thought it 'rotten'.[21]

In February 1908 Violet Hunt's literary agent J. B. Pinker advised her about placing three short stories, later published in her supernatural gothic story collection *Tales of the Uneasy* (1911). He wrote:

> 'The Coach of Death', indeed, seems to me first class, but it is only likely to appeal to something like the *Fortnightly*; and the others, though in a less degree, would also be unacceptable to most editors . . . it becomes increasingly difficult to place stories of this calibre, as most of the magazines exact something more or less conventional in plot or treatment.[22]

Hunt recalled that, after receiving Pinker's letter, she 'wrote to Mr. [H. G.] Wells, asking if he could tell me where to send them'. He answered 'Send them to the *English Review*. It's *It* this year!'[23] Hueffer often claimed that he started the *English Review* in order to print Hardy's poem 'A Sunday Morning Tragedy', which raised the controversial subject matter of a poor woman's death after her illegitimate pregnancy and a botched abortion; the poem had been rejected by an editor whose publication 'circulated amongst young people', but Hueffer placed it on the first page of the opening number.[24]

Hunt recollects that the *English Review* had been 'all that hot summer [of 1908] simmering in the minds of its promoters, Hueffer, [Arthur] Marwood, Conrad, and Wells, busily collecting artists to write and men of good will to read what they had written'.²⁵ These figures contributed to the first number and (with the exception of Marwood, who helped to finance the publication in its early stages) their work continued to feature heavily. According to Hunt, the *English Review* took the best part of a year to set up before the first number appeared: Hueffer had to sit 'patient and forlorn in the swelter of London on his nest-egg'.²⁶ On 16 October 1908 Hunt visited Hueffer to show him her stories; the editor picked out 'The Coach' for publication in the *English Review* and it appeared in the March 1909 number.²⁷ Shortly after this meeting Hunt became involved in the journal both in the office and as a contributor, beginning an affair with Hueffer that was to last for a decade. Hueffer ran the journal from his home, 84 Holland Park Avenue, which was a short walk from Hunt's home 'South Lodge' on Campden Hill Road; these became key social venues for London's literati. The management of the *English Review* was a collaborative enterprise but Hueffer, as editor, was the figurehead and key spokesperson. Women's engagements in this publication have rarely been emphasised, but another important figure in the daily running of the office was Olive Thomas, Hueffer's invaluable secretary.

Hueffer thought that there was sufficient demand for a publication that showcased the work of

> Younger lions [who] were not only roaring but making carnage of their predecessors . . . It seemed to me that if that nucleus of writers [Wells, Bennett, James, Conrad, George Meredith, Hardy, George Moore, Yeats] could be got together with what of undiscovered talent the country might hold a Movement might be started.²⁸

Although it did not independently generate a new literary movement, Hueffer's journal provided a platform that brought together a number of distinctive new writers and provided a forum for the discussion of urgent social questions; Hueffer has been credited with first identifying the talent of the now canonical modernists Ezra Pound, Wyndham Lewis – and, of course, D. H. Lawrence. Lawrence's poems appeared prominently at the start of the November 1909 number, before those of John Lazarus, a poet who is little known today but was published in two numbers of the *English Review*.²⁹ A laudatory reviewer writing in the *Schoolmaster*, Henry Yoxall, responded only to Lawrence's poems: '[a] monthly of that standing does not admit to its columns the work of mere versifiers, and I congratulate Mr. Lawrence, not only on the prominent publication of some of his poems, but on the fine quality of them'. He continues: 'Mr. Lawrence is at present a finer but weaker Walt Whitman . . . he can become something higher than Whitman ever attained to.'³⁰ Lawrence may have read this review; Jessie recalled that around this time Lawrence would sometimes write '"I'm sending you a Whitmanesque poem" when he was enclosing one of his own.'[31] To a modern reader Lawrence's poems are more forceful and linguistically and formally experimental than those of Lazarus. 'Dreams Old and Nascent' is an earnest attempt to do and say something different in poetry; it is a better representation of Hueffer's preferred submission than Lazarus's more conventional work. This highlights the nature of literary periodicals, in which there was a range of rhetorical objectives and the material need for sales. Hueffer was a poor businessman: Hunt recalls that Hueffer's system was to 'pay my contributors exactly what they ask'.[32] He could not afford to pay contributors a great deal (if he paid anything at all), but he had to fill the pages of the *English Review* in order to justify its cover price. His intention to reach a wide audience may have led him to include more popular writing to appeal to different tastes. Lazarus could have been a friend of one of the *Review*'s key contacts; he may have fitted a racial or class profile that Hueffer wished to support. Of course, Hueffer might simply have liked Lazarus's poetry.

Lazarus's 'Nell' and 'St Mary's Yard' use four-line stanzas with regular line lengths and end rhymes of *aaba* and *abba* respectively. 'Marah' (evoking the Hebrew word 'bitter', which aptly characterises its tone) has two stanzas, the central two lines of which rhyme; the speaker relates that he is unable to be nourished by waters stained by the 'tears of women' and the 'sweat of men'. 'Nell' is a polite and rather clichéd poem about the commonplace physical appearance of the speaker's London love: only her eyes (like 'grey pansies') tempt him to 'try for Paradise', but this is as near to any intimate response to her as the speaker gets. Lawrence's 'Discipline' describes a teacher's address to his 'Darling' about the difficulties of arriving at a shared understanding with his pupils, who 'strike with a blindness of fury' against him. It is more exploratory than 'Nell' in its use of natural metaphors such as roots, soil and bulbs, a cluster of similar images that recur across all the poems in this sequence. Lawrence's most sentimental poems are the two that constitute 'Baby-Movements'; the observation of the baby's 'two bare feet on my hands / Cool as syringa buds' is evocative in its simplicity. Lawrence's two-part 'Dreams Old and Nascent' is the most experimental of his five poems and is placed first in the *English Review*, just underneath the journal's large, capitalised title and the heading 'MODERN POETRY'. 'Dreams Old' has an end rhyme of *abab* and is broken into four parts. In part two the lines are so long that they run on, breaking up the stanza; this isolates up to three words at a time providing a pause in the reading and directing the reader's attention to particular lexical choices. The content of 'Dreams Old' reflects the lingering authority of Victorian literature and bestselling novels such as *Lorna Doone* and

David Copperfield to which the poem alludes; the speaker, a young teacher, notes that his schoolboys 'are all still / In a wishful dream of Lorna Doone'. A glimpse of 'Norwood Hill' out of the schoolroom window evokes 'the old romance of David and Dora' and the nostalgic speaker feels oppressed by the 'endless tapestry the past has woven' about the world. 'Dreams Nascent', the companion piece, comprises parts five to nine. It demonstrates an attempt to break free from Victorian literary influences. The stanza lengths are much more irregular and it is less concerned with rhyme in favour of keeping readers' attention on its startling abstract imagery: 'hastening, white-hot metal' is set alongside 'The whole teeming flesh of mankind' to suggest the changing visions of a modern generation of boys as they grow into twentieth-century men. 'Dreams Nascent' describes the awakening of the speaker in 'quick response' to the 'Fluent active figures of men' and 'the flow of their limbs as they move': he becomes alive to the present moment rather than remaining cloaked by the past. The organic imagery of a 'bud on the stalk of eternity' represents the prospect of natural rejuvenation in the new century: a vital, youthful humanity can anticipate 'The creation of a new-patterned dream'.

Hueffer might have considered the poem's rousing and expectant tone a suitable embodiment of his own ambitious project. In the 1913 Preface to his own *Collected Poems*, Hueffer recalled the *English Review* founders' early decision to place poetry in 'the very first place in that journal – not because it was a living force, but just because it was dead and must be treated with deference'; however, on receiving manuscripts of verse, 'much of what we read seemed to be better stuff than we had expected'. Hueffer names Yeats, De la Mare, Flint, Lawrence and Pound as having the poetic abilities of their elders Hardy and Meredith:

> gradually it has forced itself upon us that there is a new quality, a new power of impressionism that is open to poetry, and that is not so much open to prose . . It is the duty of the poet to reflect his own day as it appears to him.[33]

In this Preface Hueffer consecrates Lawrence as a significant new voice in poetry. By late 1913 Lawrence had published *Love Poems and Others* and his poems had appeared in the *English Review*, the *Nation*, the *Westminster Gazette* and the *New Statesman*; 'Snap-Dragon' had been included in Edward Marsh's anthology of *Georgian Poetry 1911–1912*. For Bourdieu, 'legitimacy' is recognition by one's peers. Hueffer assisted in legitimising the poets he names by bestowing upon them 'the recognition granted by the set of producers who produce for other producers, their competitors, i.e. by the autonomous self-sufficient world of "art for art's sake", meaning art for artists'.[34] By 1913 Hueffer saw Lawrence not as a poetic apprentice, but as an artist from whom other artists could learn.

Lawrence's literary fortunes changed dramatically in autumn 1909. He was now being published in the same review as Chesterton and was moving in similar literary circles. He was energised by Hueffer's kind offer to 'read any of the work I like to send him'.[35] In November, after engaging the help of Agnes Holt and Agnes Mason to make fair copies of heavily revised passages of his writing, Lawrence gave Hueffer the manuscript of his novel (now entitled 'Nethermere') and sought his opinion of it.[36] Lawrence had rapidly entered into a more niche, intellectual and liberal literary environment than he might have bargained for: when he revised the 'Nethermere' manuscript in autumn 1909, his writing began to record the changes in his social situation and to reflect the new literary influences brought about by his inclusion among the *English Review* set. Hueffer's crucial assistance in publishing Lawrence in the *English Review* and introducing him to London literary society has been extensively (but often inaccurately) documented.[37] By contrast, the role of Violet Hunt has been neglected. She, along with Hueffer, influenced the placement of *The White Peacock* with William Heinemann.

'the makings of a very considerable novelist'

In *The Flurried Years* (1926), Hunt discusses her prominent role in the office of the *English Review* during 1909: she was 'reader, occasional sub-editor, contributor, but above all . . . a "society hand", and touter for rich, influential subscribers'.[38] She claims that she was reader when Jessie sent Lawrence's poems to Hueffer and that he had passed her the manuscript pages, which were copied out in Jessie's hand: '[t]he editor handed me some manuscript poems written in pencil and very close'. Hunt first implies that Hueffer was the one to take initial interest in the poems, as he 'was out for new blood'; Hueffer 'was beside himself with pleasure at his discovery' of Lawrence.[39] However, in the extended 1926 US version of the memoir, *I Have This to Say: The Story of My Flurried Years*, Hunt pursues her claim that she read the poems first: Lawrence 'seemed to regard me as a sort of literary godmother ever since, as Reader, I brought his poems to Joseph Leopold's [Hueffer's] notice in *The English Review*'.[40] In 1913, Jessie would write to Hunt to consult her about the publication of 'The Rathe Primrose' (Jessie's fictional response to the portrayal of herself as Miriam in *Sons and Lovers*), so it is likely that she felt Hunt to be helpful in literary matters and recognised that she had been instrumental in supporting Lawrence's early writing.[41] In his *Life Interests* Douglas Goldring suggested that Lawrence was the 'joint' discovery of Hueffer and Hunt.[42] Whether it was Hueffer or Hunt who first read the poems, both of them advertised Lawrence in their literary circles and together they supported his approach to Heinemann.

In his 1937 memoir *Portraits from Life*, Hueffer mistakenly claims that he had first been sent 'Odour of Chrysanthemums' by Jessie and was insistent about this, even after he had read Jessie's 1935 memoir. Hueffer recalls:

> Miss E. T. in her lately published little book on the youth of Lawrence – and a very charming and serviceable little book it is – seems to be under the impression that she sent me as a first instalment only poems by Lawrence. Actually she first asked me if I would care to see anything – and then should it be poetry or prose. And I replied asking her to send both, so that she had sent me three poems about a schoolmaster's life . . . and *Odour of Chrysanthemums*.[43]

Hueffer erroneously recalls 'Odour of Chrysanthemums' as being the story that led him to Lawrence because it is a piece of working-class realism; he states that it more vividly 'captured the impact of Lawrence's personality' than the poems he actually printed. He may indeed have encouraged Lawrence's working-class writing, but he also retrospectively claims responsibility for Lawrence's later success as the realist writer of *Sons and Lovers*.

Allegedly answering his secretary's question 'You've got another genius?' with the reply 'It's a big one this time', Hueffer states that he laid 'Odour of Chrysanthemums' in the basket for accepted manuscripts. He relates how he then dressed to dine with several literary celebrities at the Pall Mall restaurant, where he announced the name of his new prodigy:

> I remarked to Mr. Wells that I had discovered another genius . . . Mr. Wells exclaimed – to someone at Lady Londonderry's table:
> 'Hurray, Fordie's discovered another genius! Called D. H. Lawrence!'
> Before the evening was finished I had two publishers asking me for the first refusal of D. H. Lawrence's first novel and, by that accident, Lawrence's name was already known in London before he even knew that any of his work had been submitted to an editor.[44]

Although literary success was heavily dependent on social networks and influential contacts who could promote a writer's name, Hueffer's entertaining account glosses over the challenges writers faced in achieving legitimacy as they negotiated the literary field. Hueffer cultivates his image as a dominant figure in Edwardian literary society by claiming that he single-handedly 'discovered' Lawrence and by implying that he was the figure publishers would approach to initiate publishing agreements. By stating that he had paved the way for Lawrence before the writer knew that any of his work had been submitted, Hueffer's account overlooks the hard work Lawrence put in to revising his literary work so that it would be acceptable in the literary marketplace and conceals the energy Lawrence spent adapting to the literary culture he was immersed in and finding his niche within it. If Hueffer had actually said in 1909 what he claims to have done in his 1937 memoir, then it would have been a flamboyant gesture to friends who had probably heard such proclamations many times before, since he relished the paternal role of literary mentor. As David Garnett recalls, 'When I was seventeen [in 1909] Ford heard that my mother was worrying about my education and wrote to her: "Send David to me for a few years, Connie, and I will teach him to write like Flaubert".'[45] In summer 1909 it was not certain that the young Lawrence would even meet Hueffer, let alone send him more of his work. It is far from clear that Jessie had even mentioned to Hueffer that Lawrence was writing a novel in the cover letter that she sent to accompany the poems. Although Hueffer's recognition and help was crucial for Lawrence in these early months, the relation between mentor and mentee would prove to be far more complex than Hueffer's romanticised account permits.

In reality, Lawrence sent 'Odour of Chrysanthemums' (along with 'Goose Fair') to Hueffer on 9 December 1909, shortly after he had written it.[46] Despite Hueffer's later appraisal of 'Odour of Chrysanthemums' as being the story that immediately drew him to Lawrence, it appears that Hueffer may at the time have actually preferred 'Goose Fair', since this was the story that was published first in the *English Review* in February 1910. 'Odour of Chrysanthemums' was set up in proof in March 1910, but new editor Austin Harrison was dissatisfied with it and returned it to Lawrence, advising him on ways to improve the story; it underwent two further layers of extensive revision prior to its publication in June 1911, long after Hueffer had departed.[47]

Given the unreliable nature of Hueffer's later accounts, it is necessary to turn instead to the letter that he wrote to Lawrence on 15 December 1909, which records his contemporary response to reading the 'Nethermere' manuscript. It served as an open letter of recommendation for the novel that Lawrence could forward to publishers; such letters would often have circulated prior to the period when aspiring authors could employ literary agents. Lawrence copied out Hueffer's letter verbatim and immediately sent it to Heinemann with a cover letter offering the novel to the publisher. Although the manuscript of Lawrence's letter to Heinemann is unlocated, Hueffer's letter in Lawrence's hand is in the University of Nottingham archives. Lawrence has written '<u>Copy</u>' diagonally at the top left hand corner and embedded the text in quotation marks (Figure 3.1).[48]

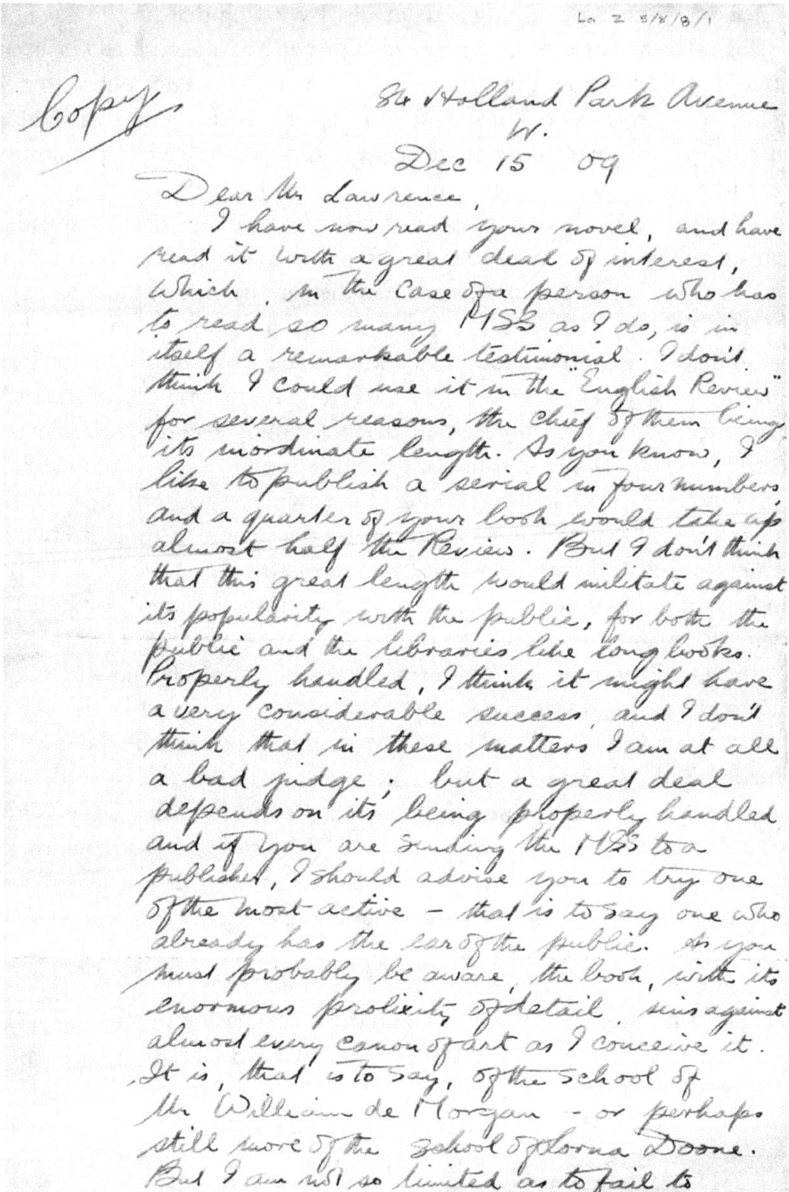

La Z 5/8/8/1

Copy

84 Holland Park Avenue
W.
Dec 15 09

Dear Mr Lawrence,

I have now read your novel, and have read it with a great deal of interest, which, in the case of a person who has to read so many MSS as I do, is in itself a remarkable testimonial. I don't think I could use it in the "English Review" for several reasons, the chief of them being its inordinate length. As you know, I like to publish a serial in four numbers and a quarter of your book would take up almost half the Review. But I don't think that this great length would militate against its popularity with the public, for both the public and the libraries like long books. Properly handled, I think it might have a very considerable success, and I don't think that in these matters I am at all a bad judge; but a great deal depends on its being properly handled and if you are sending the MSS to a publisher, I should advise you to try one of the most active – that is to say one who already has the ear of the public. As you must probably be aware, the book, with its enormous prolixity of detail, sins against almost every canon of art as I conceive it. It is, that is to say, of the school of Mr William de Morgan – or perhaps still more of the school of Lorna Doone. But I am not so limited as to fail to appreciate other schools than my own, and I can very

Figure 3.1 Copy of a letter from Ford Madox Hueffer dated 15 December 1909, written in D. H. Lawrence's hand. University of Nottingham, Manuscripts and Special Collections, La Z 5/8/8.

By reproducing the letter rather than sending the original, Lawrence would be able to reuse the recommendation to approach another publisher if Heinemann was to decline his offer. We know that he copied out references from his referees for his teaching applications, so this practice was not new to him. The very fact that Lawrence forwarded Hueffer's letter shows that he was cannier in publishing matters than he cared to admit (or he had received some sound advice). In his cover letter, Lawrence told Heinemann:

> I have just received the accompanying letter from Mr. Ford Madox Hueffer. I hasten to forward it to you, and in doing so to offer you the novel of which he speaks.
>
> It is my first. I have as yet published nothing but a scrap of verse. At the moment I feel a trifle startled and somewhat elated by Mr. Hueffer's letter, but already a grain of doubt is germinating in me.
>
> I hope you will allow me to send you the MSS. Of course I am willing to fulfil all Mr. Hueffer's injunctions. I know nothing of the publishing of books.[49]

Lawrence's cover letter reveals his position-taking in approaching a publisher; it shows his strategic cultivation of a naïve persona. This is perhaps another face-saving gesture, in which Lawrence expresses surprise and doubt at Hueffer's enthusiasm for 'Nethermere' to pre-empt and so offset the impact of possible rejection from the publisher. So apparently 'startled' was Lawrence by Hueffer's response that he talks about the novel as if it is barely his own. Lawrence knew that the publisher would be impressed by Hueffer's support of him and he naturally wished to draw attention to his association with the editor. He valued Hueffer's authority on publishing matters to the extent that he assumed Heinemann would agree with Hueffer's 'injunctions'. Lawrence was modest in his approach to Heinemann, admitting that he had only had a 'scrap of verse' published under his name; he stated that he knew 'nothing of the publishing of books'. While this final comment was intended to endear Lawrence to the publisher, it is to some extent true but partially also a case of false modesty. A ruthless publisher might have sensed that he could exploit the young author's inexperience and negotiate a good deal during the exchange of contractual agreements. At this stage, Lawrence was more concerned to secure his first publishing agreement than to haggle over the remuneration he might receive.

However, a close analysis of Hueffer's letter reveals it to be more ambivalent than Lawrence had hastily interpreted it to be; it allows us to gain an insight into a single moment in the complex negotiation between author, mentor and publisher. Hueffer begins by foregrounding his position of literary authority, commenting that the time he spent reading the manuscript was 'in itself a remarkable testimonial'.[50] Hueffer establishes his credentials so that his recommendation achieves maximum impact and his pragmatism deepens with his claim to be not 'at all a bad judge' in literary matters. Hueffer situates Lawrence in a 'school of writing' which he can understand, but from which he distances himself; he writes that the manuscript, 'with its enormous prolixity of detail, sins against almost every canon of art as I conceive it'. In other words, to Hueffer's mind it is formally artless: Lawrence would have known about the admiration Hueffer expressed for Flaubert and Maupassant in his *English Review* editorials and the two men would undoubtedly have discussed their literary values during their frequent meetings and in correspondence. Lawrence met Hueffer personally at least four times between September and mid-December 1909 and spent long evenings in the company of his circle (including Pound and Ernest and Grace Rhys). It is on the basis of the length of the manuscript that Hueffer regrets he cannot serialise the work across four numbers of the *English Review*, but he suggests that 'the public and the libraries like long books'. Hueffer clearly does not see anything immoral about 'Nethermere'; indeed, he suggests that it could attain 'popularity with the public'. He considers that the work's prolixity and potential popularity place it within 'the school of Mr William de Morgan – or perhaps still more of the school of Lorna Doone'. Lawrence's novel is placed in a category of bestselling, sentimental, romantic and stylistically outmoded literature, which was not the category of fiction Hueffer wished to promote in his modern *Review*, but – packaged correctly – it certainly had potential to capture a market elsewhere. R. D. Blackmore's novel was then far more influential than it is given credit for today. Thomas Hardy read *Lorna Doone* in 1875 and wrote to Blackmore that the latter's 'exquisite ways of describing things . . . are more after my own heart than the "presentations" of any other writer I am acquainted with'.[51] Hardy's comment uncannily echoes both Jessie's description of *Lorna Doone* as 'a story after our own hearts' and Hueffer's recollection that he memorised whole passages of the novel 'by heart' during his youth.[52] In 1882 an illustrated edition was produced and by 1893 the book reached its thirty-ninth edition. Upon its 1897 publication in sixpenny form the novel sold 100,000 copies within one week.[53] The men in Yale University's 'Modern Novels' class voted it their favourite work of fiction in both 1896 and 1906, showing that the novel continued to attract educated male readers.[54] It is male school pupils in Lawrence's poem 'Dreams Old' who are dreaming about Lorna Doone.

Hueffer had an intensive understanding of different sectors within the contemporary literary marketplace. From 19 January to 20 July 1907, he contributed to Alfred Harmsworth's *Daily Mail* Books Supplement two poems and a series of fourteen 'Literary Portraits'. He catered to the newspaper's mass audience of working and lower-middle class readers by covering a broad range of writers: Swinburne, Wells, Israel Zangwill, W. W. Jacobs, Frederic Harrison, Hilaire Belloc, W. D. Howells, Shaw, William de Morgan, Mark Twain, Father Hugh Benson, Hardy, S. R. Crockett and Marie Corelli. Hueffer had enthusiastically promoted de Morgan's *Joseph Vance: An Ill-Written Autobiography* (1906) when he reviewed it for the *Daily Mail* in 1906. It was De Morgan's first published novel and running to over 250,000 words it instantly became a bestseller in England and America.[55] De Morgan continued to generate profits for Heinemann, with a prolific output of highly melodramatic and superfluously detailed novels. Although Hueffer desired a comparably wide readership for his own novels, the *English Review* (with Conrad behind it) was to have '[n]o popular concessions! Even the rumour of such a thing in London would be, Conrad said, "like a hint of failure", and "the *Review* may have to stop, but it must not fail".'[56] Conrad knew that compromising the journal's prestige by appealing to a less intellectual readership in order to increase circulation and keep it afloat would contravene their agreed aims in forming a new publication and would reduce the contributors' standing.

In favour of 'Nethermere', Hueffer wrote that he could 'fully admire' Lawrence's 'very remarkable and poetic gifts' and that the young author had 'the makings of a very considerable novelist'. He offered Lawrence honest critical feedback whilst encouraging him to look elsewhere than the *English Review* to get his novel into print. Since Lawrence's name would not command attention, one suspects that serialisation was never intended in the first place and that the letter and its endorsement was a strategic ploy to make the manuscript stand out when circulated to potential publishers. Hueffer suggests that if the work is 'properly handled' (and this phrase is prominently repeated, to place the onus on the competency of the publisher) then 'it might have a very considerable success'. Hueffer's motives are clear: he wishes to interest commercial publishers in the potential marketability of Lawrence's works. On receiving this letter it is little wonder that Lawrence felt elated; he would have envisaged the possibility of financial success and the achievement of a professional writing career. However, he tempers his excitement, telling Heinemann: 'already a grain of doubt is germinating in me'. Lawrence hopes to come across as pliable and as willing to cooperate with the publisher so that his work meets their approval. He might have sensed the hesitancy in Hueffer's letter; the editor qualifies each positive statement he makes with a comment that allows him to retreat from any confident position-taking. In doing so he highlights the provisional nature of the literary field: repeating the phrase that he had written to Jessie in August, Hueffer emphasises that one's career is 'a matter of sheer luck' and all Lawrence can now do is approach a suitable publisher and hope to negotiate an agreement.

The overwhelming focus on Hueffer as Lawrence's first literary mentor distorts the complex nature of literary culture and commerce in the period. At no point in his letter does Hueffer state that Lawrence should offer the novel to Heinemann, since letters of recommendation had to be kept sufficiently 'open' to allow them to be used on multiple occasions. Lawrence would have known that Heinemann was 'active' and had 'the ear of the public'. He may also have taken note of Hueffer's September 1909 *English Review* editorial, which criticised Heinemann for commodifying literature by looking to publish lengthy books (which take subscribers longer to read) in order to satisfy the circulating libraries, who purchased approximately 80 per cent of the 'works of fiction and *belles-lettres* published every year'. Booksellers bought the rest.[57] We can reasonably speculate that Hueffer or Hunt (or both of them in conversation together) encouraged Lawrence to approach Heinemann. Both had extensive publishing connections and it is likely that Hunt had spoken to Lawrence in 1909 about her own ongoing publishing experiences with Heinemann.

'a neat assassin': Violet Hunt

Hunt (then aged forty-five to Hueffer's thirty-four) was an established novelist in her own right. During her career she published seventeen novels, three short story collections, two memoirs, a biography of Elizabeth Siddall, translations, collaborations (including, with Hueffer, *The Governess* [1912] and *Zeppelin Nights* [1915]) and numerous journal articles. It was during one of her gatherings at the Reform Club in Adelphi Terrace in November 1909 that Lawrence first met Pound.[58] Lawrence valued Hunt's literary knowledge and sought her advice on several occasions, particularly in relation to his plays, since Hunt was drama critic for the *Pall Mall Gazette*. Prior to this she had written for *Chapman's* magazine and *Black and White*, which Lawrence read during his schooldays.[59] In November 1910 Lawrence asked his literary acquaintance Grace Crawford to give Hunt the manuscript of his play *The Widowing of Mrs Holroyd*: 'Tell her I hope she may consider the work fit for staging, after necessary clipping and tinting.' On 13 December 1910 he wished to send *A Collier's Friday Night* to Hunt and writes again: 'what am I to do with these plays? Do tell me. I want some money.'[60] A letter from Hunt to Lawrence dated 3 February 1911 invites him to a literary society event at the 'O. P. Club' (the Savile) and informs him that she has reviewed *The White Peacock* for the *Daily Chronicle*. She states that, on submitting her review, she wrote 'a covering letter to the Editor', Robert Donald, in which she 'urged him to have the credit of being one of the first to welcome you as a great man' (see Figure 3.2).[61]

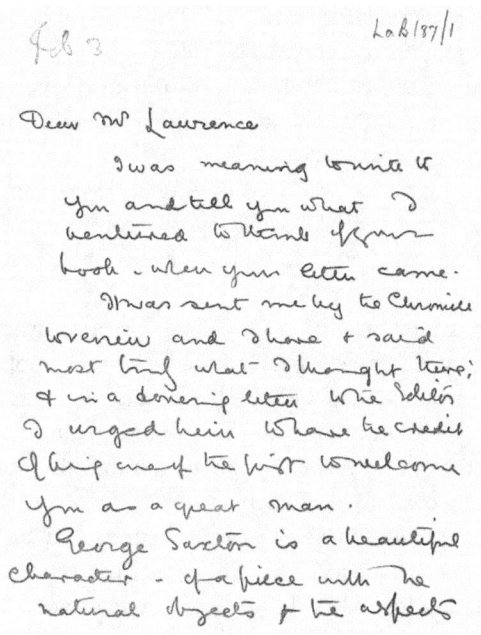

Figure 3.2 Letter from Violet Hunt to D. H. Lawrence dated 3 February 1911. University of Nottingham, Manuscripts and Special Collections, La B 187/1.

Lawrence commented that Hunt was 'very ingenious in her effort to advertise me': the review appeared on 10 February and it declared the novel to be a 'political document developed along the lines of passionate romance'.[62]

A year later Lawrence described Hunt as 'a neat assassin' in social and business affairs. He judged her to be the more dominant partner in her relationship: '[Hueffer] feels, poor fish, the hooks are through his gills this time – and they *are*. Yet he's lucky to be so well caught – she'll handle him with marvellous skill.'[63] During the time Lawrence was in Croydon Hunt had three books published by Heinemann: *The Wife of Altamont* (1908; serialised by the *English Review* from December 1909), *White Rose of Weary Leaf* (a tragic realist novel published in 1910) and *Tales of the Uneasy*; the story collection was marketed as one of Heinemann's 6s 'Popular Fiction' books alongside Lawrence's *The White Peacock* when the latter was published in London on 20 January 1911. *The White Peacock* was also listed in an advertisement for Heinemann's 'New 6s Novels' on the inside cover of *Tales of the Uneasy*, alongside titles such as Galsworthy's *The Patrician*; E. F. Benson's *Account Rendered*; J. E. Patterson's *Tillers of the Soil*; *Jane Oglander* by Mrs Belloc Lowndes; *The House of Bondage* by C. G. Compton; Jessie Leckie Herbertson's *Young Life* and Volumes I and II of

Romain Rolland's *John Christopher*. Hunt's work reveals a frank concern with the sexual psychology of the young, middle-class New Woman and a 'refusal to cooperate in the fictional idealization of romantic love and domesticity'.[64] This description would aptly apply to *The White Peacock*. Hunt was persuaded by the publisher to change the ending of *White Rose* (in which a pregnant woman was killed by bricks from a crumbling chimney stack), but Boots Circulating Library still banned the novel for its impropriety in the presentation of the protagonist Amy Stephens's adulterous relationship.[65] Hunt herself admitted that it was 'not a book for girls'.[66]

No letter from Heinemann to Lawrence agreeing to look at the manuscript of 'Nethermere' has ever been located, so we cannot judge the impact of Lawrence's correspondence with the publisher. The next available record is Hunt's recollection of hand-delivering Lawrence's manuscript to Heinemann's offices in Bedford Street at some point between the third week in December 1909 (after Lawrence wrote to Heinemann on 15 December) and mid-January 1910 (before Heinemann's business partner, Sydney Pawling, requested to see Lawrence on Friday 21 January).[67] It is likely that Lawrence left the manuscript with Hueffer in London when he returned to Eastwood at the end of the autumn term: Hunt could have taken it to Heinemann's offices from either South Lodge or the *English Review* headquarters.

Hunt's account suggests that she was a key figure in facilitating the publication of Lawrence's first novel. The details she provides about her calculated approach to the publisher on Lawrence's behalf are revealing about what kind of novel Hueffer and Hunt thought 'Nethermere' would be. Hunt's description of the publishing house, written for Frederic Whyte's 1928 memoir of William Heinemann, is worthy of analysis:

> I have now and then acted as intermediary for friends' books, and always did better for them when I succeeded in 'seeing' Heinemann than Pawling, who at once got down to brass tacks and no nonsense. Whereas Heinemann was always swayed, carried away, by his unbusinesslike appreciation of good work into accepting a masterpiece that would not earn its royalty or some lovely thing that had no money in it. . . . Pawling was always outspokenly delighted when he could shove and push Billy off to Berne or Prague or Leipzig to some Publisher's Conference, where he could gas and gup about supreme literature and do no harm, while increasing the prestige of the firm.
>
> It was during one of these absences of the Master that I happened to 'leave' the first novel of a friend of mine, Mr. D. H. Lawrence, with Mr. Pawling, left in charge, who languidly promised to read it. Three days

later Mr. Pawling summoned me and, grabbing the manuscript with a grip that masked an eagerness that my eye was not practised enough to discern through his casual manner, offered – 'Take it or leave it!' – an almost derisory sum down. Bad was the best: I had been given full powers by the humble young schoolmaster. I accepted the terms and *The White Peacock* appeared and took the town.[68]

Hunt is here recalling events that took place almost two decades earlier, but she did keep diaries throughout her life. She had already published a similar account in her 1926 memoir *I Have This to Say*:

I took [Lawrence's] first book to a publisher for him. He considered me, in this game he did not understand, a good business woman. . . . 'Billy', Mr. Heinemann, was away, talking to Book Congresses in Berne, where his coadjutors always sent the kind publisher with a soul, when he had been accepting too many worthless – as far as saleableness went – novels . . . Mr Pawling read *The White Peacock* – he read it in two days. So I think there was nothing much wrong with the book in the way of being a selling concern. Two days later I had occasion to see him about a book of my own and he said to me negligently, as he was bowing me out – 'I'll take your friend's book'. He was really jumping at it. He had a *flair* – better than Billy's even. Of course he did not let on how pleased he was to get it and I was thankful on my client's behalf to obtain the exceedingly – as things are now – humble advance that he offered.[69]

The 1926 account differs only slightly from the 1928 account: Pawling read the novel in two days rather than three, Lawrence considered Hunt to have business skills, the manuscript was considered to be a 'selling concern' and Hunt had her own literary dealings with Pawling at the time. Perhaps most importantly, Pawling is reported to have said 'I'll take your friend's book' and Hunt allegedly intervened in the settling of the terms and the advance on her 'client's' behalf. Pawling acknowledged the connection between Hunt and Lawrence and may have considered Lawrence to be an integral part of the influential *English Review* set. Of course, Hunt could have couched Pawling's response in this way in order to strongly imply that her influence lay behind the acceptance of the novel, but we know that Lawrence considered her to be a fine businesswoman and that he had a history of persuading carefully selected women to take charge of his literary transactions.

After the manuscript had been accepted in late January 1910, Lawrence revised it extensively and by 11 April 1910 he had added an entirely new part three.⁷⁰ *The White Peacock* turned out to be a rather different novel to 'Nethermere' and the third part of the novel emphasises the tragic plight of George in a naturalistic manner, following Lawrence's reading of French authors such as Zola and Balzac. Shortly after the novel's publication he reflected in a letter to Heinemann's reader Frederick Atkinson that his revisions might have 'forfeited' its saleability, but that he might attain a 'small but individual name':

> I do not expect a great deal from it in the financial way. I feel that I have forfeited such expectations, and I do not mind, seeing that I could not help myself. But I had hoped, and I think justifiably, that the book would break me an entrance into the jungle of literature; that it would give me a small but individual name by which I should be known; and that it might bring me a bit of monthly work to eke out my lamentable state.⁷¹

Critics and biographers have never discussed Hunt's strategic actions in getting Lawrence's manuscript noticed by Pawling and she has been increasingly erased in contemporary accounts. Harry T. Moore writes that 'Miss Hunt . . . carried the manuscript of *The White Peacock* to the publishers' and he also acknowledges that she wrote 'exaggeratedly of the book'.⁷² Andrew Robertson mentions Hunt's delivery of the manuscript in a single sentence: '[t]he manuscript was delivered personally by Violet Hunt, novelist and short story writer, who lived with Ford'.⁷³ John Worthen simply states that 'Heinemann very naturally asked to see the manuscript'.⁷⁴ It is possible that Hunt delivered the manuscript before Heinemann asked to see it; she may have pressed Lawrence's case, since only a month had elapsed between the date of Lawrence's letter and his first visit to Heinemann's offices.

Examining the individual roles that exist within publishing houses is essential to gain a clearer insight into how the book was perceived by the publisher and the way in which it was marketed to attract a specific audience, yet critics rarely distinguish between these roles. Helen Baron, for example, incorrectly states that Pawling was Heinemann's 'new reader'.⁷⁵ In fact, Pawling owned a 45 per cent share in the business and had an extensive knowledge of the marketplace: he was the nephew of Charles Mudie and had worked for 'Mudie's Select Library' for sixteen years prior to his partnership with Heinemann in 1893. Heinemann had trained with the scholarly publisher Trübner and began his business independently in 1890 before he started working with Pawling.⁷⁶ With this background, Pawling would have known what kind of books the libraries would accept and what type of literature would be in high demand in the bookshops. Taste was constantly evolving in the commercial literary marketplace, so individuals like Pawling had not only to apply their commercial knowledge but also to anticipate shifts in the market. The dominance of the circulating libraries meant that novels were often written to the tastes of their subscribers who were mainly middle-class women. However, the death of the three-decker in favour of a single volume after 1894 meant that many consumers could afford to buy their own copies rather than depend on libraries. Consequently readers sought literature that appealed to their own interests, and authors had the opportunity to write different novels from those that Mudie would have accepted. These factors contributed towards the segmentation of the market.

Hunt must have thought that Lawrence's novel would attract Pawling's interest for its potential saleability; she would have known what kind of literature he liked because he was at that time dealing with the publication of her own work. The eagerness with which the shrewd and experienced Pawling accepted the novel ('He was really jumping at it') indicates that he considered the work a good proposition: a high quality novel that might sell.[77] Pawling would have seen Lawrence as a young novelist whom the firm could rely upon to deliver further novels and greater profit. Lawrence was offered a 15 per cent royalty on sales, at a time when 10 to 15 per cent was the norm. Hunt considered that Lawrence had been given a poor contract because her own *White Rose* had brought her a generous £100 advance and a 20 per cent royalty on the 6s price up to 5,000 copies, with 25 per cent thereafter.[78] However, her contract had been negotiated by Pinker and, helpfully, she was a personal friend of 'Billy' Heinemann.

As Hunt suggests, Heinemann was the likeable figurehead of the company; he was a generous innovator with international contacts and cosmopolitan interests. Pawling 'carried with him that atmosphere of the solid respectability of the House of Mudie' that was attractive to booksellers and which 'count[ed] for so much when thrown into the scales against the sometimes daring methods' of Heinemann himself.[79] The different skills and backgrounds of the two men combined to create a publishing house whose 'direction was endowed with taste, as well as flair for what would sell': this is the reason Hunt had aimed to publish her own work with Heinemann, following the advice given to her some years previously by another of the house's authors, William Somerset Maugham, who had gone over to Heinemann in 1902 with his novel *Mrs Craddock*.[80]

Hunt, then, was acting in Lawrence's best interests: she had enough confidence in the quality of his novel to recommend it to her friend's company, and to see it appear alongside her work in the same imprint. She may have read the novel in manuscript along with Hueffer and been attracted by its many literary allusions to the Pre-Raphaelites. She was the daughter of the painter Alfred

W. Hunt and grew up in the Rossetti circle; she shared several characteristics with the older Lettie Beardsall. Lawrence added aspects of Hunt's personality to the character of Lettie in his February–April 1910 rewrite (the new part three). The elder Lettie is a member of the 'Women's League';[81] Hunt was an active suffragist and founding member of the Women Writers' Suffrage League. Lettie acts maternally toward the 'Pound' figure who appears in part three: the character is described as having 'under her wing a young literary fellow, who affected the "Doady" style – Dora Copperfield's "Doady". He had bunches of half-curly hair and a romantic black cravat'.[82] Details from Hunt's two accounts can be corroborated: it was indeed Pawling who corresponded with Lawrence about the novel's publication (despite Lawrence having written directly to Heinemann to offer him the novel on 15 December 1909). On 19 January 1910, Lawrence responded to Pawling's request to meet him in person. Four days later he told Louie: '[m]y novel is practically accepted ... I am to alter a bit in parts, then the thing will come out, and I shall have royalties'.[83] As he did when summoning Hunt and outlining the terms of his offer, Pawling moved quickly to secure the novel and with his Mudie's experience in mind Lawrence was asked to censor his work to satisfy the tender sensibilities of 'the old ladies of Croydon'. By 11 April 1910 Lawrence wrote to Pawling that he had

> removed all the offensive morsels, all the damns, the devils and the sweat ... My own skin is not super-sensitive, so I can hardly judge what will make delicate people dither. But to my fancy, it is now all quite suitable even for the proverbial jeune fille – a kind of exquisite scented soap, in fact.[84]

Madame Magazine

The White Peacock was marketed as a novel for fashionable middle-class women. On 4 February 1911 it appeared in the 'Books Received' list in *Madame* magazine, alongside ten other books by mostly – apparently – female authors whose names are no longer familiar (such titles include *Marie Clare* by Marguerite Ardoux; *The Third Wife* by Herbert Flowerdew; *Boudoir Poems* by Muriel Edgar; *When Woman Loves* by R. Wilson and *The Bourgeois Queen of Paris* by Janet M. Clark). On 26 August Lawrence's novel was discussed in a brief but laudatory hitherto-unknown review in the magazine. The anonymous reviewer stated:

> If the object in a book is to create a reading-public for future work, the author of the above novel has achieved success, for the strongest impression that would be left upon the mind of most readers would be the determination to see the next work of D. H. Lawrence. The characters are drawn

with the utmost skill, and as they are real, primitive characters, this has been no light task. The book is a very strong work, curiously mingling the most delicately romantic with the vulgar real. The descriptive powers of the writer are quite remarkable, especially welcome, as that sort of writing is lost sight of in the present-day novel.[85]

The review is so positive that it may prompt us to question whether there had been a background influence working in support of Lawrence. *Madame* was a sister paper of the nationalistic magazine *The Throne*, owned by Réné Byles, a notoriously skilful publicist who Lawrence had lunch with on 3 July 1910.[86] Hunt claimed that she 'interviewed [Lawrence] in *The Throne*', but the only reference to him or his work in this little-known magazine during 1911 and 1912 is a notice of *The Trespasser* as one of the 'BOOKS WE CAN RECOMMEND' on 15 August 1912.[87] Given her comment and the evidence we have that she was promoting Lawrence to her friends in the publishing industry at this time, it is plausible that Hunt may have influenced the review in *Madame*. She was a pervasive presence within its pages during these years: St. John Adcock, who wrote the column 'Feminism in Bookland', considered her to be 'One of our leading woman writers'. Her heavily illustrated 'BRILLIANT NEW SERIAL', 'The Celebrity's Daughter', appeared in the magazine from 15 April 1912.[88] The glossy 3d magazine described itself as 'An Illustrated Journal of Fashion, Social Events and the Drama' and 'the brightest of women's fashion weeklies'. It is not difficult to imagine why Lawrence's novel (with its discussion of fashionable cultural trends and the French drama of Sarah Bernhardt, to whom Lettie is likened[89]) was considered apt material for the readership of *Madame*. So while Hueffer's assistance from autumn 1909 was undoubtedly crucial, Hunt's hitherto overlooked endorsement of Lawrence is also significant and provides further evidence of his engagement with women as facilitators of the publication of his earliest work. The next chapter will consider the similarly practical but more prolonged support Edward Garnett provided from August 1911. Garnett turned out to be a more suitable mentor for Lawrence as he developed his interests in writing a more risqué romantic – even erotic – novel.

Notes

1. Crichton, '"An Interview with Lawrence", Kyle S. Crichton' (1981), p. 216.
2. E. T. 156.
3. E. T. 157.

4. Lawrence asked McLeod 'to get him a lot of sermon paper at Boots' (which he used when writing 'Nethermere') and gave an 'anxious demand to let him know' if the writing was good (Harry T. Moore, *The Priest of Love: A Life of D. H. Lawrence* (1975), pp. 90–1). Lawrence met Corke through Mason in late 1908, but they became close from September 1909.
5. Violet Hunt, *The Flurried Years* (1926), p. 47.
6. E. T. 158.
7. E. T. 156; 158.
8. Hueffer, 'The Political and Diplomatic' (1908): 162–3.
9. E. T. 157.
10. Ford, *Portraits from Life*, p. 70.
11. *L*, I, 139; E. T. 158.
12. E. T. 158.
13. *English Review*, iii (November 1909). Lawrence's poems appear on pp. 561–5. The articles were authored by J. A. Hobson, H. W. Nevinson, G. P. Gooch and E. S. P. Haynes, respectively.
14. In *Austin Harrison and the* English Review (2008), Martha S. Vogeler implies that Harrison was employed to edit the journal from December 1909 (pp. 61–2). Max Saunders, however, states that 'The last issue that Ford put together was the one for February 1910 . . . though under Harrison it continued to carry pieces that Ford had selected.' *Ford Madox Ford: A Dual Life* (1996), p. 252.
15. Hueffer, 'The Functions of the Arts in the Republic: I. Literature' (1908): 159.
16. Douglas Goldring reproduces the key aims of Hueffer's project, discussed with Joseph Conrad: *South Lodge; Reminiscences of Violet Hunt, Ford Madox Ford and the English Review Circle* (1943), p. 24.
17. Mark S. Morrisson, 'The Myth of the Whole and Ford's *English Review*' (2001), p. 32.
18. Mark S. Morrisson, *The Public Face of Modernism: Little Magazines, Audiences, and Reception, 1905–1920* (2001), pp. 32; 38.
19. Morrisson, *The Public Face of Modernism*, p. 41.
20. See Walter Edwards Houghton, *The Wellesley Index to Victorian Periodicals, 1824–1900* (1972), pp. 173–83; and Alvin Sullivan, *British Literary Magazines* (1983), Vol. III, pp. 131–5. Harris was replaced as editor by W. L. Courtney in 1894.
21. *L*, II, 22.
22. James B. Pinker Letter to Violet Hunt, 28 February, 1908 (Cornell University, Kroch Library, Ford Madox Ford Collection). Quoted in Morrisson, *The Public Face of Modernism*, p. 44.

23. Hunt, *The Flurried Years*, p. 19.
24. See Saunders, *Ford: A Dual Life*, p. 242; 548 fn. 9. Ford named the publication as the *Cornhill*: Ford Madox Ford, *Mightier than the Sword* (1938), p. 132.
25. Hunt, *The Flurried Years*, p. 18.
26. Ibid., p. 24.
27. Hunt, *The Flurried Years*, p. 21. See also Saunders, *Ford: A Dual Life*, p. 247; Violet Hunt, 'The Coach' (1909): 665–80.
28. Ford, *Return to Yesterday*, p. 377.
29. John Lazarus, 'Saturday Love Song' (1909): 194; 'Three Poems' sequence [alongside Lawrence] (1909): 566–8. Lazarus's 'Ferrer's Funeral Hymn' appears in the *New Age*, v (28 October 1909): 473. Poets who previously occupied this position include Bennett, Rachel Annand Taylor, Pound, Rupert Brooke, Laurence Binyon, F. S. Flint, Galsworthy, Hardy and Emile Verhaeren.
30. Henry Yoxall, 'Books and Pictures' (1909): lxxvi.
31. *L*, I, 151 (letter conjecturally dated to early 1910) and E. T. 122.
32. Hunt, *The Flurried Years*, p. 29.
33. Ford Madox Hueffer, *Collected Poems of Ford Madox Hueffer*. First published by Max Goschen in 1913, though dated 1914. The copy I consulted was a 1916 Martin Secker edition, p. 24. I follow Saunders in using 1913 as the date of first publication (*Ford: A Dual Life*, p. 495).
34. Bourdieu, *The Field of Cultural Production: Essays on Art and Literature*, p. 51.
35. *L*, I, 138.
36. *L*, I, 144.
37. Saunders reproduces Hueffer's inaccurate account: *Ford: A Dual Life*, pp. 298; 248.
38. Hunt, *The Flurried Years*, p. 28.
39. Ibid., p. 47.
40. Violet Hunt, *I Have This to Say: The Story of my Flurried Years* (1926), pp. 257–8.
41. Jessie also approached Garnett about the publication of her manuscript: *L*, I, 525; 551.
42. Douglas Goldring, *Life Interests* (1948), p. 83.
43. Ford, *Portraits from Life*, p. 72.
44. Ibid., p. 71.
45. David Garnett, *Great Friends: Portraits of Seventeen Writers* (1979), p. 50.
46. *L*, I, 147.
47. *L*, I, 150; 179; 246. Lydia Lawrence writes to her sister Lettice Berry on 11 July 1910 about 'Odour': 'It is to be in the August number of the

"Review'" (MS UN La Ac 2/8/8/1, D. H. Lawrence Collection. Manuscripts and Special Collections. University of Nottingham). On 6 April 1911 Harrison had written to Lawrence 'I am looking forward to see "Chrysanthemums" with all its old atmosphere and the old ending, and less of the early talk' (MS UN LaB 188). Harrison's letter is reproduced in *L*, I, 254 fn. 3.
48. This element of the transcription is not reproduced in *L*, VIII, 2–3, nor does the editor note that Lawrence copied out the letter.
49. *L*, I, 148–9.
50. *L*, VIII, 2–3.
51. Hardy to Blackmore, 8 June 1875. Richard L. Purdy and Michael Millgate, *The Collected Letters of Thomas Hardy: Volume I, 1840–1892* (1978), p. 37.
52. Lawrence 're-enacted' the novel's scenes on the 'Annesley Hills': E. T. 96; Ford Madox Ford, 'The Reader' (1924): 503–4. Hueffer mentions his familiarity with *Lorna Doone* in his *Ancient Lights and Certain New Reflections* (1911), p. 180.
53. Waldo Hilary Dunn, *R. D. Blackmore* (1956), pp. 126–46.
54. See Pamela Knight's 'Introduction' to R. D. Blackmore, *Lorna Doone* (2004), vii.
55. A. M. W. Stirling, *William de Morgan and his Wife* (1922), pp. 230–60.
56. Hunt, *The Flurried Years*, p. 27. Ford had written in the historical romance sub-genre in his *Fifth Queen* trilogy (1906–8). His collaborations with Conrad in writing *The Inheritors* (1901 – Hueffer's only book published by Heinemann until 1934 and *It Was the Nightingale*) and *Romance* (1903) were (in Conrad's words) attempts to write in 'the genre that is currently very much in vogue with the public' (Letter dated 8 November 1903). Frederick R. Karl and Laurence Davies, *The Collected Letters of Joseph Conrad: Volume 3, 1903–1907* (1988), p. 76.
57. Ford Madox Hueffer, 'The Critical Attitude: The Two Shilling Novel' (1909): 321.
58. *L*, I, 144–5.
59. See Hunt, *The Flurried Years*, p. 26. Lawrence shared copies of *Black and White* with Jessie's father: E. T. 25.
60. *L*, I, 188; 199; 381.
61. UN MS La B 187/1–2.
62. *L*, I, 227–8. For Hunt's review see Draper, 38–9.
63. *L*, I, 230; 364.
64. Marie Secor, 'Violet Hunt, Novelist: A Reintroduction' (1976): 25–6.
65. Barbara Belford, *Violet: The Story of the Irrepressible Violet Hunt and Her Circle of Lovers and Friends – Ford Madox Ford, H. G. Wells, Somerset Maugham, and Henry James* (1990), p. 136.

66. Unpublished letter of Violet Hunt, owned by Olin Library, Cornell University, Ithaca, New York. Quoted by Secor, 'Violet Hunt, Novelist: A Reintroduction', p. 29.
67. See also *L*, VIII, 3 for Lawrence's 19 January 1910 note to Pawling, confirming their meeting.
68. Hunt quoted in Frederic Whyte, *William Heinemann: A Memoir* (1928), pp. 229–30.
69. Hunt, *I Have This to Say*, pp. 257–8.
70. *L*, I, 158.
71. *L*, I, 222.
72. Moore, *The Life and Works of D. H. Lawrence*, p. 39.
73. *WP*, xxvi.
74. *EY*, 222.
75. *PM*, xxv.
76. Anon., 'Mr Sydney Pawling' (1923), p. 12.
77. Hunt, *I Have This to Say*, pp. 257–8.
78. Belford, *Violet*, p. 136.
79. This comment was related to Whyte by Mr E. C. Houston, an acquaintance of Henry Le Caron, who published the political memoir *Twenty-Five Years in the Secret Service* (1892) with Heinemann. *William Heinemann*, p. 77.
80. Hunt, quoted in Whyte, *William Heinemann*, p. 229; Belford, *Violet*, p. 136.
81. *WP*, 297.
82. *WP*, 305, *cf.* Lawrence's depiction of Pound's appearance in *L*, I, 165.
83. *L*, I, 152.
84. *WP*, xxviii; *L*, I, 158.
85. Anon., 'What to Read' (1911): 348.
86. *L*, I, 167. Hueffer recalls Byles's skills as a publicist in Ford, *Return to Yesterday*, pp. 238–65.
87. Hunt, *I Have This To Say*, pp. 257–8; Frank A. Mumby, 'Mainly About Books' (1912): 308.
88. *Madame* (18 November 1911): 290; (15 April 1912): 17.
89. *WP*, 30.

4

'My dear Garnett . . . why do you take so much trouble for me?': Edward Garnett, 'Friend and Protector'

Edward Garnett was one of the most important literary friends Lawrence ever made. From August 1911 to November 1914 he offered Lawrence practical editorial advice and emotional support, publication opportunities and career guidance, as well as introductions to a range of professional contacts. Although Garnett's support of Lawrence lessened after spring 1914, the last publication he helped to edit and market during Lawrence's early career was *The Prussian Officer and Other Stories*, published by Duckworth on 26 November that year. Since they were not often bestsellers, short stories in volume format were usually only published by those whose name had attained a degree of recognition, so this publication was a key milestone for Lawrence in the attainment of his professional career. Garnett's crucial role as one of Lawrence's early literary mentors has long been acknowledged. John Worthen observes that 'Garnett's support, practical advice and influence at Duckworths made all the difference to Lawrence's prospects.'[1] Reviewing Lawrence's career from the vantage point of 1913, Mark Kinkead-Weekes describes Garnett as 'an ideal father-figure' or 'a much older brother' with whom Lawrence could share his deepest concerns about his life and work.[2] When they met in 1911 Lawrence was twenty-six and Garnett was aged forty-three. Garnett came from an intellectual rather than monied middle-class background and he romanticised his mother's Anglo-Irish nationality, believing himself to be a natural outsider. In his own time Garnett was renowned for the level of work he carried out on behalf of the authors for whom he was responsible: surveying the literary scene between 1901 and 1917, Frank Swinnerton notes that 'among all English readers, [Garnett] was considered pre-eminent'.[3]

However, contemporary critical appreciation of the role Garnett played varies. Jean Moorcroft Wilson's 2015 biography of Edward Thomas recognises that 'Garnett's support of Thomas was of crucial importance to him in 1904 and the following decade', but it does not go into detail about the extent of the guidance Garnett offered.[4] Pierre Coustillas's 2012 biography of George Gissing unfairly considers Garnett in 1895 to have been 'a young man of twenty-seven and scanty experience'. Coustillas states that Garnett is now 'mainly remembered as the husband of Constance Garnett and as a publisher's reader to several successive firms'.[5] Helen Smith's biography *An Uncommon Reader: A Life of Edward Garnett, Mentor and Editor of Literary Genius* (2017) does much to contest this view, making full use of archival materials to uncover the extent of Garnett's appreciation of new talent. His intensive support of Joseph Conrad from 1894 (and until that author's death in 1924) has been fully appreciated by Conrad scholars. Cedric Watts observes that as well as reading manuscripts with a sharp eye for originality and distinction, Garnett strove to get those manuscripts into print; he would meet and correspond with authors, 'encouraging, cajoling, criticising; he would urge them to read works which he felt might provide artistic challenge and sustenance, would introduce his favourite authors to others'.[6] As Garnett's 'favourite author' (at least in 1913), Lawrence was an appreciative beneficiary of this attentiveness.[7]

Garnett's role in Lawrence's career, like that of Conrad, was wide-ranging. During their friendship Garnett sent several of Lawrence's short stories, sketches, plays and poems to a variety of publication outlets and he advised Lawrence on which books he should review for the *English Review*. Apart from persuading Duckworth to accept *The Trespasser* and *Sons and Lovers*, Garnett was, for example, influential in getting the poems 'Violets' and 'Lightning' and the sketch 'A Miner at Home' published in the *Nation* (in November 1911 and March 1912 respectively) and by 8 March 1912 he sent the short story 'The Harrassed Angel' to Mitchell Kennerley's US magazine *Forum* (it was published as 'The Soiled Rose' in March 1913 and as 'The Shades of Spring' in *The Prussian Officer* collection). He was not often successful in getting Lawrence's work into print, which makes his persistence even more admirable. Critical discussion of Garnett has too often focused on what is generally perceived as his destructive role in cutting the manuscript of *Sons and Lovers* by one-tenth in order to shorten it to what was a more standard length for a published novel and to reduce its sexual content. Novels became shorter in the early twentieth century to accommodate the new norm of a one-volume format. The original *Sons and Lovers* manuscript ran to 180,000 words, whereas the standard length would have been 120,000, or *c*.400 pages.[8] Garnett had to satisfy his employer Duckworth and fulfil his role as a professional reader by making the novel acceptable for the literary marketplace, but that does not mean that he condoned literary censorship. On the contrary, as an ambitious creative writer himself Garnett notoriously opposed censorship and this detail has often been overlooked in assessments of him as the editor who 'botched, censored, and butchered' *Sons and Lovers*.⁹ This chapter rejects a narrow view of Garnett and takes account of his work not only as a professional publisher's reader, but also as a respected literary critic and writer who was broad-minded and progressive. Lawrence repeatedly expressed his gratitude to Garnett for his assistance and the decision to dedicate *Sons and Lovers* 'To Edward Garnett' shows his appreciation for the work Garnett had carried out on his behalf; he inscribed Garnett's copy 'To my friend and protector in love and literature Edward Garnett from the Author'.¹⁰ The inscription alerts us to the fact that we cannot entirely separate Garnett's friendship with Lawrence and his early acceptance of Lawrence and Frieda's relationship from his role as editor and his 'investment' in *Sons and Lovers*; the investment was both personal and professional. On 21 May 1912 Lawrence wrote to Garnett that 'Frieda sort of clings to the idea of you, as the only man in England who would be a refuge.'¹¹

Specifically, this chapter examines Garnett's background and his earliest interactions with Lawrence before Lawrence made the transition from full-time elementary school teacher to professional writer. It discusses the commercial negotiations that took place between Lawrence and the publishing houses of Heinemann and Duckworth to examine how *The Trespasser* came to be published by Duckworth at Garnett's instigation. By taking on *The Trespasser*, Garnett helped Lawrence to negotiate the fine line between poetic 'erotic' writing and outspoken sexual or pornographic writing which would have been detrimental to his early career as a novelist. By understanding Garnett's background more fully, we begin to acquire a more nuanced sense of his relationship with Lawrence and the nature of Garnett's attraction to Lawrence's work, which in turn helps us to better understand how Lawrence's career, authorial identity and comprehension of the literary marketplace was shaped by Garnett's mentorship. The chapter will draw to a close at the point when Lawrence began to distance himself from Hueffer: a time when his dealings with Heinemann also became more difficult and when he sought Garnett's advice about the publication of the novel that was to become *The Trespasser*. Rather than seeking to provide an overview of all Garnett's engagements with Lawrence's work my intention is to focus in detail on a very specific turning point in Lawrence's early career to provide a response to the question that Lawrence put to Garnett on 17 April 1912: 'Why do you take so much trouble for me?'¹²

Edward Garnett: Publisher's Reader

Garnett at T. Fisher Unwin, 1887–99

When Garnett started his career in 1887 at the age of nineteen he carried out general office tasks for T. Fisher Unwin, but he quickly moved on to the role of reader on a weekly salary of ten shillings. When a manuscript was submitted to a firm it was screened by a 'gatekeeper' reader; if it passed this process then it was sent to at least one other reader who would produce a report before figures and terms were discussed, generally with the input of the head of the firm. According to the level of responsibility they held, readers reported on the literary worth and commercial potential of manuscripts and took on editorial work; they might also write publicity blurbs and create advertising flyers before duplicating them, using, for example, technology such as the new cyclostyle copier machine which had been invented in London in 1890. During his time at Unwin Garnett's colleagues and fellow readers were W. H. Chesson, Vaughan Nash and, from winter 1896 until 1902, G. K. Chesterton. There were other positions within available. At Unwin T. Werner Laurie was General Manager before he started his own publishing company in 1904 and A. D. Marks (later director of The Quality Press) was Trade Manager.[13]

Thirty-four-year-old Thomas Fisher Unwin established his publishing house in 1882 when he bought out Marshall, Japp and Co (whose list largely consisted of nonfiction) for £1,000. The business returned relatively small average annual profits of between £600 and £700 until 1900; by 1912 it made returns of £6,000.[14] In comparison, Heinemann's profits in 1900 (a decade after its foundation) were a healthy £4,848; by 1912 the figure declined to £3,557, before reaching £5,406 a year later.[15] By 1917 Unwin had published twenty-seven series and became known for his support of new writers. Publishers had begun launching inexpensive books in collectible series to tempt readers to buy and build up their own libraries rather than borrow reading matter from public and subscription libraries. Hueffer's first book, *The Brown Owl* (1891), was published as the first volume in Unwin's 'Children's Library' series when Hueffer was eighteen; Garnett had been the reader who recommended its publication, having been urged to do so by Hueffer's artist grandfather, Ford Madox Brown. Hueffer was paid £10 for the copyright, which was a normal arrangement in the years before a royalty system became general practice at the turn of the century. He would have made a great deal more with royalty terms since the book had gone into a tenth edition by 1904, but for the publisher this was a sound investment and it showed good judgement on the part of the young Garnett.[16] Peter Keating explains that the royalty system was an American phenomenon; it was 'hardly known in Britain before the 1880s' but was introduced gradually thereafter. In 1903 H. G. Wells called for legislation to prevent authors from selling the copyright of their books to publishers outright.[17] The royalty system benefited everyone involved, serving to 'check unscrupulous publishers, protect unpractical authors, give both sides an interest in a book's success, and therefore improve relations between publishers and authors'.[18] Despite his support for writers in their early careers, Unwin was notorious for refusing to increase the pay of those whose careers took off, so writers such as John Galsworthy, Somerset Maugham, Conrad, George Moore and Hueffer left Unwin as they made their names; many of Unwin's authors moved on to Heinemann. To balance the risk of publishing unknown writers whom he would have to advertise sufficiently to introduce them to the public and on whose work he may not have broken even, Unwin was one of the chief exponents (alongside G. Bell and Sons) of colonial editions. Unwin purchased the novels of other publishers in the form of flat sheets; he had the sheets bound before selling them in his 'Colonial Libraries' series to booksellers in the dominions.[19] Unwin developed his relations with the international market when he acted as an early form of literary agent by serialising fiction for publication in America, charging a commission fee of 10 per cent.[20] Members of publishing firms regularly acted as talent scouts for their American connections, which is how Garnett (possibly on Hueffer's recommendation) first came into contact with Lawrence.

A long time before this connection, however, Garnett was developing his career by helping to launch Unwin's very successful 'Pseudonym Library' series (1890–6), which ran to fifty-two pocket-sized paper or cloth volumes. Garnett asked the company traveller to sell the volumes to railway booksellers, since their low price of 1s 6d or 2s for a new title dramatically undercut the 3s 6d or 6s fee for a reprint edition of a three-decker, as well as competing with a 2s yellowback (volumes of which were mainly stereotyped reprints of fiction novels, including sensation fiction, adventure stories, handbooks and biographies).[21] The Pseudonym Library series published work by writers who were then little-known, such as Edith Nesbit, John Buchan, Ouida, Vernon Lee, Mark Rutherford and Olive Schreiner. It also published collections of Russian short stories and works by other foreign writers, including Giovanni Verga's *Cavalleria Rusticana: And Other Tales of Sicilian Peasant Life* (1893), which Lawrence would go on to translate and publish with Jonathan Cape in 1928. The mystery surrounding the authorship of the books was a clever marketing ploy: it intrigued readers who were left guessing about whether or not they were reading an author they were familiar with, at the same time as it allowed Unwin to try out the work of new writers whose names would not have been recognised by the general public. The concept encouraged unknown writers to submit manuscripts; known authors would be less interested in publishing their work under a pseudonym since it would bring them no public recognition and it also allowed the author's gender to remain ambiguous.[22] When the author became better known and wanted to claim credit for the work, the writer's identity could be revealed by a press interview or review, which sparked further interest in the volume. The Pseudonym Library included John Galsworthy's first book, a collection of short adventure stories entitled *From the*

Four Winds (1897) released under the pseudonym 'John Sinjohn'. The edition ran to 500 copies, but Galsworthy had to pay for its publication. It marked the start of a friendship between Garnett and Galsworthy that lasted for over a decade. Unwin also published several of W. B. Yeats's early works, including his short autobiographical novel *John Sherman*, which appeared under the pen name 'Ganconagh' in March 1891.[23] That month, Garnett negotiated a pay rise for himself from £2/6d to £4 per week and took on further responsibilities in the firm. In the summer, the twenty-five-year-old Yeats asked Garnett and Constance to read the manuscript of his verse drama *The Countess Kathleen*, which Garnett considered 'most original'.[24] In September 1892 500 copies were published in Unwin's 'Cameo Series' (a poetry library).

The partner series to the Pseudonym Library was the 'Autonym Library'. It was intended for writers whose names were better known and enabled the publisher to advertise the strength of his list. On the advice of Clement Shorter (editor of the monthly *English Illustrated Magazine*, who had commissioned from George Gissing several stories and sketches), Unwin approached Gissing in January 1895 about publishing a book in the Autonym Library. Although Gissing was notoriously bad at negotiating good terms with publishers (he often undersold himself, or stuck with poor publishers from a mistaken sense of loyalty), in financial terms his career was just beginning to take off.[25] Unwin paid £5 per 1,000 words for the sale of all rights to America, Britain and the colonies even before his work had been seen by the firm's readers. Neither Garnett nor Chesson commended the 33,000-word typescript of *Sleeping Fires* that Gissing had written specifically for the Autonym Library. Coustillas is particularly offended on behalf of his biographical subject by Garnett's reader's report; he comments that '[w]ith a cocksureness which sometimes consorts with callow youth, [Garnett] ran head on into Gissing's admittedly unambitious achievement and pulled it to pieces'.[26] Garnett compared the work unfavourably to Gissing's three-decker *New Grub Street* (Smith, Elder, 1891), concluding:

> We think TFU ought seriously to consider what is the value of a story like *Sleeping Fires*. Of course Gissing's name has a certain marketable value, but we feel that a strong effort ought to be made to get good work out of him and that he ought not to get rid of work which very likely would be refused by every other publisher. 'Sleeping Fires' we consider would prove a very bad bargain for The Autonym, in the long run, even if the name did sell a few extra thousand copies.[27]

Garnett may have been aggrieved that Unwin had negotiated a costly deal for what he felt was an inadequate work before he had received his readers' advice. He acknowledges that Gissing had accumulated some cultural capital and that his name would help the book to sell, but considers that this is not enough to excuse a story so 'horribly dull', which might serve only to discredit the Series and therefore prove to be a 'bad bargain'. In his comment 'we feel that a strong effort ought to be made to get good work out of him', Garnett implicitly criticises Unwin for his over-enthusiastic approach to Gissing and, characteristically, uses 'we' in order to sound more authoritative, as if he is the spokesperson of the firm of 'TFU', or at least representative of its small team of readers. Chesson's report was less damning: '[t]he defect of the quality is obvious: it is *artificial*', but it 'must be treated with respect and therefore it would be agreeable to have a Gissing story in the "half crown" series [of which] this is a fair enough specimen for the purpose'.[28] Chesson self-deprecatingly referred to himself as 'Mr Unwin's receiver and weeder of MSS', but Unwin must have agreed with his judgement and decided not to lose face by backing out of the agreement; he bought the work for a generous £150.[29] This case demonstrates the tensions that existed within publishing firms when the advice of an experienced reader (who would have to work with the author on editorial and marketing matters) was not followed. The authority inevitably rested with the owner of the firm, which proved challenging to an ambitious, dedicated and self-confident reader such as Garnett.

Aubrey Beardsley was commissioned to design an advertising poster for both series. He was at that time illustrating both *The Yellow Book* (which took its name from the covers in which controversial French novels were published) and *The Savoy* (1896) which was published by Leonard Smithers who also issued pornographic books.[30] The poster image of the so-called 'Beardsley Woman' browsing a bookstall played on bourgeois fears of the middle-class woman reader as a consumer of potentially immoral works. Contemporaneous reviewers frequently saw in the independent, sensual and modern 'Beardsley Woman' signs of corruption, sexual deviance and emancipation.[31] Significantly, the cover designs for *The Yellow Book*'s first and second volumes each featured a New Woman figure glancing over a selection of untitled books. The marketing of the Pseudonym and Autonym series was thereby connected with avant-garde and decadent publications, making a statement that the series targeted a similar readership that challenged conservative social codes.

Although he was known to be prudent, Unwin paid generous sums for work in which he believed, spending £1,500 to publish Olive Schreiner's 25,000-word 6s novel *Trooper Peter Halket of Mashonaland* (1897) which attacked the British South Africa Company and accused colonialist Cecil Rhodes of murdering Matabele envoys.[32] Unwin was 'an intelligent man with probably more understanding of nonfiction than of fiction, a tyrant in the office, capable of exasperating meanness in money matters, and an idealist in matters of social reform'.[33] He published periodicals with cosmopolitan and internationalist agendas, such as the multilingual *Cosmopolis: an International Review* (1896–8) and the *Independent Review* (1903–7). His 'Reformer's Bookshelf' series included Edward Carpenter's *Towards Democracy* (1892) which had initially been published in Manchester and London by The Labour Press in 1883; Lawrence gave this book to Helen Corke while in Croydon. She read Carpenter's *Love's Coming of Age* after her friendship with Lawrence ended and began a correspondence with Carpenter.[34] Like *The Trespasser*, *Towards Democracy* was taken on by Mitchell Kennerley in 1912, but Carpenter had to enlist the help of the Society of Authors to claim his unpaid royalties. Lawrence faced similar financial problems with Kennerley in 1914. In 'The Bad Side of Books' Lawrence recalled that Kennerley sent him a £20 royalty cheque for his American edition of *Sons and Lovers* but there was 'an alteration in the date on the cheque, and the bank would not cash it'.[35] Unwin was also to have published Carpenter's *Love's Coming of Age* but he cancelled his contract in the wake of the Wilde trial in 1895. Since he was senior reader at this time Garnett was likely to have been the reader who initially advised publication, although it is not known if he was involved in revoking the contract. It was that senior position which brought Garnett into contact with Conrad.

When Conrad submitted the manuscript of *Almayer's Folly* to T. Fisher Unwin in 1894 he hoped that it might be published in the Pseudonym Library under the name 'Kamudi', but it exceeded the Series word limit of 36,000 words. In January 1895, three months before the novel's publication, Garnett advised Conrad to 'follow his own path and disregard the public's taste'. Conrad responded, 'But I won't live in an attic!'[36] Garnett supported Conrad's aesthetic principles, judging that having a prestigious author who did not 'sell' added cultural capital to Unwin's list. Conrad accepted a £20 advance with no royalties, but Unwin spent generously on advertisements and the 6s novel received long notices in the prestigious *Saturday Review* and *Athenaeum*. *Almayer's Folly*, however, took seven years to reach its third impression.[37] Although Unwin lost heavily on Conrad he remained open to wage negotiations with his senior reader. During further discussions about his pay in early 1895, Constance wrote that Garnett was 'guaranteed not less than £350 a year'.[38] The Garnetts were becoming financially comfortable: by March, Constance had published six volumes of translations in just over a year, earning from Heinemann approximately £30 to £40 per volume and she inherited £1,000 which she used to commission the building of the Cearne in Edenbridge, Kent.[39]

Literature and social purity

While Unwin published bestselling writers (such as 'John Oliver Hobbes' [Pearl Craigie], S. R. Crockett, H. de Vere Stacpole and Ethel M. Dell) he also published politically contentious works. As reader, Garnett was shaping the firm's reputation during the time when social purity groups targeted literature. The 1857 Obscene Publications Act had made the publication and sale of obscene writing illegal and it extended the remit of the police to intervene and target publishers. The Society for the Suppression of Vice (1802–85) was succeeded in 1889 by the Public Morality Council, founded by the Bishop of London. These organisations acted as pressure groups lobbying the government to act against the corruption of – in the words of the Benjamin 'Hicklin Ruling' of 1868 – 'those who are open to such immoral influences'; the ruling sought to devise a common law definition of obscenity.[40] These actions contributed towards creating a climate of censorship that lasted long into the twentieth century. In one of the best-known cases of the period, the literary sub-committee of the National Vigilance Association (founded in 1885) pursued the publisher Henry Vizetelly, who published eighteen 2s volumes of English translations of Zola's work between 1884 and 1889.[41] Katherine Mullin has observed that Vizetelly specifically advertised the Zola translations as erotic literature and hoped to reap the financial benefits of selling fiction marketed as risqué, but he was prosecuted in 1888 for obscene libel and fined £100. A year later when he reissued Zola's work he was imprisoned and fined £200. Receiving moral censure was a sign of 'creative martyrdom, struggle and rebellion'; it could either offer greater sales figures, or damage writers' and publishers' reputations. In this case, it was the publisher who took the risk and paid a steep price for doing so.[42]

Vizetelly also published George Moore's *A Modern Lover* (1883) and *A Mummer's Wife* (1885). Moore, like Vizetelly, was an assiduous self-publicist who for a time actively associated himself with Zola; as well as having written prefaces to some of Vizetelly's editions of Zola, Moore wrote to Zola in 1882 offering to produce an English translation of *L'Assommoir*. In 1891 Moore collaborated with Alexander Teixeira de Mattos on the translation of a dramatisation of Zola's *Thérèse Raquin*, which was staged at the Royalty Theatre, Soho, on 9 October 1891.[43] Moore's novels were withheld by Mudie's because of their frank exploration of sexual desire. *A Modern Lover* 'gained an immediate reputation for immorality' and *A Mummer's Wife* 'appalled the critics', so that 'only the boldest of publishers would deal with him'.[44] *A Modern Lover* was removed from library circulation because 'two ladies in the country' complained about a scene that involved the nudity of a character as she posed for the artist protagonist (similarly, Heinemann made Lawrence censor a passage in *The White Peacock* that referred to Lady Chrystabel having Annabel 'in her bedroom while she drew Greek statues' of him[45]). Moore wrote an article responding to the action, which was printed in the *Pall Mall Gazette* on 10 December 1884. His pamphlet *Literature at Nurse, or, Circulating Morals* (1885) mocked the prudery and censorship of the circulating libraries and objected to the proposition that realist novels could exert a harmful influence on young female readers.[46] The controversy offered Moore greater exposure and notoriety as a provocative writer and his sales did not suffer: at the time of writing the pamphlet, *A Mummer's Wife* was already in its fourth edition. *Esther Waters* (published by Walter Scott in 1894, following Vizetelly's death) was banned by W. H. Smith's circulating libraries a month after its publication. A prominent review had observed that Moore was 'hampered by the trammels of Zolaism', but the novel's notoriety as a cause célèbre for debates about libraries and literary censorship boosted sales and brought Moore financial security.[47]

By 1896 Moore was a frequent contributor to Unwin's periodical *Cosmopolis*. That year, Moore agreed to publish his next novel with Unwin: it was to be *Evelyn Innes* (1898). The heroine of *Evelyn Innes* sings in a Wagnerian opera; like Helena Verden in Lawrence's *The Trespasser*, Evelyn is a musician who takes an unsuitable man as her lover. Provocative literary responses to Wagner's music were prevalent in the later nineteenth century, especially among French writers; Baudelaire wrote 'Richard Wagner et Tannhäuser à Paris' (1861) which was followed by Mallarmé's 'Hommage à Richard Wagner' (1885), Verlaine's 'Parsifal' (1886) and Huysman's 'L'Ouverture de Tannhäuser' (1893). During a period when he renewed his acquaintance with (and attraction to) Yeats in 1895, Moore published a homoerotic fantasy imagining himself as 'the prey of' Wagner, 'that dark, sensual-eyed Bohemian'.[48] As Howard J. Booth observes, Moore was also an influence on Lawrence's early work, with *A Modern Lover* acting as an intertext for Lawrence's story 'A Modern Lover' of 1910.[49] Lawrence read several of Moore's books and lent *Evelyn Innes* to Helen Corke in October 1909.[50] Significantly, George Neville recalled that after Lawrence had read *Esther Waters* he told him that he 'wanted to write on matters of sex . . . deeper than anybody had ever gone so far'.[51] Moore thought that Garnett had read *Evelyn Innes* while he was working for Unwin.[52] If Garnett had already worked on this novel and dealt with authors such as Moore who had been notoriously outspoken on the subject of female sexuality then he would be undaunted at the prospect of editing Lawrence's 'erotic' manuscript for commercial publication in 1911.

Despite Garnett's eye for talent, by the end of 1899 Unwin dispensed with his services due to their 'differences in temperament and outlook'.[53] A. D. Marks suggested that Garnett found it difficult to get on with Unwin, 'a cold, humourless man, who liked to pose as the great and omniscient publisher, the patron of authors, who were exceptionally fortunate to be published by him'.[54] In private Conrad and Garnett sarcastically referred to Unwin as the 'Enlightened Patron of Letters'.[55] Douglas Goldring, however, wrote about Garnett in similar terms: '[h]is manner to all the "rising" authors present was so heavily patronising as to suggest that they had no business to "rise" without his consent and approval', adding, 'he would have liked to patronize even Ford'.[56] Garnett was replaced by Will H. Dircks, who had previously worked for Walter Scott, pioneers in the reprinting of the classics.

The professionalisation of publishing

Publishing, then, was a complex, competitive, international business, in which the financial stakes were high and strong professional relationships were crucial. During the 1890s new London publishing firms proliferated. These included Hutchinson, The Bodley Head (both founded in 1887), J. M. Dent (1888), Methuen (1889), Heinemann, Edward Arnold (both 1890), John Lane (1892),[57] Grant Richards (1897) and Duckworth (1898). Fifty-eight publishing firms signed a minute book to be recorded as founding members of the Publishers Association in 1895, which aimed to establish common practices and principles among publishers.[58] The 'big three' elected officers rotated between Charles Longman, John Murray and Frederick Macmillan until 1904, when Heinemann became vice-president. By 1910 there were ninety-three members.[59] The Publishers Association was partly formed in response to the foundation of the Society of Authors in 1884, which had seen a rise in membership numbers from sixty-eight at its foundation to 2,500 in 1914.[60] Among its greater achievements came in 1886 when the Society campaigned for America to adopt the Copyright Act, which would prevent the work of British authors from being pirated in America. A copyright agreement was passed in 1891 with the Chace Act; after this date authors would be paid for the same work by both their British and American publishers, in addition to being remunerated for any printing of the work in magazines or periodicals that each publisher owned. Publishers were forced to modernise and become more enterprising, but the professionalisation of the field and the increasing variety of firms meant that there were more opportunities available to new writers. By September 1911 Lawrence had a grasp of the shape of different publishers' lists. He wrote to Louie that she should advise their old College friend Dolcie Rutter, an aspiring writer (and fellow former member of the 'Society for the Study of Social Questions'):

> If she wants to do fiction, she'd better try Wm Heinemann or Methuen – or if its anything racy, John Long; if it's essays, Duckworth or Martin

Secker or Dent; if its Drama – well, drama's a bit risky; if its philosophy – a complete Montaigne, for instance – then 'The Open Court' [a British subsidiary of a Chicago publishing house] – or Macmillan.[61]

Figures from a study of the long-established international publishing house Macmillan (founded in London in 1843 and New York in 1869) demonstrate the extent to which publishing was a business conducted socially, with the commercially astute and well-connected author attaining most success. Edith Wharton built up a close personal relationship with Frederick Macmillan, who published nineteen of her titles over twenty years and offered her generous terms. She was one of the authors whose manuscripts were immediately accepted on trust without the advice of a house reader; Macmillan's records show that out of a total of 657 manuscripts received in the year 1900, sixty-two titles were eventually accepted and of these twenty-three manuscripts (including Rudyard Kipling's *Kim*) were taken on trust.[62] Becoming a Macmillan author was a mark of prestige: the firm prided itself on the quality of its list, which included Henry James, Mrs Humphry Ward and Margaret Oliphant. They offered high quality production values and good terms under the royalty system, although this did not guarantee the author a good financial return: James's annual income from the novels he published with Macmillan between 1896 and 1909 averaged just £12 and he had to sustain his career by a private income.[63] Unlike much newer and smaller firms such as Unwin or Duckworth, Macmillan's usual strategy was to publish high yield books over the long term rather than accepting the risk of unknown writers. One exception was the first novel of Maurice Hewlett, *The Forest Lovers* (1898), a medieval romance which brought the firm remarkable sales success. Alongside other bestsellers such as F. Marion Crawford, Hewlett became a stalwart of the list who could sell 50,000 copies and was routinely offered a 25 per cent royalty and an advance of at least £500.[64]

Garnett at Heinemann, 1900–1901

By 15 February 1900 Garnett was unofficially engaged in reading manuscripts at Heinemann, but the employment was uncertain and offered only one or two days of work per week.[65] Readers at the firm were either on the staff or freelance and they included Daniel Conner, Frederick Atkinson (who had been introduced to Heinemann by George Moore) and Walter de la Mare, who replaced Atkinson in January 1912. The influential *Sunday Times* critic Edmund Gosse had been (from *c*.1894) the firm's chief adviser and reader; he edited Heinemann's 'International Library' of novels translated into English and was appointed Librarian to the House of Lords in 1904.[66] Garnett may have been the reader who accepted Conrad and Hueffer's *The Inheritors* (1901) for Heinemann, since it was he who had introduced Conrad and Hueffer to one another in 1898. Unwin and Garnett appear as minor characters in the novel, portrayed as the miserly publisher Polehampton and his reader Lea. The narrator states that 'You would probably find traces of Lea's influence in the beginnings of every writer of about my decade ... He had given me the material help that a publisher's reader could give, until his professional reputation was endangered.'[67] Perhaps it was Garnett's unwavering assistance of writers such as Conrad while he was at Unwin (and particularly his insistence that Conrad be given the freedom to pursue his artistic proclivities over commercial considerations) that 'endangered' his 'professional reputation' as reader from Unwin's perspective; Garnett appears to have taken more responsibility in the firm than Unwin could tolerate.

Garnett had been at Heinemann for less than eighteen months when he wrote to his mother Olivia on 5 July 1901 about his plans to resign 'in two to three months time ... I daresay I shall do better in the long run by leaving Heinemann as for a very responsible position he holds out practically a clerk's pay.' On the same date he wrote to his father that

> as Pawling's protégé I have, from the first, been looked upon by Heinemann with some jealousy, and he has now taken the opportunity of putting his own man in my place ... I have worked too for the extremely small sum of 3£ to 3£10/- a week.[68]

This pay would return a yearly income of little more than Gissing had received for *Sleeping Fires* (although it was still more than the average annual wage of a qualified full-time schoolteacher, which in 1900-1 was £128 for a man and £86 for a woman).[69] In the letter to his father Garnett enclosed Heinemann's letter of dismissal, in which the publisher agreed that the salary he could afford to pay Garnett was 'hardly adequate to your qualifications and your work', but, he continued:

> I am also aware that I require soon – and shall require even more in the future – a certain editorial assistance which is somewhat outside your lines. Under these circumstances I cannot afford further to burden any 'reading budget' by offering you a salary such as I should like to offer you. This consideration has led us to revise the whole question of reading, paragraphing, editing, etc. and we have come to the conclusion that it will suit our purposes best to remould our arrangements entirely. Under our new arrangement we could I fear even less than in the past offer you what

is so unquestionably your due, and we think therefore that it will be best if you at your own convenience and in your own time dispose of your work elsewhere. . . . we beg to thank you very cordially for the efficient, original, and devoted manner in which you have conducted our affairs. Your relations with our authors have certainly been entirely satisfactory to ourselves.[70]

Heinemann switches from the use of the singular 'I' to 'we', implying that Pawling was party to the decision to 'remould our arrangements', but Garnett considered that the tensions between Heinemann and Pawling over the degree of authority each partner had in the business was the main factor. Heinemann had the greater share at 55 per cent and may have resented Pawling's attempt to slip Garnett into the firm through the side door. Despite noting Garnett's good work, Heinemann implies that he is not quite up to the 'editorial assistance' the firm's restructuring demands. At Unwin, Garnett had been a senior reader and editor. The emphasis on editorial *assistance* 'which is somewhat outside your lines' and Heinemann's reference to his limited 'reading budget' belies Garnett's conviction that he held a 'very responsible position' in the firm. Heinemann did not seem to be a firm that would support his career ambitions.

Perhaps the editorial support to which Heinemann refers had to do with translation work. Constance wrote that Heinemann had given translated manuscripts to her husband, who did not know the original languages and expected him to make revisions (thereby presuming that Constance would provide her labour for free): '[f]irst it was a terribly tedious Universal History from the German which took us both some weeks of work – now it is a novel from the Italian, execrably translated'.[71] The low payment for their work created an ongoing dispute between Heinemann and both Garnetts: by 1915 Constance had been publishing her Russian translations with Heinemann for twenty years and had been, in her own words, 'uniformly praised by all the critics . . . Yet I am actually being paid less for what I am doing for you now than for the work I did when I had no name and no experience.'[72] In an attempt to sever Garnett's employment Heinemann notes that he would have to reduce Garnett's pay even further if he were to remain. The use of the word 'burden' in connection with the reader's task and the final insult that Garnett should 'dispose' of his work elsewhere would be enough to offend any employee. To add to the slight, Heinemann's business was buoyant: in 1900 it achieved a net profit margin of 7 per cent.[73] By 1903, Heinemann had dealt with 459 authors and had a total of 766 titles in print.[74] Heinemann concedes by recognising Garnett's 'efficient, original, and devoted' work for the firm; it might have been this concession to Garnett's strengths, tempered by the rather moderate admission that his 'relations with our authors' had been 'entirely satisfactory', that caused Garnett to reason that he was dismissed because of Heinemann's jealousy of his abilities.

Garnett at Duckworth, October 1901–15

Garnett secured another position in less than three months. On 4 October 1901 he wrote to his father that he was to be employed as a reader at Duckworth on the same terms as he had at Heinemann: 'I have also settled with them to start a certain series, which, if successful, will bring me some money, and also give literary work to several friends.' In a separate letter of the same date, Constance expressed her delight at her husband's new position: '[t]here are so few houses in which Edward could possibly be employed that one could hardly expect him to find a vacancy at once'.[75] Like Heinemann's admission that Garnett's work was 'original', Constance's comment suggests that there was something unique about Garnett's attitude to the role of reader. Perhaps he was guilty of overstepping the mark drawn by publishers who had a clear idea of the structure and hierarchy of their employees. As a much smaller firm, however, Duckworth needed a reader who was not shy of taking control and being accountable for business matters. Garnett was a valued reader there for the next fourteen years.

Gerald Duckworth (1870–1937) was two years younger than Garnett. He had previously gained publishing experience working for J. M. Dent and Company (founded in 1888) and it was there that he met A. R. Waller, who became his business partner at Duckworth; Waller left in 1901 to become Secretary to the Syndics of Cambridge University Press and he was replaced by George Harry Milsted, who had entered the firm a year earlier as an apprentice. The team was therefore just 'Duckworth–Milsted–Garnett' until 1904, when Jonathan Cape began as Town Traveller, before becoming Manager in 1909; that year A. J. Griffiths joined the firm as London Traveller.[76] Duckworth's first list was established in May 1898; that year he published August Strindberg's play *The Father*, James's novella *In the Cage*, *Jocelyn* by 'John Sinjohn' (Galsworthy) and his stepfather Leslie Stephen's *Studies of a Biographer*.

Duckworth seems to have founded the publishing house as a gentlemanly pursuit rather than for the love of books. A later employee remembered him as a 'clubman' whose 'interest in books, anyway as a medium for reading, was as slender as that of any man I have ever encountered'.[77] Now given the relatively free hand that he had long sought, Garnett established the 'Greenback Library' series in which the first title was W. H. Hudson's Southern American romance stories *El Ombú*; Garnett had initially read the manuscript for Heinemann, who rejected it thinking that it would not sell.[78] Volumes that appeared alongside

Hudson's included *Success* (1902) by R. B. Cunninghame Graham and *Stories from De Maupassant* (1903) translated by E. M. (Elsie Martindale, Hueffer's first wife) with a Preface by Hueffer. Garnett also edited the 'Popular Library of Art' shilling series for which Hueffer contributed three short monographs: *Rossetti: A Critical Essay on his Art* (1902), *Hans Holbein* (1905) and *The Pre-Raphaelite Brotherhood* (1907). For its first nine numbers until August 1909 the *English Review* was one of the firm's journals. During 1911, the year in which Garnett approached Lawrence, Duckworth was publishing work such as Thomas Sturge Moore's plays *A Sicilian Idyll* and *Judith*, George Bourne's *Memoirs of a Surrey Labourer* and Galsworthy's plays (such as *The Silver Box* and in 1912, *The Pigeon*). The 'Modern Plays Series' meant drama was a significant feature of the firm's list in 1912 and titles included Ibsen's *Love's Comedy*, Chekhov's *Plays* and Eden Phillpotts's *The Secret Woman*. It is not surprising, therefore, that Garnett took an interest in Lawrence's plays as early as October 1911.[79]

In defence of the 'sex novel'

Following the model of the 'public bookman' (and to earn extra income), alongside his work as a reader Garnett reviewed books and wrote articles with a specific focus on emerging writers. Yet most significantly in terms of his support of Lawrence, Garnett was a notable figure in the fight against censorship. He wrote a Preface entitled 'The Sex Novel' to accompany Maud Churton Braby's first novel *Downward: 'A Slice of Life'* (1910). Braby went on to write further marriage problem novels from a feminist perspective (such as *The Honey of Romance: Being the Tragic Love-Story of a Publisher's Wife* [Werner Laurie, 1915]) and marital advice books (including *Modern Marriage and How to Bear It* [T. Werner Laurie, 1908]). She 'advocated better sex education for girls, a "preliminary canter" for women before marriage, and "wild oats" for wives'.[80] Garnett's Preface was written from 'the point of view of "a publisher's reader" who is much interested in the modest claim of the Circulating Libraries to sit in judgement on the morals of all the new volumes that pass through their hands'. Garnett makes it clear that he is not acquainted with Braby, has not read for the house of Werner Laurie and is not judging the novel on its artistic merits; the Preface is a discussion of censorship and its negative impact on women writers. For Garnett,

> the spirit of a Censorship never alters: it is always 'orthodox', and it is always to be seen energetically defending the big battalions. For this reason alone any publisher's reader who is worth his salt takes a kindly interest in the fate of books that are on the side of the minority.[81]

The 'sex novel', Garnett explains, is a term that had been coined 'twenty years ago' by 'masculine reviewers', who were 'perturbed and scared' about threats to the institution of marriage. Garnett quotes a passage from *Downward* in which the female protagonist, Dolly (an unmarried mother), eloquently and humorously defends herself against a suitor's accusation that she is impure. Garnett praises the sincerity of the dialogue and demonstrates his experience as a reader by identifying areas of the text that had been censored and edited prior to publication. He argues that library censorship 'foster[s] conventional morality' and incentivises 'bad art': he states that the 'middle-class Press' is comprised of 'masculine critics' who have tried 'to freeze the "sex novel" out of existence'. In his view, women's freedom of expression has been limited and they have been constrained to write 'immature' and 'over-emotional' fiction in the knowledge that any work that is more outspoken risks being censored, restricted, banned or prevented from being published. For Garnett, the

> sex novel, even when it is not good art, is a document, a piece of polemics, a special diagnosis of a state of social unrest of a vast class of women who are placed in a radically false situation to men by the defects of our social organization.

He calls for women to put forward a 'forcible expression of the whole series of problems, social, economic and sexual' that underlie their demand for Suffrage, but acknowledges the difficulties they face in doing so. As well as outlining his support for the suffrage, Garnett differentiates himself from the majority opinion of the male-dominated press. He emphasises that he is speaking from the vantage point of a publisher's reader, who might otherwise be expected to operate from within the bounds of the institution of publishing.

Garnett's argument was timely. At a meeting held at W. H. Smith and Son in the Strand on 30 November 1909, a group comprising representatives from six of the major circulating libraries (W. H. Smith and Son, Boots Booklovers' Library, Day's, Mudie's, Cawthorn and Hutt and *The Times* Book Club) agreed to form a Circulating Libraries Association.[82] In January 1910 the Association issued a circular to all publishers which stated that their objective was to withhold from circulation 'any book which, by reason of the personally scandalous, libellous, immoral, or otherwise disagreeable nature of its contents, is in our opinion likely to prove offensive to any considerable section of our subscribers'.[83] They asked publishers to send to the Association copies of all new fiction at least one week before publication so that an official reading committee could classify the books as: (a) satisfactory, (b) doubtful and (c) objectionable. The libraries concerned had to agree not to circulate any book considered objectionable by any three members of the association. *The Times* reported on 2 December 1909 that the libraries were exhorted to 'do their best to make the distribution of any book considered doubtful . . . as small as possible'.[84] Despite Garnett's work to safeguard it from censure, *Sons and Lovers* later became one of the many books classified as 'doubtful' by the CLA. This meant that the book was subject to a form of censorship of which the public was unaware; it could be stocked at the library but not on the open shelves and a reader could only borrow it if they requested it from a librarian and paid the highest rate of subscription to obtain books 'on demand'. This procedure meant that, to borrow the book, the reader had to be relatively affluent and well-informed about literary reviews. As Nicola Wilson suggests, the implication was that such readers were less susceptible to moral corruption.[85] It was both 'literary' and popular fiction that was deemed 'objectionable' by the Circulating Libraries Association, which blurred the boundaries between 'pornographic' work and high art. Work by the bestselling sex novelist Victoria Cross (the pseudonym for Vivian Cory Griffin, who was published by John Long, specialist in the publication of the sensational 'sex novel'), for example, was classified '(c)', and, in a private document produced by Smith and Son after the First World War, the list of banned books included *Esther Waters* and three other works by Moore, as well as Lawrence's *The Prussian Officer and Other Stories* and *The Rainbow*, Theodore Dreiser's *The Genius* (1915), Upton Sinclair's *Sylvia's Marriage* (1915) and Joyce's *A Portrait of the Artist as a Young Man* (1916).[86] Given these constraints it is no wonder that writers, publishers, printers and booksellers became fearful and confused about what they could afford to send into the public domain.

Both subscription libraries and state-funded public libraries were concerned about the effects of literature on their clientele. H. G. Wells's 'sex problem' novel *Ann Veronica* (T. Fisher Unwin, 1909) featured an independent, educated New Woman who sought sexual freedom. Macmillan had refused to publish it because 'the plot develops on lines that would be exceedingly distasteful to the public which buys books published by our firm'; the book was denounced in the press as 'poisonous' and many public libraries refused to stock it.[87] A cartoon by 'Littlejohns' entitled 'The Censorship' on the front cover of the 3 February 1910 number of the *New Age* reacts to the library debate and shows its allegiance to those who oppose censorship by showing a copy of the publication atop a burning pyre of notoriously censored books, including *Ann Veronica* and Garnett's play *The Breaking Point* (1907). The other books shown are Harley Granville-Barker's play *Waste* (1907) and Shaw's plays *Mrs Warren's Profession* (written 1898) and *The Shewing-Up of Blanco Posnet* (1909). All three plays had been refused a licence to be staged in England and in 1911 Shaw published *Blanco Posnet* with a Preface detailing his anger towards the social purity movement and the English public. Also on the pyre are Hardy's novel *Jude the Obscure* (1895) and Henry James's travel essays *Italian Hours* (1909). In the image an elderly middle-class man wearing what appears to be a clerical collar averts his eyes from the heap of noxious reading matter while his well-dressed, faceless supporters, thronging the grand entrance to a 'free library', spectate from a distance; amusingly, ornamental cattle set in the stone pillars of the library peer at the pyre as if gratified that it is contaminated books rather than animal carcasses that are feeding the fire.

Opposing censorship

As a publisher's reader, critic and censored creative writer, Garnett occupied a unique position in being able to understand and respond to the complexities of the literary marketplace from different perspectives. Garnett was recognised as a key figure in anti-censorship debates following the notoriety he gained in 1907, when his play *The Breaking Point* was refused a licence to be staged at the Haymarket Theatre on the grounds of its alleged indecency. Before a play could be staged in England, the theatre manager had to submit the manuscript for approval by the Lord Chamberlain, who employed an Examiner or 'Reader' of Plays, who for a non-returnable fee would write a report on its suitability for obtaining a licence and list any necessary amendments to the script.[88] The legal procedure was still based on the 1843 Theatres Act and the case of *The Breaking Point* sparked 'much discussion . . . as to whether the office of Censor ought to be abolished or not'.[89] The play (which features the suicide by drowning of a young middle-class woman made pregnant by a married man and torn between love for her father and her lover) was considered in intellectual quarters to be 'quite free from offence', so that the action of the Examiner, George Redford, was deemed incomprehensible.[90]

Duckworth published the play and drew attention to the controversy it generated by entitling it *A Censured Play: The Breaking Point*. Garnett's 'Letter to the Censor' prefaces the volume and so Garnett publicly opposed the action of a fellow professional reader who had censored his creative work. Writing about the debate in the *Academy*, St John Hankin considered Garnett to be 'a writer of pluck and determination, who is not at all afraid of the Censor, and is quite equal to nailing Mr Redford's ears to the pump'.[91] It was perhaps this intermediate position that Garnett held in being an informed 'insider' to the institutions of publishing and yet working against regulatory constraints that attracted writers to him; his work on behalf of other authors paid off in the form of a network of connections he could draw on when he needed support for his own fictional projects. Granville-Barker and Shaw were among a group of seventy-one writers and public figures who rallied in defence of Garnett by signing an open letter printed in *The Times* in October 1907 opposing British stage censorship. Granville-Barker's play *Waste* (about the death of a woman – the lover of a politician – from a botched backstreet abortion) had also been refused a licence in 1907, but before this, a licence for Shaw's *Mrs Warren's Profession* had been turned down in 1898. Shaw published *Mrs Warren's Profession* in *Plays Pleasant and Unpleasant* (Grant Richards, 1898) with a Preface attacking censorship. He wrote a new Preface, 'The Author's Apology' for the first separate publication of *Mrs Warren's Profession* (Grant Richards, 1902); these outspoken prefaces likely influenced Garnett. Shaw's play about a female brothel owner and former prostitute was finally staged in New York in 1905 to the distress of some members of the audience, such as the American social purity leader Anthony Comstock who branded Shaw an 'Irish Smut Dealer'.[92] Garnett was correct in his judgement that literature and drama about the social, economic and sexual problems faced by women were likely to be suppressed by sections of society that resisted women's suffrage and campaigns for equal rights.

Following a deputation to the Home Office in February 1908 where a petition against censorship was handed to the Home Secretary Herbert Gladstone, it was decided that a Joint Select Committee would meet between July and November 1909 to take testimonies from authors and to re-examine the laws of stage censorship. No changes were made to the system and dramatists had to wait until 1968 for a radical alteration to the procedure.[93] Garnett wrote a strident eleven-page essay on 'The Censorship of Public Opinion', printed in the *Fortnightly Review* in July 1909; he had also been invited to deliver a paper on the topic of censorship at the Playgoers Club. The essay stated that 'a censorship must necessarily embody and crystallise the ideas and prejudices of the average person; whereas it is the aim of art to transcend those ideas and prejudices'.[94] Garnett's conception of art was, then, that of a 'purist' (to use Peter McDonald's terminology) who presented a challenge to the middle-class playgoer, or what Garnett called 'the conventional-minded man'. He continued: 'I assert that, especially for young or little known dramatists there is no real freedom to-day in plays that present any deep picture of the relations of love between men and women.'[95] Lawrence would write to Garnett on 2 May 1913 using similar terms to describe his new novel 'The Sisters':

> It was meant to be for the 'jeunes filles', but already it has fallen from grace. I can only write what I feel pretty strongly about: and that, at present, is the relations between men and women. After all, it is *the* problem of today, the establishment of a new relation, or the re-adjustment of the old one, between men and women.[96]

The Breaking Point was performed at the private members-only Stage Society in April 1908. Although Lawrence praised *The Breaking Point* to Garnett as 'a fine, clean moulded tragedy' when Garnett sent the volume to him in October 1911, Lawrence confessed to Louie that he did not 'care for Garnett's plays – they are not alive'.[97] James Moran observes that, despite this opinion, Lawrence still 'wanted to impress Garnett, and drew upon *The Breaking Point* during a renewed bout of playwriting' during 1912–13 when he wrote *The Married Man*, *The Fight for Barbara* and *The Daughter-in-Law*.[98] Garnett's other plays include *The Feud* (A. H. Bullen, 1909) which was performed by Annie Horniman's Company at the Manchester Gaiety Theatre in April 1909, where his *Lords and Masters*, written under the pseudonym James Byrne, was also staged in May 1911. Ben Iden Payne, to whom Garnett introduced Lawrence in April 1912, directed both plays. Garnett was keen to encourage Lawrence to try breaking into theatre just as Garnett's friends Galsworthy and Yeats had done; Maugham also turned to plays as an additional source of income, but Conrad had far less interest in the theatre.[99] Lawrence thought the prospect of his own works reaching the stage 'ripping'.[100] Before turning to plays Garnett wrote novels, such as *The Paradox Club* and *Light and Shadow* (both published by his new employer, Unwin, in 1888 and 1889 respectively) and a volume of prose poems, *An Imaged World* (Dent, 1894), but all his fictional work received poor reviews. Lawrence observed that Garnett 'ate his heart out trying to be a writer', which perhaps indicates why he was so helpful to others who shared his ambitions.[101]

Garnett's first approach to Lawrence

Garnett first approached Lawrence on 25 August 1911, requesting from him several short stories to send to the New York publishing house, the Century Company, for whom Garnett acted as English literary representative from 1911 to 1912.[102] He must have built up connections with the Company while working for Unwin, who was publishing *The Century Illustrated Monthly Magazine* by 1893.[103] As the Company's primary publication, *The Century* had been highly regarded during the 1880s and 1890s when it found success with a series of articles on the history of the Civil War. The series ran for three years from November 1884 and doubled the magazine's circulation to 250,000, returning one million dollars. The readership declined in the early twentieth century due to increased competition and Garnett appears never to have succeeded in placing any of his chosen authors' work.

On 10 September Lawrence sent Garnett two short stories (the 'rather lurid' 'Intimacy' and one other – possibly 'The Old Adam' or 'The Fly in the

Ointment') and politely suggested that 'if, anytime, you would give me a word of criticism on my MSS, I should go with surer feet'.[104] Lawrence had initially mistaken Garnett for his father Richard, who edited the twenty-volume *International Library of Famous Literature* (1899) that the Lawrence family had owned and revered. Garnett complied with Lawrence's request: although the stories Lawrence had sent were unsuitable and he needed to 'write something more objective, more ordinary', he offered advice about 'Intimacy' (later revised as 'The Witch à la Mode') and read another story, 'Two Marriages', which Lawrence had tried to make 'sufficiently emotional, and moral, and – oh, American!'[105] The suggestion that Lawrence needed to enhance the morality of the story indicates the conventional nature of the *Century*, which had to uphold sound values to ensure that it satisfied a general readership. Lawrence wrote 'Two Marriages' (later entitled 'Daughters of the Vicar') with the idea that it could be divided into three parts for the purposes of serialisation. Lawrence was sufficiently encouraged by Garnett's approach to suggest having the manuscript typed, which would have been a costly investment. Garnett invited Lawrence to lunch on Wednesday 4 October; the meeting was arranged around Lawrence's lunch hour at school and he was to call for Garnett at Duckworth's office on Henrietta Street. Lawrence commented that Garnett was 'curious to see what sort of animal I am – and I'm willing to be seen'.[106]

It is highly likely that the venue for their meeting was the Mont Blanc restaurant on Gerrard Street in Soho, a seven-minute walk away from Henrietta Street. From the time he became reader for Duckworth in 1901 Garnett held weekly lunches there on Tuesdays and Wednesdays. Regular attendees included Thomas Seccombe, R. A. Scott-James, Stephen Reynolds, Edward Thomas, W. H. Davies, Hilaire Belloc, Muirhead Bone, Hueffer, Perceval Gibbon, 'occasionally Galsworthy and rarely Joseph Conrad'.[107] Lawrence was aware of what was at stake if he failed to impress Garnett. A week after the publication of *The White Peacock* back in January 1911 he told Louie what he had learned about the mechanisms of the literary marketplace:

> The publisher sends a copy of the book to the office of the newspaper or magazine, together with a slip saying when the book is to be issued. If the publisher has puffed the book behind scenes, at his club, where he meets the big newspaper men – or if the writer has friends among the literary circles and clubs – or influence – then the book has been talked about, so the editor pounces upon it and writes it up in reviews. If the book has no friends, and the publisher, knowing there is no chance of *Scarlet Pimpernel* sales, does not trouble much, then the best book in the world might fall dead. It gets handed to the hack-man for a twelve line review.[108]

Baroness Orczy's *The Scarlet Pimpernel* (Hutchinson, 1905) had gone into its twenty-fourth impression within two years of publication.

Lawrence must have made a good impression during the meeting: he informed Louie that he had been invited to Garnett's Kent residence, the Cearne, on the weekend commencing Friday 13 October and that Garnett had told him he would 'try and get me published a vol of verse, for Spring – and would also get the three plays placed, for publishing'.[109] Lawrence had sent *The Widowing of Mrs Holroyd* to Garnett, but at that point Hueffer had mislaid *A Collier's Friday Night* and *The Merry-Go-Round*. Garnett evidently got Lawrence thinking quite soon about the various needs of the marketplace and about potential outlets for his work, both creative and journalistic. In November 1911 Garnett arranged for Lawrence to meet Scott-James (literary editor of the *Daily News* from 1902 to 1912) at the Cearne; Lawrence hoped that Garnett would only show Scott-James those poems that were 'quite respectable, and black and white'.[110] He began to feel hopeful that 'this Spring will give me a bit of a reputation' and worked hard to secure his beneficial new connection by 'getting verse ready to take to Garnett on Friday'.[111] The meeting had an awkward interlude, however:

> While Garnett and I were having lunch who should come in the place but Atkinson, Heinemann's man. Garnett doesn't like Heinemann's people, so he was beastly sarky with him. I hate Atkinson – I don't go to Heinemanns because I don't like the sneering, affected little fellow. But he made me promise to call there. I did last Thursday. It appears my contract with Heinemann was for yearly payment – so the *Peacock* money is not justly due till February. They owe me £40 – and Atkinson said they'd send me on a cheque. It's not come yet . . . I am afraid I have offended Heinemann's people mortally. I haven't done a stroke of Paul for months – don't want to touch it. They are mad, and they are sneery. I don't like them.[112]

Lawrence's ready allegiance with Garnett is seen in his emulation of Garnett's attitude to 'Heinemann's people', particularly his reader Atkinson, whom Lawrence now professes to hate; there is no indication of this aversion to Atkinson in his previous letters. In July 1910 Lawrence had attempted to get Atkinson on his side, asking him to '[i]ntercede with Pawling for me, will you? . . . in his presence I feel like an extinguished glow-worm under a lamp-post: when I think of writing to him, the stopper dives into the neck of my bottle of words'.[113] The elaborate language Lawrence used when writing to the 'affected' Atkinson is far removed from the informal tone he adopted almost immediately with Garnett; it is a sign that Lawrence did not feel as comfortable with Atkinson as he did with Garnett.

Garnett had likely informed Lawrence of his previous employment at Heinemann, perhaps embellishing his account to get Lawrence on his side in the hope that he might take him over to Duckworth. If this is the case, then their conversation must have tainted Lawrence's opinion of Heinemann: in the space of a few sentences Lawrence twice repeats that he does not like the people who work for Heinemann. Nevertheless, he is understandably 'afraid' that he has 'offended' them by being seen with a rival firm's reader and making no progress with 'Paul Morel', the novel that he was contractually obliged to offer to Heinemann. After all, it was not yet certain that Garnett would be of assistance to Lawrence and he might have slighted the only firm that was interested in publishing his work. That Atkinson made him 'promise to call' at the office is an indication that Atkinson was concerned that Lawrence might be planning to defect to Duckworth. Lawrence became relatively adept at managing and smoothing over tensions in his interactions with others whose social position might benefit his work.

'The Saga of Siegmund': the 'love-novel'

Lawrence was first introduced to Helen Corke, the woman who would provide the subject matter of his second novel, through his friend and fellow schoolteacher Agnes Mason during winter 1908–9. Lawrence and Corke began to spend more time together in autumn 1909 after he learned that her married lover Herbert Macartney (a violinist in the Covent Garden orchestra) had committed suicide on 7 August 1909, shortly after Macartney had returned from a holiday with Corke at Freshwater on the Isle of Wight. Lawrence encouraged Corke to write about the tragedy and her memories of Macartney and she began 'The Letter' in early September, before beginning an account of the holiday, 'The Freshwater Diary', on 26 November. Lawrence shared his writing with Corke (he read his poems to her, allowed her to read *A Collier's Friday Night* and asked her for help in revising 'Nethermere'); then at an unspecified date between 9 January and 25 March 1910 Lawrence read 'The Freshwater Diary' and urged Corke to allow him to expand its 'prose poems' into a novel.[114] Jessie recalled that Lawrence wrote to her 'very much disturbed, saying that he had to write the story of Siegmund' and he did so 'in feverish haste'.[115] His excitement about having sourced the material for another tragic romance novel coalesced with his sexual attraction to Corke and his disturbance at the extent of Macartney's emotional torment.

Lawrence read *Evelyn Innes* and *Ann Veronica* before he began the 'Saga', in what seems like an effort to gain knowledge about the ways in which well-regarded authors had approached the genre of the 'love-novel', as he termed it.[116] He wrote 'The Saga of Siegmund' (the first version of *The Trespasser*) in just four months: the first version was completed by 4 August 1910. Lawrence then sent it to Hueffer. It may not be a coincidence that from October 1909, the month after he met Hueffer, Lawrence actively sought out German literature; he would have wanted to learn more about the literary background of his mentor in order to write work that might appeal to him. In October 1909 Lawrence and Helen Corke read a 'little ragged copy of German lyric verse'; Lawrence also read Heine and Goethe to her.[117] On 15 October Lawrence saw (and was disappointed by) a performance of Wagner's *Tristan and Isolde* at the Grand Theatre, Croydon. In June and July 1910 Lawrence read Gerhart Hauptmann's plays *Elga* (1905) and *Einsame Menschen* of 1891. Hueffer had given Lawrence a copy of his poems, *High Germany: Eleven Sets of Verse* (1911), which Lawrence lent to Corke. In November 1911 Lawrence went to Covent Garden 'to hear *Siegfried* – Wagner – one of the *Ring* cycle that I had not heard'.[118] Lawrence included many allusions to Wagner in *The Trespasser*. Hueffer's father Franz Hüffer was from 1879 a music critic for *The Times* who was credited with bringing the craze for Wagner to England. Hüffer wrote two books on Wagner – *Richard Wagner and the Music of the Future* (1874) and *Wagner* (1881) – and he translated the *Correspondence of Wagner and Liszt* (1889). Hüffer also started the journal *Musical World* in order to champion the work of the composer, but in 1915 his son felt 'considerably out of sympathy with Wagner's music'.[119] Hueffer did not tell Lawrence his opinion of the 'Saga' manuscript until 9 September 1910. If Lawrence had hoped to interest Hueffer in his work then he had misunderstood his mentor's literary tastes: Corke noted that 'Hueffer's criticism of the *Saga* has been taken very much to heart ... The work is too molten, says the critic – by which I suppose he means too much the stuff of life itself'.[120]

Lawrence reported to Louie that Hueffer considered the novel to be 'a rotten work of genius, one fourth of which is the stuff of masterpiece. He belongs to the opposite school of novelists to me: he says prose *must* be impersonal, like Turgenev or Flaubert. I say no.'[121] This sounds like an accurate paraphrase of what Hueffer might have said; as well as that recurrent term 'genius', he used the word 'school' of novelists twice in his November 1909 letter to Lawrence about *The White Peacock*. Pawling wrote to Lawrence 'curtly to say that I owed it him on promise to have sent him the MSS of the second novel by the end of August', but Hueffer had taken the 'Saga' manuscript to read in Germany. Lawrence asked him to 'send the thing to Heinemann, but I can get no answer. So the publisher is at outs with me.'[122] Heinemann had long vocalised his dislike of 'parasitic' literary agents and 'middlemen' who got in the way of his relationships and negotiations with authors, so on this occasion it may have irritated the publisher that Hueffer (and then Garnett) was acting as an intermediary in Lawrence's affairs.[123]

It was not until shortly before 18 October that Pawling acknowledged receipt of the manuscript, because on that date Lawrence wrote a fretful reply:

> It contains, I know, some rattling good stuff. But if the whole is not to your taste, I shall not mind, for I am not in the least anxious to publish that book. . . . I do want, to overhaul the book considerably as soon as you care to return it to me. I am not anxious to publish it, and if you are of like mind, we can let the thing stay, and I will give you – with no inter-mediary this time – my third novel, 'Paul Morel', which is plotted out very interestingly (to me), and about one-eighth of which is written. 'Paul Morel' will be a novel – not a florid prose poem, or a decorated idyll running to seed in realism: but a restrained, *somewhat* impersonal novel.[124]

Lawrence begins on a positive note: the work contains 'rattling good stuff' (as Hueffer had said, one fourth of it is masterpiece), but if Pawling should not like its 'florid prose poem' style then there is a thoroughly different 'plotted . . . restrained, *somewhat* impersonal' novel on the way.[125] Lawrence seems also to have noted Hueffer's words about his preferred 'school of novelists' being those writers of 'impersonal' novels, such as Flaubert, and shorter, more concise fiction, such as the writing of Turgenev; Lawrence may have wondered whether Pawling was of a like mind. In any case, he would provide him with the option and retain the publisher's interest in his work. He emphasises his eagerness to please, stressing his keenness to 'overhaul the book considerably' or set it by for the future. He implicitly invokes Hueffer in his reference to the intermediary who had held up the passage of the manuscript to Pawling, but Hueffer's support of his writing had been brought into question. He had not liked 'Saga' and his appreciation of *The White Peacock* had been lukewarm. Later, Hueffer may have written a more negative review of *The White Peacock* than Lawrence expected. On 9 February 1911 Lawrence wrote to Hunt: 'Mr Hueffer says he's reviewed me. If that was he in the *Standard* – and it was in his "Jove-abdicated-in-disgust" tone – I'll never forgive him.'[126]

It could have been the thought of this review and the receipt of a long letter from Hueffer that prompted Lawrence to write to Atkinson on 11 February to inform him of his wish to suppress the book. It was Hueffer's sense that the book was erotic enough to damage Lawrence's reputation that led him to withhold it from Heinemann. Offering his reasons, he declared:

> I have been thinking about the 'Siegmund' book, which has been sunk in my consciousness for some time. You are going to tell me some nasty

things about it. I guess I have told them, most of them, to myself – amid acute inner blushes. The book is execrable bad art: it has no idea of progressive action, but arranges gorgeous tableaux-vivants which have not any connection one with the other: it is 'chargé' . . . its purple passages glisten sicklily: it is, finally, pornographic.'[127]

Lawrence knew the word 'pornographic' would alarm Atkinson and settle any quarrel over his withdrawal of the manuscript. In his 1938 memoir, Hueffer recalls his reaction to Lawrence's manuscript: '[i]t was a *Trespassers* much – oh, but much! – more phallic than is the book as it stands . . . Lawrence had come under the subterranean fashionable influences that made for Free Love as a social and moral arcanum.'[128] Hueffer's comment suggests that Lawrence was particularly receptive at this time and easily influenced by literary trends. One of the possible identities he was considering forging at that time was that of the 'erotic' writer. In the middle of writing 'Saga' Lawrence had reflected on and discussed the opportunities for publishing erotic work for a non-mainstream audience. In June 1910 he apparently suggested to Pound (who wanted to write 'an account of the mystic cult of love – the dionysian rites, and so on – from earliest days to the present') that Pound might write his book in French and publish it in Paris, because 'no damned publisher in London dare publish it'.[129]

Although Douglas Goldring has suggested that Hueffer was ambivalent about Yeats, it was Hueffer who introduced Lawrence to Yeats in 1909. Yeats was another of the poets whose work Lawrence read to Corke in their early acquaintance; Lawrence had met Yeats and other 'celebrities' at the home of Ernest and Grace Rhys in March 1910 just before he began work on the novel.[130] This was the evening when Pound (if Ernest Rhys's account is to be believed) ate a vase of red tulips and performed, 'in a resonant, histrionic voice', his 'Ballad of the Goodly Fere'. Yeats read his poem 'That the Night Come', about a woman that 'lived in storm and strife, / Her soul had such desire'. Members of the 1890s Rhymers' Club were in attendance and poets influenced by Yeats's monologues on the 'new art of bringing music and poetry together' intoned their verse to the sound of 'mysterious' instruments.[131] Perhaps it was these poetic, dramatic and musical circles that formed the 'subterranean fashionable influences' to which Hueffer referred in 1938, although Garnett's unconventional marital arrangements might also have been behind Hueffer's comments on 'Free Love': Constance openly accepted her husband's relationship with the artist Nellie Heath from *c.*1902. After his receipt of Hueffer's 'great long letter', Lawrence, suffering from 'acute inner blushes', quite soon arrived at the conclusion that he had acted rashly in opposing Hueffer's September 1910 opinion of the manuscript. A period of silence from the publisher made Lawrence fear for his 'tender reputation' if Heinemann were to proceed.[132]

From Hueffer to Garnett, from Heinemann to Duckworth

After being spotted with Garnett, Lawrence attended a meeting with Heinemann on 20 October and found him to be

> much sweeter. It is very remarkable. Last week they were sneering and detestable: today they are of the honeycomb. Heinemann wants to publish the verses . . . he wants me definitely to promise the next novel – the one that is half done ['Paul Morel'] – for March.[133]

If Heinemann was to have the first refusal of 'Paul Morel' and the poetry, Garnett expressed interest in seeing the manuscript of 'Saga' which was still with Heinemann (by 4 December the 'erotic MSS' had been returned by Heinemann and Lawrence sent the package straight on to Garnett).[134] With Garnett's encouragement, Lawrence began to consider anew the possibility of revising the manuscript for publication. Garnett had already read 'Intimacy' which, like the 'Saga', focused on the theme of passionate love and used Corke as the model for its central female character, Margaret Varley. Lawrence had noted on 16 October that Garnett 'praises me for my sensuous feeling in my writing', so he had good reason to think that Garnett would approve of the novel.[135] The growing influence of Garnett on Lawrence and the extent to which Lawrence came to align himself with Garnett over Hueffer can be detected in the following letter to Garnett regarding the potential publication of the 'Saga', dated 18 December 1911:

> Your letter concerning the Siegmund book is very exciting. I will tell you just what Hueffer said, then you will see the attitude his kind will take up. 'The book' he said 'is a rotten work of genius. It has no construction or form – it is execrably bad art, being all variations on a theme. Also it is erotic – not that I, personally, mind that, but an erotic work *must* be good art, which this is not'.
>
> I sent it to 'our friend with the monocle'. He wrote to me, after three months: 'I have read part of the book. I don't care for it, but we will publish it.'
>
> I wrote back to him 'No, I won't have the book published. Return it to me.'

> That is about fifteen months ago. I wrote to Hueffer saying: 'The novel called "The Saga of Siegmund" I have determined not to publish.' He replied to me 'You are quite right not to publish that book – it would damage your reputation, perhaps permanently.'
>
> When I was last up at Heinemanns, two months ago, I asked Atkinson to send me the MS. . . .
>
> Is Hueffer's opinion worth anything, do you think? Is the book *so* erotic? I don't want to be talked about in an *Anne Veronica* [sic] fashion.
>
> If you offer the thing to Duckworth, do not, I beg you, ask for an advance on royalties. Do not present me as a beggar. Do not tell him I am poor. Heinemann owes me £50 in February – I have enough money to tide me over till he pays – and that fifty will, at home, last me six months. I do not want an advance – let me be presented to Duckworth as a respectable person. . . .
>
> We will, then, discuss the book on Wednesday. I shall change the title. Shall I call it 'The Livanters' – is that a correct noun from the verb 'To Livant'. To me, it doesn't look an ugly word, nor a disreputable one.[136]

Firstly, Lawrence demonstrates his departure from Hueffer's influence and his allegiance to Garnett by differentiating Hueffer's tastes from his own ('you will see the attitude his kind will take up'). It had become apparent to Lawrence that he would never be one of Hueffer's 'kind'. Hueffer himself commented that 'one day [Lawrence] brought me half the MS. of *The Trespassers* [sic] – and that was the end'.[137] A breach in their relations had occurred after just one year. Lawrence asks Garnett whether he thinks Hueffer's opinion is 'worth anything'. In recent years Garnett and Hueffer had had several disagreements, so Garnett would not have taken Hueffer's views at face value. Reflecting on his estimation of Hueffer's 'gorgeous embroideries' early on in his career, for example, Garnett confided to his sister that as Hueffer 'never could stand criticism our relations practically ceased before the war'.[138] On hearing of Garnett's death in 1937, Hueffer wrote to Stanley Unwin that Garnett 'was a pretty vindictive foe of one – or rather of what I stood for'.[139] Since Hueffer had been a teenager in the family circle whom Garnett assisted into publication on several occasions, Garnett (five years older than Hueffer) could lay claim to at least equal literary authority. Yet Hueffer's much greater success as a creative writer would have led him to contest this standing as the years went by. As Helen Smith explains, the pair already had a history of competing over the level of literary influence each had on Joseph Conrad, so that in their association with one another 'the personal and the professional were inextricably linked'.[140] The way in which Lawrence draws a dividing line between Hueffer's 'kind' and his own echoes Hueffer's conviction that he and Lawrence belonged to different 'schools', just as Garnett was against what Hueffer 'stood for'. It seems that all parties would go on to perceive that Garnett was the more natural mentor for a writer such as Lawrence.

If Garnett's previous letter concerning 'the Siegmund book' had been 'very exciting' then Lawrence must have felt he was already being taken under Garnett's wing. Forgetting all that Hueffer had done for him in autumn 1909, Lawrence flatters Garnett by allowing him to discredit Hueffer. He shares in-jokes with Garnett (just as Garnett did with Conrad), such as the reference to Atkinson as 'our friend with the monocle'. The way Lawrence dramatises the proceedings of trying to get his novel published, using dialogue to mimic the voices of Hueffer and Atkinson, is intended to entertain Garnett. The humour glosses over the more serious issue at stake: the risk inherent in publishing the work and the amount of revision and editorial advice it would take to get the novel into a form suitable for publication. Lawrence infers that he has been ill-treated by Heinemann over the novel: Atkinson had only read part of it and offered no substantive criticism. Lawrence indicates his willingness to be introduced to Duckworth, suggesting, offhandedly, that Garnett might 'offer the thing to Duckworth'. Evidently Heinemann wanted to keep Lawrence on their books, but they had dallied. Lawrence began to find himself in some demand: in the space of fifteen months between June 1911 and September 1912 he received more approaches from publishers. In June 1911 after having read 'Odour of Chrysanthemums' in the *English Review* Martin Secker wrote to ask Lawrence whether he would be interested in publishing a volume of short stories with his firm; again in July 1912 he asked whether Lawrence would offer him a novel. On 17 September 1912 Fisher Unwin acting on the advice of Austin Harrison asked Lawrence for 'a good strong novel', and two days later Hutchinson offered an advance of £110 on receipt of a novel manuscript.[141] Naturally Garnett, with Duckworth's interests in mind, advised against these propositions.

Hueffer had acted with the best of intentions for Lawrence in the knowledge of the difficulties facing an impecunious young author – and one who was working in a position of moral influence as a teacher – trying to publish an erotic novel. He would rather have seen Lawrence continuing to produce clean, romantic schoolmaster poetry, or working-class realism like 'Odour of Chrysanthemums' for which he knew there was a safe market. The situation concerning censorship was more acute in 1911 than it had ever been, so Hueffer was right to fear for the reputations of both Lawrence and Heinemann. It is no coincidence that the stranglehold on fiction about women's desire and sexual independence was most vehement in the year that saw the largest suffragist demonstration in London on 17 June 1911. *The Times* reported a five-mile procession of 40,000 people; Lawrence wrote to Louie on 14 June to ask whether she could join him there.[142] On 7 June 1911 the publisher John Long wrote to G. Herbert Thring, Secretary of the Society of Authors, that '[t]he condition of the fiction market . . . has . . . during the last few years, undergone a great change, with the result that books which were freely circulated a year ago on the bookstalls are now banned'.[143] In 1912 Heinemann's offices were visited by the police who, acting on court orders, burnt on their stove the remaining stock of Charles E. Vivian's recently published novel *Passion Fruit*, which had been successfully prosecuted on charges of obscenity.[144] Another novel published by Heinemann in May 1912, Upton Sinclair's *Love's Pilgrimage* (dedicated to 'those throughout the world who are fighting for the emancipation of woman'), was banned in W. H. Smith and Son's libraries. It was on account of this last action that De la Mare wrote to Garnett in July 1912 that it was likely Heinemann would refuse 'Paul Morel' because 'the Libraries would ban the book as it stands'.[145]

With this context in mind, Lawrence's letter offers us an insight into the type of novelist he wanted to be at this time, while revealing his fears about being judged a 'disreputable' author. His class anxieties come to the fore; Lawrence begs Garnett not to 'present me as a beggar. Do not tell him I am poor . . . let me be presented to Duckworth as a respectable person.' On the face of it Lawrence did not want Duckworth to think that he would pester him for money, but there may be a deeper anxiety at play here. His concern to be seen as 'a respectable person' seems inextricably linked with his final comment about changing the title of the novel to 'The Livanters': 'it doesn't look an ugly word, nor a disreputable one'. In this age of the author as public figure, Lawrence conflates his identity with his book, as if the one will have an impact on the other. Lawrence's background left him more vulnerable to being labelled a pornographer, just as Shaw's nationality had been invoked when he was branded an 'Irish Smut Dealer'. In Lawrence's opinion, if Duckworth thought of Lawrence as a 'respectable person' then he might be more likely to judge the book decent rather than 'rotten' or 'subterranean'.

The letter reveals that, although 'Saga' might have been deemed to take a 'pornographic' line according to the classifications of the period, it is clear that Lawrence did not want to be categorised as a sensational sex novelist, like the popular Victoria Cross. Neither did he want to write a thematically driven novel that directly interrogated women's issues, in the style of Maud Churton Braby. By December 1911 he did not 'want to be talked about in an *Anne Veronica* fashion' like Wells, nor to court the level of controversy attained by Moore, Shaw and Garnett. With *The Trespasser*, he hoped to consolidate the 'small but individual name' that *The White Peacock* had brought him by producing a tragic romance that appealed to the educated and broadminded middle-class woman reader with aesthetic literary tastes (women like his correspondents at the time: Rachel Annand Taylor, Violet Hunt, Grace Crawford and Helen Corke).

Garnett's advice

Garnett discussed the book with Lawrence and on 30 December Lawrence began to revise the manuscript using notes that Garnett had made on the reverse of its pages; by 7 January 1912 they had agreed to change the title to *The Trespasser*.[146] That month Lawrence declared to Garnett his wish that 'the *Trespasser* were to be issued privately, to a few folk who had understanding'.[147] Lawrence knew that commercial British publishers would have no choice but to censor work that tested the boundaries of how sex and desire could be represented in fiction. He fleetingly and fancifully envisaged *The Trespasser* as appealing to a coterie audience, although he knew that was implausible since private publication would not earn him the money and public recognition he needed. Lawrence could have made this comment to Garnett knowing about his reputation as a defender of the 'sex novel' and hoping that Garnett would empathise with him; the comment about appealing to the 'few folk' with 'understanding' acts as a reminder of their shared literary values. As Elizabeth Mansfield observes, Lawrence transferred 296 pages of the 'Saga' manuscript into the final manuscript of 485 pages and the pages he transferred often received little further revision.[148] This suggests that Garnett was far less concerned than was Hueffer about the erotic material in the 'Saga' and *The Trespasser* is not markedly censored. If anything, it is more direct in its treatment of sex. Corke would have agreed: she recorded in her autobiography that on reading the published novel she found that 'the eroticism of one imaginary scene has been heightened' in comparison to how she remembered reading it in manuscript.[149] Lawrence dwelt on and heavily revised a passage which appears to describe the first time the lovers have sex. The first version ('MS I', written between *c.*11 April 1910 and 4 August 1910), in which Helena was originally named 'Sieglinde', reads:

> 'I wonder what next Monday will bring us.'
> Siegmund gripped her hard.
> 'Quick curtain,' he said joyously, ~~magnificent~~ proud with conquest. Sieglinde prepared the meal. It was her joy to do it for him. She had no joy, save to give him joy. He seemed to have such a splendid, even

a magnificent capacity for happiness. Sieglinde knew that he drew this marvel of unbounded happiness from her, ~~even~~ as he drew music from his violin, ~~and~~ so it was her passion to render him his happiness to its fullest, to its exquisite perfection. She only asked that he would take her and lure her to his need. If he bruised her in making his music, as sometimes he hurt his violin, she was glad. She could think of nothing more exquisite than being hurt by him while he rang out from her his passionate, ~~transcendent~~ music of happiness. And Siegmund knew, and all the evening long he felt himself swinging with powerful, furious harmonies in an overture of passion. The fire music ~~went on~~ accumulated, movement by movement, ~~and~~ while Siegmund and Sieglinde breathed ~~with a little awe and dread.~~ with a tension that was almost dread. The climax was coming grand and inevitable. It seemed as if they would ~~be enveloped in sheet~~ have to step into strong, white flame. Such great happiness needed courage, and they looked into each others eyes.

The climax came, when their hearts were nearly bursten; it passed slowly, then their hearts sang the exquisite flickering fire music, sang and repeated the pure calm beauty of joy, dimly, and more dimly, continuing down their sleep. (MS I, pp. 111–12).

Viewing herself as Siegmund's instrument, Sieglinde is self-sacrificial and subservient, even masochistic. Being 'bruised' by him is 'exquisite' to her if it will give him pleasure. The reader is unsure whether to interpret this as a literal bruising by the 'powerful, furious' Siegmund, caught up in the throes of a long-awaited passion, or merely a metaphor which indicates the agony of their mutual emotional dependence. The description of passion is coded; Lawrence uses musical terminology to make the scene more poetic than corporeal (it is the 'fire music' that overcomes the couple and accumulates into an inevitable, rhythmic 'climax'). We do not know for sure whether Garnett focused Lawrence's attention on this scene, but in revision it becomes progressively less florid and abstract. This is consistent with the advice he gave on the so-called 'Stranger' scene, in which Lawrence was directed to add in 'little realistic touches', to be 'more ordinary & natural & slip in the pregnant things at moments'.[150] Lawrence makes significant cuts to the second version ('MS II'), rewritten in January 1912:

'I wonder what next Monday will bring us.'
'Quick curtain,' he answered joyously. He was looking down and smiling at her with such ~~delight~~ careless happiness, that she loved him. He was wonderful to her. She loved him, was jealous of every particle of him that

evaded her. She wanted to sacrifice to him, make herself as a burning altar to him: and she wanted to possess him.

The hours that would be purely their own came too slowly for her. That night, she met his love with love as blazing as his own. They were not themselves, but transfigured into in pure, fiery love, passion for which they themselves merely held located, like the burning bush. They far transcended their own beings. It was a wonderful night to achieve. (MS II, p. 115).

Helena is still self-sacrificial, but in revision the language becomes more religious than musical. Helena sees herself as a 'burning altar' at which Siegmund will worship; before, she wanted him to take her, to 'lure her', but now she wants 'to possess him' out of love. In the rewritten passage their passion is equally matched because she takes a more active role: 'she met his love with love as blazing as his own'. Whereas in the first version 'he rang out from her his passionate, transcendent music of happiness', in the second, the sexual encounter causes them both to 'transcen[d] their own beings'.

The published version retains much of the second manuscript version but is far less positive about the relationship. It reads:

'I wonder what next Monday will bring us.'
'Quick curtain,' he answered joyously. He was looking down and smiling at her with such careless happiness that she loved him. He was wonderful to her. She loved him, was jealous of every particle of him that evaded her. She wanted to sacrifice to him, make herself a burning altar to him, and she wanted to possess him.

The hours that would be purely their own came too slowly for her. That night she met his passion with love. It was not his passion she wanted, actually. But she desired that he should want *her* madly, and that he should have all – everything. It was a wonderful night to him. It restored in him the full 'will to live.' But she felt it destroyed her. Her soul seemed blasted. (*The Trespasser*, first edn, 68).

In the final version, Helena does not want his 'passion' – the sex act itself – but craves his desire for her and is therefore willing to give him 'everything'. It is a wonderful night for *him*, but it destroys Helena's 'soul'. Lawrence indicates the restorative power of sex for Siegmund but characterises Helena as detached and deceptive. Lawrence's revision often reproduced, rather than eradicated, passages Hueffer might have deemed 'erotic' and so we cannot state that either Lawrence or Garnett – or Duckworth – were concerned enough about the threat of censorship to take significant action during the revision. Given the delicate environment and although the tragic romance novel was then in vogue, it is very fortunate that Lawrence got away with directly inferring the act of extra-marital sexual consummation narrated from a woman's perspective in 1912. Since it was not as widely reviewed as *The White Peacock* and Lawrence was still little-known, the book slipped under the radar of the censors.

Heinemann became increasingly concerned that Lawrence was defecting to Duckworth: the firm 'tried to soft-sawder me into not giving the second, love-novel which they practically refused, to Duckworth'.[151] Lawrence suspected that Heinemann rejected 'Paul Morel' in July 1912 'because he was cross with me for going to Duckworth'; Heinemann, however, claimed that he refused it because the novel's 'want of reticence' would have ruled out the circulating libraries, and 'there is practically no market for fiction outside of them'.[152] Heinemann may ultimately have regretted that he did not act to secure *The Trespasser* before Garnett came on the scene, because although the reception of the novel following its publication on 23 May 1912 was relatively limited, it was largely very positive. Most reviews did, however, advise caution along the lines of the comment made by a reviewer at the *Westminster Gazette* that the book should 'not to be put into the hands of the timid or the frivolous'.[153] It was also said that Mr Lawrence did not know 'the value of the decent fig-leaf'.[154] In the *Nation*, a joint review of *The Trespasser* alongside *Marriage* by H. G. Wells called attention to Lawrence's book as being 'too full of anatomy' which could leave the reader 'repelled'; the reviewer also stated that the novel 'reminds one of the exotic writers of the nineties'.[155] Hueffer would have agreed.

The Trespasser went into a second impression two months after publication, but Lawrence was never confident about the book, neither from an aesthetic perspective nor as a saleable novel, even though the £50 advance he received supported him for months. On 10 December 1912 Lawrence wrote a rather curt response to a recent letter from Hueffer:

> Thanks for your full opinions on the *Trespasser*. I agree with you heartily. I rather hate the book. It seems a bit messy to me. But whether it injures my reputation or not, it has brought me enough money to carry me – so modestly, as you may guess – through a winter here on the Lake Garda. One must publish to live.[156]

Lawrence's terse sentences and the brevity of this letter are uncharacteristic of his correspondence, so that the 'thanks for your full opinions' seems disingenuous. He was by now weary of defending his reputation and more assertive in standing his ground against critical judgements. Luckily, Garnett's advice proved to be percipient: the novel had not damaged Lawrence's reputation and in Garnett he had found a sympathetic and industrious friend who offered him a connection to Duckworth as well as to a variety of other publication outlets.

'Why do you take so much trouble for me?'

I have noted just a fraction of the works and authors with whom Garnett came into contact between 1887 and 1913, but it is clear that he had a unique insight into the changing literary marketplace and by the time he met Lawrence he was an experienced, well-established and respected figure in literary circles. He relished his roles as publisher's reader and literary critic, writing in 1907 that

> we have not had a single novelist of insight to-day who has analysed or mirrored the life of the great manufacturing centres, of the relations of the 'classes' to the industrial population, from Birmingham to Newcastle. Consider that from modern fiction we can gather more knowledge about the life of the Kaffirs, the Malays, the Hindus, than about the life of the Yorkshire miners, the Lancashire mill-hands or the Staffordshire 'Black Country'.[157]

Garnett recognised that Lawrence was a writer who could bring to fiction a unique 'insight' into working-class life in Nottinghamshire; the writing that we know Lawrence shared with Garnett during their earliest acquaintance (such as the dialect poems and the Eastwood plays) demonstrated that he could provide the sympathetic analysis of life in a miner's family that Hueffer and Garnett had called for. According to Garnett, as 'the son of a miner' Lawrence 'possessed the rough force, the directness and "the guts", which his young contemporaries of the intelligentsia lacked'.[158] In autumn 1911 Lawrence wrote three new dialect ballads at the Cearne ('The Collier's Wife', 'Whether or Not' and 'The Drained Cup') under the watchful eye of his new mentor. Garnett greatly admired the dialect poetry of Robert Burns (writing in 1909 that 'none of our poets are more daring and unconventional than Burns') and Lawrence shared this reverence, declaring in December 1912 that he would write a novel based on the life of Burns but would turn the Scot into 'a Derbyshire man' because 'he seems a good deal like myself'.[159] It was Garnett who encouraged Lawrence in February and March 1912 to write his series of journalistic essays responding to the national coal strike, which had begun in nearby Alfreton, Derbyshire. Shortly after Duckworth had accepted 'Paul Morel', in August 1912 Lawrence informed Garnett that he had thought of a novel 'purely of the common people' (this abandoned project was to have been called 'Scargill Street').[160]

Alongside these writings on working-class life, Lawrence continued to explore in depth the passionate relations between men and women that so fascinated Garnett. Unlike Hueffer, Garnett did not dissuade Lawrence from writing on the topic of female sexuality and Lawrence soon wrote several more risqué stories after his work on *The Trespasser*, including 'New Eve and Old Adam', 'Once–' and probably a rewritten version of 'Delilah and Mr Bircumshaw'. He commented incisively that 'their moral tone would not agree with my countrymen' and he was right. In August he received a letter from Austin Harrison refusing a story: Lawrence thought his stories were 'too "steaming"' for Harrison.[161] Garnett may even have *encouraged* Lawrence to write about sex and sensuality. When Lawrence wrote his most explicit final novel, *Lady Chatterley's Lover*, he remembered his old mentor's literary values. In March 1928 Lawrence wrote to Laurence Pollinger, 'personally of course [Garnett]'ll like "John Thomas"'.[162] In August 1928 Lawrence asked David Garnett if Edward would like a copy, as

> [i]n my early days your father said to me 'I should welcome a description of the whole act' – which has stayed in my mind till I wrote this book . . . I always look on the Cearne as my jumping-off point into the world *and* your father as my first backer.[163]

The inscription in Garnett's copy reiterates this memory and gestures towards their disagreements: 'To Edward Garnett who sowed the first seed of this book, years ago, at the Cearne – and may not like the full fruit.'[164] Louie associated the Cearne with sexual impropriety because of its inhabitants' open marriage and she wrote that Garnett had suggested 'that "Sex" was necessary for the development of [Lawrence's] authorship'.[165] Our image of Garnett as Lawrence's censor, then, must be revised to reflect the more complex reality of his standing in early twentieth-century literary society.

Lawrence and Garnett believed that art should challenge readers' existing preconceptions about issues such as sex and sexuality to extend the vision of readers and shift the parameters of social attitudes. Lawrence's writing was shaped by the advice of his mentors, together with a growing understanding through first-hand experience of a literary marketplace that was unstable, reactionary and closely monitored by official and self-appointed bodies. The constraints faced by publishers and editors in the period make it clear why Garnett had to intervene in making Lawrence's work suitable for publication and so we cannot view him as a blundering philistine who carved up

Lawrence's work to deleterious effect. Garnett's notorious battle with censorship, his high standards for literature, his attempts to become a creative writer, his anti-institutional sentiments, unconventional marital arrangements and his advocacy of the rights of women to claim their sexual independence help us to understand how it was that he and Lawrence got on so well. It was, however, his practical commitment to Lawrence's work as a professional author at such a crucial time in his career that led him to overlook Hueffer and commemorate Garnett as his 'first backer'.

Notes

1. Worthen, *D. H. Lawrence: A Literary Life*, p. 18.
2. *TE*, 27.
3. Frank Swinnerton, *Background with Chorus* (1956), p. 115.
4. Jean Moorcroft Wilson, *Edward Thomas: From Adlestrop to Arras* (2015), p. 133.
5. Pierre Coustillas, *The Heroic Life of George Gissing, Part II: 1888–1897* (2012), p. 229. Garnett married Constance Black in August 1889.
6. Cedric Watts, *Joseph Conrad: A Literary Life* (1989), p. 53.
7. In a letter dated 2 November 1913 W. H. Hudson writes to Garnett: 'I had just read your favourite author's *Sons and Lovers*. A very good book except in that portion where he relapses into the old sty – the neck-sucking and wallowing in sweating flesh.' Edward Garnett (ed.), *Letters from W. H. Hudson to Edward Garnett* (1925), p. 130.
8. George Jefferson, *Edward Garnett: A Life in Literature* (1982), p. 150.
9. These words are used by Helen Baron, 'Some Theoretical Issues Raised by Editing *Sons and Lovers*' (1995), p. 76.
10. Carolyn G. Heilbrun, *The Garnett Family: The History of a Literary Family* (1961), p. 149.
11. *L*, I, 410.
12. *L*, I, 383.
13. Stanley Unwin, *The Truth about a Publisher* (1960), p. 84.
14. Julie F. Codell, 'Unwin, Thomas Fisher (1848–1935)' (2015).
15. John St John, *William Heinemann: A Century of Publishing 1890–1990* (1990), p. 58; 87.
16. Helmut E. Gerber (ed.), *George Moore in Transition: Letters to T. Fisher Unwin and Lena Milman, 1894–1910* (1968), p. 28.
17. H. G. Wells, *Mankind in the Making* (1903), p. 383, quoted in Keating, *The Haunted Study*, p. 18.
18. Keating, *The Haunted Study*, p. 18.

19. Unwin, *The Truth about a Publisher*, p. 90.
20. Codell, 'Unwin, Thomas Fisher (1848–1935)'.
21. Heilbrun, *The Garnett Family*, p. 71.
22. Troy J. Bassett finds that, of the known identities, out of eleven male authors, seven took male pseudonyms, one used initials, and three wrote their names in Greek or Russian characters; out of the twenty-six female authors, seven took male pseudonyms, thirteen took female pseudonyms and six took gender-neutral pseudonyms. 'T. Fisher Unwin's Pseudonym Library: Literary Marketing and Authorial Identity' (2004): 143–60.
23. Jefferson, *Edward Garnett*, p. 45.
24. Garnett, letter to his father, 14 July 1891 quoted in Richard Garnett, *Constance Garnett: A Heroic Life* (1991), p. 71.
25. Coustillas, *The Heroic Life of George Gissing*, p. 211.
26. Ibid., p. 229.
27. Garnett's reader's report quoted and transcribed by Coustillas, ibid., p. 230.
28. Chesson's reader's report quoted by Coustillas, ibid., pp. 230–1.
29. Chesson's comment is quoted in Ugo Mursia, *Scritti Conradiani* (1983), p. 30.
30. See James G. Nelson, *Publisher to the Decadents: Leonard Smithers in the Careers of Beardsley, Wilde, Dowson* (2000).
31. See Allison Pease, *Modernism, Mass Culture, and the Aesthetics of Obscenity* (2000), p. 93.
32. Codell, 'Unwin, Thomas Fisher (1848–1935)'; figure of £1,500 reported by Unwin, *The Truth about a Publisher*, p. 89.
33. Gerber, *George Moore in Transition: Letters to T. Fisher Unwin and Lena Milman, 1894–1910*, p. 26.
34. Sheila Rowbotham, *Edward Carpenter: A Life of Liberty and Love* (2008), p. 275; 329; 342–3.
35. *IR*, 75–8; 77.
36. Cited by McDonald, *British Literary Culture and Publishing Practice*, pp. 24–5.
37. Watts, *Joseph Conrad: A Literary Life*, p. 51.
38. Letter from Constance to Olive Garnett (24 January 1895), quoted in Garnett, *Constance Garnett*, p. 145.
39. Garnett, *Constance Garnett*, pp. 145–6.
40. Walter Kendrick, *The Secret Museum: Pornography in Modern Culture* (1987), pp. 121–3.
41. See Anthony Cummins, 'Émile Zola's Cheap English Dress: The Vizetelly Translations, Late-Victorian Print Culture, and the Crisis of Literary Value' (2009): 108–32.

42. Katherine Mullin, 'Pernicious Literature: Vigilance in the Age of Zola (1886–1899)' (2013), p. 50.
43. Gerber, *George Moore in Transition: Letters to T. Fisher Unwin and Lena Milman, 1894–1910*, p. 123. Moore both praised Zola and came to emphatically reject his influence in numerous reviews and letters, particularly during the period 1885–96.
44. See David Skilton's 'Introduction' to George Moore, *Esther Waters*, viii–xiii.
45. *WP*, xxxv.
46. George Moore, 'A New Censorship of Literature' (1884): 1–2; and Moore, *Literature at Nurse, or, Circulating Morals* (1885).
47. Anon., 'George Moore, Esther Waters' (1894): 4.
48. George Moore, 'A Reaction' (1895): 42–3. Adrian Frazier, *George Moore, 1852–1933* (2000), pp. 260–1.
49. Howard J. Booth, 'Same-Sex Desire, Cross-Gender Identification and Asexuality in D. H. Lawrence's Early Short Fiction' (2011): 37–57.
50. In November 1909 Lawrence wrote to Blanche Jennings that he wanted to 'get hold of one of George Moore's – *Evelyn Innes* or another'; in January 1910 he informed her that 'You can get *Evelyn Innes* and *Sister Theresa* for 4 1/2d each – Fisher Unwin, I believe. Send me *Esther Waters*, will you.' In February 1913 Lawrence and Frieda read Moore's autobiography, *Salve*. *L*, I, 142; 154; 512. For Corke's shared reading practices with Lawrence, see *T*, 9–10.
51. Neville, *A Memoir of D. H. Lawrence*, p. 83.
52. Moore wrote to Garnett on 17 October 1908 with his idea that Garnett 'may have received the proofs of *Evelyn Innes* from Fisher Unwin'. Helmut E. Gerber, ed. *George Moore on Parnassus: Letters (1900–1933) to Secretaries, Publishers, Printers, Agents, Literati, Friends and Acquaintances* (1988), p. 152.
53. This is Jefferson's opinion about the dismissal, *Edward Garnett*, p. 71.
54. A. D. Marks is quoted in Philip Unwin, *The Publishing Unwins* (1972), p. 46.
55. Watts, *Conrad: A Literary Life*, p. 51.
56. Goldring, *South Lodge*, p. 171.
57. Lane had been co-founder (with Elkin Mathews) of The Bodley Head before they split. Lane retained the imprint and retitled the business in his own name.
58. R. J. L. Kingsford, *The Publishers Association, 1896–1946* (1970), p. 216.
59. Iain Stevenson, *Bookmakers: British Publishing in the Twentieth Century* (2010), pp. 13–14; Keating, *The Haunted Study*, p. 59.
60. Hepburn, *The Author's Empty Purse and the Rise of the Literary Agent*, p. 42.

61. *L*, I, 306.
62. See Shafquat Towheed's Introduction to his edited volume *The Correspondence of Edith Wharton and Macmillan, 1901–1930* (2007), p. 27.
63. Michael Anesko, *Friction with the Market* (1986), p. 172.
64. Towheed, *The Correspondence of Edith Wharton and Macmillan*, pp. 23–4.
65. Garnett, *Constance Garnett*, p. 181.
66. St John, *William Heinemann*, p. 14.
67. Conrad and Hueffer, *The Inheritors*, p. 67.
68. Unpublished MS letters (Hilton Hall) quoted in Jefferson, *Edward Garnett*, p. 75.
69. Paul Bolton, 'Education: Historical Statistics', report commissioned by the Library of the House of Commons, dated 27 November 2012. Lawrence expected to earn £95 a year in 1908 but this was his first post and he had a teacher's certificate rather than a degree.
70. Letter from Heinemann to Garnett, quoted in St John, *William Heinemann*, p. 61.
71. Constance to Garnett's father, letter dated 27 August 1900, quoted in Garnett, *Constance Garnett*, p. 192.
72. Letter from Constance to Heinemann, 5 April 1915 (Heinemann archive, Octopus Publishing Group Library), quoted in Garnett, *Constance Garnett*, p. 265.
73. Stevenson, *Bookmakers: British Publishing in the Twentieth Century*, p. 6.
74. St John, *William Heinemann*, p. 58.
75. Letters to Dr Richard Garnett, quoted in Garnett, *Constance Garnett*, p. 198.
76. Anon., *Fifty Years 1898–1948* (1948), pp. 8–9; 11.
77. Anthony Powell, *To Keep the Ball Rolling: The Memoirs of Anthony Powell. II* (1978), p. 6.
78. Garnett, *Constance Garnett*, p. 198.
79. *L*, I, 309.
80. Sandra Kemp, Charlotte Mitchell and David Trotter (eds), 'Introduction' to *The Oxford Companion to Edwardian Fiction* (1997), xiv.
81. Edward Garnett, 'The "Sex Novel"' (1910), unpaginated.
82. See Nicola Wilson, 'Circulating Morals (1900–1915)' (2013), p. 58.
83. Anon., 'Censorship of Books' (1910): 28 (cited by Wilson, 'Circulating Morals', p. 58).
84. Anon., 'Circulating Libraries Association: The Question of Improper Books' (1909): 12.
85. Wilson, 'Circulating Morals', pp. 64–5.
86. Ibid., pp. 63–4.

87. Frederick Macmillan to H. G. Wells, 19 October 1908; quoted in Lovat Dickson, *H. G. Wells: His Turbulent Life and Times* (1971), p. 166; John St Loe Strachey, 'A Poisonous Book' (1909): 846–7.
88. Steve Nicholson, *The Censorship of British Drama 1900–1968. Vol. I: 1900–1932* (2003), p. 4. Irish theatres were not required to submit plays to the Lord Chamberlain's office.
89. S. H. Strong, 'The Breaking Point' (1908): 227.
90. Ibid.
91. St John Hankin, 'The Censorship of Plays Again' (1907): 39.
92. See 'Bernard Shaw's Defensive Laughter', Celia Marshik, *British Modernism and Censorship* (2009), pp. 46–87; 54.
93. On the 1909 government enquiry, Nicholson, *The Censorship of British Drama 1900–1968*, pp. 46–79.
94. Edward Garnett, 'The Censorship of Public Opinion' (1909): 137–48.
95. Garnett, 'The Censorship of Public Opinion', p. 144.
96. *L*, I, 546.
97. *L*, I, 317; 326.
98. James Moran, *The Theatre of D. H. Lawrence* (2015), pp. 52–66.
99. Yeats wrote twenty-six plays. Galsworthy was known for his social problem plays, such as *Justice* (1910), which exposed the double standards of the social justice system. Maugham had nine plays published by Heinemann in 1912–13. Conrad wrote three plays (adaptations of some of his fictional work) and it was not until late in his career that he showed interest in the theatre: see Richard J. Hand, *The Theatre of Joseph Conrad* (2005).
100. *L*, I, 384.
101. Crichton, '"An Interview with Lawrence", Kyle S. Crichton', p. 217.
102. *L*, I, 297.
103. 'Unwin has a strong and close alliance with publishers of the United States . . . Unwin is publisher of the *Century*.' Anon., 'London Publishers: Mr T. Fisher Unwin', (1893): 51–2; 52.
104. *L*, I, 301. *PO*, xxii.
105. *L*, I, 307.
106. *L*, I, 308.
107. Garnett, *Letters from W. H. Hudson to Edward Garnett*, pp. 1–2.
108. *L*, I, 223; fn. 1.
109. *L*, I, 309.
110. *L*, I, 323. Scott-James reflected on meeting Lawrence at the Cearne in his obituary of Edward Garnett in *The Spectator* (26 February 1937): 22.
111. *L*, I, 310.
112. Ibid.

113. *L*, I, 170.
114. The chronology provided here is the one given in *T*. For Lawrence's reference to 'The Freshwater Diary' as containing 'prose poems' (as cited by Helen Corke), see *T*, 8.
115. E. T. 181.
116. He read *Ann Veronica* before 28 January 1910 and thought it 'not very good': *L*, I, 154. In the same letter he told Blanche she could get Moore's novels in 4½d editions published by Unwin. The phrase 'love-novel' was used by Lawrence to classify *The Trespasser* in January 1912: *L*, I, 355–6.
117. *T*, 6; Corke, *D. H. Lawrence: The Croydon Years*, p. 5.
118. *L*, I, 140; 164; 171; 359; 327.
119. Saunders, *Ford: A Dual Life*, p. 20. For Wagnerian allusions in *The Trespasser*, see *T*, 325–7. In July 1910 at a literary event at Holland Park Avenue Lawrence met Hueffer's relatives: the poet and editor of the Pre-Raphaelite Brotherhood publication the *Germ* William Rossetti (brother of Dante Gabriel and Christina Rossetti) and Hueffer's sister Juliet, who was a 'Wagnerian contralto of great ability and heard at Covent Garden' (Saunders, p. 100). Hueffer's mother, Catherine Madox Brown, was an artist and model associated with the Pre-Raphaelites; Ezra Pound termed Lawrence's early love poems 'pre-raphaelitish slush' in his review of *Love Poems and Others* (1913). For Hueffer's comment on Wagner see his *When Blood is Their Argument: An Analysis of Prussian Culture* (1915), p. 66.
120. Helen Corke, *In Our Infancy: An Autobiography* (1975), p. 201.
121. *L*, I, 178.
122. *L*, I, 182–3.
123. See St John, *William Heinemann*, pp. 93–5 for an extract of Heinemann's attack on literary agents printed in *The Author* in 1901. He called the middleman 'a parasite' in a letter to the *Athenaeum* in 1893.
124. *L*, VIII, 4.
125. I argue here that 'florid prose poem' refers to 'Saga' rather than *The White Peacock*. Critical opinion is divided: Michael Bell (*D. H. Lawrence: Language and Being* (1992), p. 14) and John Worthen (*EY*, 261) have ascribed the 'decorated idyll' description to 'Saga', but Andrew Robertson assigns the description to *WP* (*WP*, xxxiv).
126. *L*, I, 228, fn. 3.
127. *L*, I, 229.
128. Ford, *Mightier than the Sword*, p. 121.
129. *L*, I, 165–6.
130. *L*, I, 130. Goldring writes about Hueffer's opinion of Yeats in *South Lodge*, p. 49.

131. Ernest Rhys, *Everyman Remembers* (1931), pp. 253–4.
132. *L*, I, 276. 'The coincidence of correspondence from Hueffer and Lawrence's use of words like "pornographic" and "erotic" is noticeable' (*T*, 15–16).
133. *L*, I, 317.
134. *L*, I, 317; 330.
135. *L*, I, 315.
136. *L*, I, 339–40.
137. Ford, *Mightier than the Sword*, p. 121.
138. Edward Garnett to Olive Garnett, 9 December 1924, unpublished letter, Harry Ransom Center, University of Texas at Austin. Quoted by Helen Smith, 'Opposing Orbits: Ford, Edward Garnett, and the Battle for Conrad' (2007), p. 81.
139. Ford Madox Ford to Stanley Unwin, 24 January 1937 (letter misdated by Ford as Garnett died on 19 February), Allen and Unwin Archive, University of Reading. Quoted by Smith, 'Opposing Orbits', p. 79.
140. Smith, 'Opposing Orbits', p. 90.
141. *L*, I, 275; 433; 458.
142. *L*, I, 277, fn. 1.
143. John Long to G. Herbert Thring, 7 June 1911. BL, Soc. of Authors. MS Add 56978.
144. St John, *William Heinemann*, p. 47.
145. *L*, I, 424, fn. 1.
146. *L*, I, 343; 345.
147. *L*, I, 353.
148. *T*, 32.
149. Corke, *In Our Infancy*, p. 216.
150. Garnett's comment is reproduced in *T*, Appendix 4, 323.
151. *L*, I, 355–6.
152. *L*, I, 455; 421, fn. 4.
153. *Westminster Gazette* (8 June 1912): 18.
154. Anon., '*The Trespasser* by D. H. Lawrence' (1912): 950.
155. Anon., '"Marriage" and Another' (1912): 152–4.
156. *L*, I, 485.
157. Garnett, 'The Novel of the Week' [review of Arnold Bennett's *Anna of the Five Towns*] (1907): 642.
158. Edward Garnett, 'D. H. Lawrence: His Posthumous Papers' [review of *Phoenix*], (1936): 155.
159. Garnett, 'The Censorship of Public Opinion', p. 139; *L*, I, 487.
160. *L*, I, 431; 466.

161. *L*, I, 420; 430.
162. *L*, VI, 343.
163. *L*, VI, 520.
164. Quoted in Heilbrun, *The Garnett Family*, p. 161.
165. Private family letter dated 14 January 1962, cited in *L*, I, 16.

PART III

LITERARY COMMERCE (1910–14)

5

'A green fresh poet': Self-Fashioning, Networking and Marketing the Contemporary Poet

It is a marker of Lawrence's canny negotiation of the marketplace that he managed to maintain a distinctive reputation and avoid the stigma attached to commercialism and self-promotion that was necessary when engaging in the business of publishing and sustaining a career. It also helped, of course, that he was practical, thrifty and courageous enough to accept financial instability and work around his penurious circumstances. Finding plenty of evidence to support their readings, critics have generally maintained the idea that Lawrence was sceptical of marketing tactics and reluctant to engage with the fashioning of his authorial identity, so there has been a lack of interrogation of these aspects of Lawrence's professional career. In this respect, Lawrence studies has not yet caught up with a broader discussion within modernist studies about the promotional activities and marketing of modernist writers which has led to an examination of wider material culture in the period across a variety of media. For example, Lawrence's fashionable late journalism and his public spat with the former Conservative Home Secretary Sir William Joynson-Hicks ('Jix') – which resulted in the publication of the outspoken pamphlet 'Pornography and Obscenity' (1929) in Faber and Faber's 'Criterion Miscellany' series – are instances of his energetic involvement with the public sphere which have been overlooked and yet they demonstrate his ability to both mimic the discourse of newspaper journalism and interrogate popular modes of thought on issues such as sex, gender relations and censorship. In defence of his so-called 'obscene' work in the late 1920s he courted the controversy that had afforded his name notoriety since 1915.

Patrick Collier has been instrumental in highlighting the significance of the 'print marketplace' as 'part of the intellectual matrix in which modernism took shape'; he examines the interactions of T. S. Eliot, Woolf, Joyce, Rose Macaulay and Rebecca West with the newspaper press to examine the role that journalism played in shaping their careers.[1] Similarly, in *Modernism and the*

Culture of Celebrity (2005) Aaron Jaffe explores the ways in which modernist authors advertised their names and yet attempted to distance themselves from self-promotion, using archival evidence to trace local instances of collaboration, editing, networking and reviewing 'a the careers of an array of writers (principally the 'men of 1914': Eliot, Joyce, Pound and Wyndham Lewis). Lawrence is notably absent from these studies. Arguing that publicity, promotion and engaging with the public were unavoidable if sales were to be made and careers sustained and aiming to highlight Lawrence's understanding of these circumstances from the very beginning of his career, the two remaining chapters examine how he negotiated self-fashioning and engaged with those who sought to introduce him to the reading public. Working with Marysa Demoor's definition, I describe 'self-fashioning' as the way in which an individual chooses to 'self-mythologise', to 'construct an identity in and through language and represent it "before an audience"'.[2] Yet since the literary field is a sociological phenomenon formed by networks of associations it is also important to consider how others helped to fashion and publicise Lawrence's authorial identity. This chapter traces two key instances of promotional activities concerning the marketing of the contemporary poet. Firstly, we return to consider the period in 1910, concurrent with the production of manuscripts such as 'A Modern Lover' and 'The Saga of Siegmund', when Lawrence was attracted to a particular kind of esoteric poetry which corresponds with the work of the Scottish poet Rachel Annand Taylor, with whom he was in close contact. Lawrence delivered a paper on her to the Croydon branch of the English Association in November 1910, which was intended to inflame the audience by drawing on details of her personal life. Later, Lawrence fashioned his own poetic identity when he was invited to contribute a poem ('Snap-Dragon') to Edward Marsh's anthology *Georgian Poetry 1911–1912*. In 1913 Katherine Mansfield asked Lawrence to review the anthology for the magazine *Rhythm*; his laudatory review, 'The Georgian Renaissance', was published in the March 1913 number. Lawrence knew that his affiliation with the 'Georgian poets' was at that time beneficial for his early professional career and consciously aligning himself with the 'new men' of contemporary poetry allowed him to promote *Love Poems and Others*, which was due to be published in the same month in which the review appeared.

'Rachel Annand Taylor' (1910), 'a green fresh poet'

Lawrence first met Rachel Annand Taylor (1876–1960) in 1910 (probably on 10 March), at a gathering of poets at the home of Ernest and Grace Rhys in Hampstead.[3] On occasions such as these, Yeats intoned his poetry accompanied by the music of Florence Farr, and Pound performed eccentrically, on one instance reputedly eating a vase of tulips: dramatic enactments of poetic identities were the order of these evenings.[4] Taylor attended Aberdeen Training Centre for Teachers from 1894 to 1897, before marrying Alexander Taylor (a Classics teacher in Dundee) in 1901. The Bodley Head published her first volume, *Poems*, in 1904. By the time Lawrence met her she had known Yeats for at least five years: she and her husband arranged for him to give a lecture in Dundee in late 1905. Taylor wrote to her former Professor H. J. C. Grierson in January 1906 that they had 'had to educate Dundee into knowing who Yeats was', but 'the lecture turned out a great success'.[5] Yeats was interested in Taylor's work, too: he wrote to Grierson on 12 October 1909 enclosing 5s for a copy of her latest poetry collection, *Rose and Vine* (Elkin Mathews, 1909).[6]

Lawrence had been introduced to the Rhyses through Hueffer on 14 November 1909 and read from a notebook at one of their poetry evenings on 18 December. On 20 November Lawrence reported to Louie that Hueffer 'says I ought to get out a volume of verse, so you see how busy I am'.[7] One of the most significant of Lawrence's poetic experimentations dating from this month was the nine-part sequence 'A Life History in Harmonies and Discords', which is an attempt, through musical cadence, colour and pattern, to make high art out of autobiographical experience and personal conflict. In Lawrence's 'Last Harmony' of the sequence, his speaker watches pairs of 'stepping feet trace a strange design / . . . I trace a pattern, mine or thine / . . . Pains that were clotted over mine.'[8] As Taylor advises in her poem 'XI: The Passion-Flower', 'Let Music, Colour, decorated Verse, / Meditate, each like some sad lutanist, / This Paten, and the marvels it uncovers, / Identities of joy and anguish'.[9] Since the publication in 2018 of the third volume of the Cambridge University Press edition of Lawrence's uncollected poems and early versions it is now possible to discern the extent of Lawrence's experimentation with esoteric and erotic poetry at this time. Christopher Pollnitz identifies 'a shift into sexual realism' in the poetry around November 1909 and into the next six months of 1910. Poems such as 'Amour' and 'Dream' (dated to *c.* November 1909) are, for Pollnitz, 'precursors of the more explicit poetry of 1910' which reflect Lawrence's 'criss-crossy' affairs.[10] Lawrence briefly considered marrying Agnes Holt, who could not condone pre-marital sexual intimacy, began a tortuous physical relationship with Jessie Chambers at Whitsun in 1910 until he broke off their informal engagement on 1 August, had a dalliance with married mother Alice Dax in March when she visited him in Croydon to see a production of Richard Strauss's *Elektra* and became ever more attracted to a troubled Helen Corke. Lawrence's relationships, the writing of the 'erotic'

'Saga of Siegmund' (for which novel Lawrence suggested 'The Man and the Dreaming Woman' as a potential title as late as April 1912) and the new circle of poets to whom Lawrence was reading all shaped his poetry and he reports a particular fascination with Taylor's work.[11]

Lawrence had read three of Taylor's poems ('The Epilogue of the Dreaming Women', 'The First Time' and 'The Mask of Proteus') in the October 1909 number of Hueffer's *English Review* and thought them 'exceedingly good'.[12] In a letter dated 15 November Lawrence tells her he would 'put you first among the poets of today'.[13] There are correspondences between poems such as 'The Epilogue of the Dreaming Women' and Lawrence's poem 'Liaison' (later revised and entitled 'The Yew Tree on the Downs'), for which Pollnitz provides the date of first composition as *c*. September 1910. Its setting is based on a visit Lawrence made with Corke to a yew tree near Purley several times, firstly in July 1910 and then again in August or September.[14] Both poets use the same conceit of the speaker's enclosure. Taylor's speaker, representative of female muses who 'feed the gods with spice and canticles', wishes to be clothed 'In veils mysterious and delicate / Clothe us again, in beautiful broideries'. Instead of 'idle words', Taylor's muses ask the gods for 'graven thuribles . . . mercies, cruelties, and exultations, / Give the long trances of the breaking heart / . . . Give cloud and flame, give trances, exultations'.[15] Lawrence's speaker desires enclosure with a lover

> under the tree, where the leaf cloths
> Curtain us in, so dark
> . . .
> Under the yew-tree tent
> Darkness is loveliest; wherein I could sear
> You like frankincense into scent,
>
> Fill full this vaulted hole with the odour
> Of you, as the sulphur primroses.[16]

'The Epilogue of the Dreaming Women' is the last in a sequence of poems in Taylor's latest collection, *The Hours of Fiammetta*. In her Preface to the collection, Taylor describes her poetry as the 'music of bewilderment' which tells the story of 'the acolyte, the priestess, the clairvoyante of the unknown gods' who 'troubles and quickens the soul of man'.[17] The first poem in the sequence, 'The Prologue of the Dreaming Women', describes how these women 'carry spices to the gods. / Sacred and soft as lotos-flowers / Are those long languorous hands of ours'. Using similar floral imagery and sultry phrasing, Lawrence's aroused speaker in 'Liaison' puts his 'mouth / Among the loose, languorous primroses, / And flower-dust filling my moustache a fine drouth / Keen on my lips imposes'. He implores his lover to 'Kiss but the dust then off my lips . . . You will kiss to wholesome flame from the fire / That smouldering, wears me down to ash'. Lawrence's poem also recalls Pound's 'La Fraisne' ('The Ash Tree'), which was initially to have been the title of Pound's first poetry collection, *A Lume Spento*, a volume that similarly reflects the haunting spiritualism of the period in which poets demonstrated the exalted nature of their souls. Pound's poem is set in 'The Ash Wood of Malvern' and his tortured speaker has 'curled mid the boles of the ash wood, / I have hidden my face where the oak / Spread his leaves over me'.[18] Corke recalled the occasion when Pound gave Lawrence a 'proof copy of his book of poems *A Lume Spento* and he attended one of those séances where the poems of W. B. Yeats were intoned, to the mystification of a devoted company. Lawrence parodied the performance most unkindly.'[19] As a newcomer to the circle, Lawrence naturally drew upon the poetry he encountered at the Rhys's poetry evenings. His poetry is more erotic than Taylor's, however, because it is less abstract. Taylor's poetry often refrains from depicting external reality and seeks to achieve its effects more implicitly and symbolically, using shapes, colours and textures, whereas Lawrence's poetry is often based on his own immediate sexual circumstances and physical environments. Although he experimented with this spiritual style of poetry he also viewed it with a degree of ironic detachment. At some level he was showing himself that he had the ability to produce poetry like this if it might find favour with the 'Swells' and be accommodated in the limited marketplace for poetry; introducing the erotic element was an intervention that allowed him to explore the pressing sexual tensions within himself – and Siegmund – and depart from 'sickly sentimentalis[m]'.[20]

Lawrence must have read *The Hours of Fiammetta* in September 1910, the same month in which it was published, since he informed Taylor on 30 September 1910 that he had been invited to speak at the Croydon branch of the English Association and had chosen to give a paper on her. It is his first known letter to Taylor, an excerpt of which is produced here:

Our 'English Association' ~~prosy~~ vague, middle-class Croydonians mostly ladies, lingering remnants of the Pre-Raphaelites – asked me to give a paper on 'A Living Poet'.
 'I will give you,' I said, 'Rachel Annand Taylor.'
 'Excuse me,' they said, 'but how do you spell it.'
I have got the *Fiammetta* (*I* can't even spell her) sequence. I admire them, and wish to goodness I had your art.

> 'This is deep Hell to be expressionless.'
> I have to devote myself to prose. Please, if you are bold enough, persuade somebody to buy my novel *The White Peacock* which Heinemann will publish directly. – (a bit of advertisement.)
> But to come to the point. I have only got *Fiammetta* (esoteric creature): if I can't borrow *Rose and Vine* I'll buy it (this is poverty, believe me); but isn't there another, earlier volume? Shall I need it? – would you lend it to me?
> Those old ladies would love me to describe you to them, but I won't. I will keep you vaguely in upper air, as a poetess should be.
> You said you would ask me to come and see you. Why did you not?[21]

The opening line is not overtly dismissive of the intellect and tastes of his perceived audience of 'old ladies', but the pejorative reference to the 'remnants of the Pre-Raphaelites' suggests that they will not be particularly discerning or critical. Lawrence's manner is arch, but *The White Peacock* was aimed at a similar kind of readership; even its title foregrounds its association with aestheticism. Books such as *The Green Carnation* – anonymously published in 1894 but written by the journalist and satirist Robert Hichens and based on his friend Lord Alfred Douglas's relationship with Oscar Wilde – were a *succès de scandale* at the turn of the century. In quoting 'This is deep Hell to be expressionless', the opening line from Douglas's 'Silence' in his recently published *Sonnets* (1909), Lawrence implicitly shows himself to be a reader of aesthetic poetry and someone well-placed to talk about Taylor. His playful approach was also rather strategic. He flatters her in order to ask several favours: that she may look out for the publication of *The White Peacock* and advertise it among her literary friends, that she should lend him the earlier volumes of her poetry and invite him to her home.

Lawrence's extant letters to Taylor are excessively florid and contrived. He consciously takes the part of the suffering artist and makes known to her the shifts in his personae:

> Your muted, slyly malicious manner makes me obstreperous. If it were Violet Hunt I should be witty (sic), and if it were Elizabeth Martindale – I should be sweet and refined. But your slow, soft burning like almost invisible alcohol, with a yellow tip of cynicism now and again makes me crackle like burning straw. I'm afraid I was a nuisance: if so, don't ask me again.[22]

Lawrence demonstrates his awareness that literary culture requires one to present modified versions of oneself to please different parties; the literary world seems to him artificial, but necessarily so, for the sake of social connections and promotional activities. He implies that he can be a social chameleon. Emphasising his unsettled and fluid approach to self-fashioning in a flippant and devil-may-care manner, Lawrence reveals his inexperience and hesitancy. The description of Taylor as 'muted, slyly malicious' and intoxicating 'like almost invisible alcohol' shows Lawrence conflating Taylor's personality with that of her Dreaming Woman whose withdrawal troubles male souls. Lawrence put a great deal of work into pleasing others and almost four decades later Taylor recorded her memories of his visit: '[h]e was a terrific snob, he was definitely a cad, yet in this early period he was touching, he was so artlessly trying to find his way'. Disquietingly, she continues: '[h]e suddenly laughed, and said "Oh, I'll probably die of drink like my father" . . . I felt . . . that he was so neurotically unstable that he would collapse before he made an impression.'[23] His mother was gravely ill with abdominal cancer, which accounts for his emotional instability. Lawrence appears to have been at a crossroads, attempting to fashion a poetic identity for himself by considering the stances and positioning of others; giving the paper allowed him to appraise Taylor's poetic identity as a means of tentatively exploring his own. Taylor invited Lawrence to visit her on Saturday 15 October. During this visit he found out more about her life and work; she also lent him *Poems* and gave him the address of her friend Adrian Berrington so that Lawrence could write and request to borrow his copy of *Rose and Vine*.[24]

Bruce Steele suggests that Lawrence delivered his paper on Thursday 17 November 1910. The number of attendees is unknown and the manuscript prepared for the event (written during the first two weeks of November) is extant.[25] Since the text was orally delivered we cannot know how much he embellished, revised or omitted aspects of the written document. There are, however, two surviving accounts of the occasion. Philip F. T. Smith, Headteacher at Davidson Road School, recalls that the English Association was

> patronised by many of the intelligentsia including members of the Education Authority, mostly ladies. The Chief Director at the time was a scholar with a profound academic record. He was a most influential and sympathetic supporter of Lawrence's literary ambitions and he suggested that on his introduction it might be useful if Lawrence would attend a meeting and provide a reading for discussion. Lawrence agreed, and apparently chose and read a medieval romance, the text of which included some embarrassing situations and erotic conversations. I was not present . . . but the next day was interviewed by the offended official. . . . did I approve of his choice of subject? . . . Lawrence lost a very good friend

[in the Director]. . . . I can imagine his grim satisfaction at the efforts of his audience of superior intellects to preserve an unconcerned interest in his performance.[26]

While Smith mistakenly remembers the subject of the paper to have been a 'medieval romance', the classification is relevant: Lawrence stressed the influence of medieval romance on Taylor's sensual poetry, selections from which he read out. Smith perceived that Lawrence would have wanted to coerce his audience of 'superior intellects' into a strong reaction to the poetry; his account suggests that Lawrence put on a particularly memorable 'performance' and caused offence. Lawrence's performativity was remembered by another of his teaching colleagues, Stewart A. Robertson:

> I took Lawrence once to a meeting of a private literary society . . . Lawrence, then in a Rossetti stage, could not understand my liking for verses which 'only spoke' and whose words had neither colour nor cadence nor resonance. Lawrence's choice was Rachel Annand Taylor. A thrill went around the circle as he said, with Clara Butt intonations, 'Rachel Annand Taylor has red hair, squirrel-red hair,' and went on to chant her jeweled verbosities. His introductory sentence was characteristic, he was obsessed by the physical aspects of persons and places.[27]

Robertson viewed Lawrence as being influenced by literary fashions (he was in a 'Rossetti stage'), suggesting that he selected Taylor because of their shared poetic interests and appreciation of 'cadence' and 'resonance'.[28] Lawrence's musical delivery of his paper – intoning it in the style of the English contralto singer Clara Butt – was surely influenced by his experiences of the theatrical and musical poetic performances of figures such as Pound and Yeats. David Garnett noted Lawrence's talent for mimicry: 'he had once seen Yeats or Ezra Pound for half an hour in a drawing room, and straightaway Yeats or Pound appeared before you'.[29] The disorientation Lawrence experienced when engaging with his teaching circle after being present at the gatherings of literary society must have been at once uncomfortable and amusing and it contributed towards the ironic stance he adopted towards both worlds.

Lawrence's desire to give a memorable oral performance and to shock or 'thrill' his audience by invoking the 'physical aspects of persons' can be traced in the script of his paper. If Lawrence delivered the paper more or less as it is written then it is the work of a confident speaker, although Ernest Rhys gave another impression of the way Lawrence read at a poetry evening (an occasion when he 'rose nervously but very deliberately' and read with his back to the company).³⁰ Despite having assured Taylor that he would not 'describe' her to the audience but keep her 'vaguely in upper air', the textual evidence indicates that he did not plan to keep these promises. He opens the paper by mentioning Taylor's age and outlining the breakdown of her marriage: she is 'not more than thirty; she has been married and her husband has left her: she lives in Chelsea, visits Professor Gilbert Murray in Oxford, and says strange, ironic things of many literary people, in a plaintive, peculiar fashion'. In fact, Taylor was thirty-four; Lawrence stresses her youthfulness to emphasise that she is 'not ripe yet to be gathered as fruit for lectures and papers'. Sardonically, he notes that '[i]t is impossible to appreciate the verse of a green fresh poet. He must be sun-dried by time and sunshine of favourable criticism, like muscatels and prunes.'³¹ By using the pronoun 'he' it is as if he is talking from personal experience rather than describing Taylor's critical fortunes. His gesture in paying critical attention to her work contains an implicit claim for his own work to be taken seriously. The audience would likely have known that Lawrence, too, was an *English Review* poet; his poems 'Sigh No More', 'Tired of the Boat' and 'Ah, Muriel!' had just been published in the October 1910 number of the journal, now under Austin Harrison's editorship. A deletion explicitly predicts the audience's response to position them as critics who will find 'green' poets distasteful: 'you will not be prepared to bow and listen with respect touched with reverence'.³² Lawrence plays up to the Pre-Raphaelite theatricality that he had earlier disparaged and lightly mocks the pseudo-sophistication of his Croydon audience.

New Journalism

Lawrence begins the paper by using the popular 'personal interview' technique of New Journalism, mimicking its provocative and gossipy register to provoke a reaction from the audience. In stories such as 'The Death of the Lion' (1894) and 'John Delavoy' (1898), Henry James satirised the belief of modern authors that in order to succeed one must be profiled by journalists. Due to the boom in printed matter the 1870s and 1880s witnessed forms of promotion that we now identify as the beginnings of modern advertising techniques. In 1853 a tax on advertisements in journals and newspapers was lifted and by the 1880s many advertising agencies had been founded; advertisers began to replace black and white engravings with photographic reproduction and colour.³³ These changes affected the production and consumption of the printed word and consequently the notion of authorship. As Demoor observes, 'the name of the author and the identity of the author attached to that name had become the foremost marketing strategy by 1900'.³⁴ Richard

Salmon notes that through media such as 'advertising, journalism, and photography, authors, like the texts which they produce, are marketed as commodities, as products to be circulated and consumed'.[35] The public became attuned to reading about the lives of authors and this was largely due to the 'Americanisation' of British journalism from the 1880s. W. T. Stead and T. P. O'Connor pioneered the adoption of New Journalism in Britain. The new style of journalism had begun to flourish in America during the 1860s and it came to dominate the British newspaper press by the end of the decade, to the dismay of 'serious' journalists such as W. E. Henley.[36] Stead (editor of the *Pall Mall Gazette* for seven years from 1883) was a major proponent of the personal interview which often included photographs of the artist at home: 'autobiographical and even confessional writings were, he thought, what the public unwittingly craved' and in 1884 alone he published over 100 interviews in the *Gazette*.[37] For O'Connor, 'personalities, not politics, sold newspapers'; he considered that the best way to attract readers was with the use of 'a "personal tone" involving detailed description of a public figure's appearance, clothes, habits, home, and lifestyle'.[38] According to its critics, New Journalism often contravened the 'bounds of good taste'; it included women's pages and interviews with 'second-rate burlesque actresses' who lived in 'palm-treed flat[s] with Liberty draperies', as well as features on sensational crimes and the latest divorce court scandals.[39] The 'author at home' feature of popular journalism, 'an informal conversation with the writer in a domestic setting – was an effective way of converting the artist into a literary celebrity for public consumption'. It responded to the 'desire for peeps into the boudoirs and drawing-rooms of the polite world'.[40]

Lawrence sensationalised Taylor as a sensual female poet. He originally wrote that she 'has left her husband'; the revision, making her passive in the breakdown of her marriage, is useful for Lawrence in his later construction of her as a lovelorn and solitary 'romanticist'. Using lexis derived from Taylor's own poetry, he writes that 'she cherishes a yew-darkened garden in her soul where she can remain withdrawn, sublimating experience into odours'. She now lives alone in fashionable Chelsea amongst literary figures about whom she tells 'strange' stories; the newly single poet visits Gilbert Murray, which stresses aestheticism's connection to Oxford and classical study. Although emotionally stricken, Taylor is, then, an independent, well-connected and perhaps transgressive educated woman. After reading aloud four of her 'love songs' ('Desire', 'Surrender', 'Unrealised' and 'Renunciation'), Lawrence stated that the fourth poem contains 'the story of Mrs Taylor's married life'. The conventions of the personal interview form demanded that the interviewer should refer to the subject as though they were familiar friends and so Lawrence 'interviews' Taylor using an appropriately intimate rhetorical style when he quotes from the conversation they reportedly shared:

> 'There is nothing more tormenting' I said to her, 'than to be loved overmuch.'
> 'Yes, one thing more tormenting' she replied.
> 'And what's that?' I asked her.
> 'To love,' she said, very quietly.[41]

The presentation of private dialogue, paired with the esoteric love poetry, may be the type of 'erotic conversation' that offended the 'official' who had invited Lawrence to speak. 'Rachel Annand Taylor' was first published in edited form by Ada Clarke and Stuart Gelder in *Young Lorenzo: Early Life of D. H. Lawrence* (G. Orioli, 1932), but Taylor threatened legal action to suppress the paper from being re-published in Secker's English edition of *Early Life of D. H. Lawrence* (1932). It may have been Lawrence's insensitive discussion of her divorce that prompted her complaint: Taylor's husband suffered from mental illness and was institutionalised, which appears to have been the cause of the divorce.[42]

As Robertson recalled, Lawrence describes Taylor's appearance:

> [she is] all that could be desired of a poetess: in appearance, purely Rossettian: slim, svelte; big, beautiful bushes of reddish hair hanging over her eyes, which peer from the warm shadow; delicate colouring, scarlet, small, shut mouth; a dark, plain dress with a big boss of a brooch on her bosom, a curious, carven witch's brooch; then long white languorous hands of the correct subtle radiance. All that a poetess should be.[43]

Lawrence seems almost mocking, either of the way in which Taylor has fashioned her identity as a particular kind of poetess, or of the necessity for her to fashion herself in this manner in order to be marketed as appealing to a readership interested in all things 'Rossettian'. He implicitly satirises all parties: authors (as creators), the literary marketplace (as the arena that produces commodities and facilitates commerce) and readers (as consumers and arbiters of 'taste'). The author conflates herself with her poetry, which is as mysterious and sensual as her 'scarlet' mouth and her 'bosom', highlighted by a brooch worn in Scotland as a charm against witchcraft. Taylor had her portrait painted by the Dundee-born artist John McKirdy Duncan in 1907; appropriately, Duncan's usual choice of subject matter was rooted in the Celtic Revival and the Pre-Raphaelite tradition. The portrait may have been commissioned by her husband: her wedding ring is prominently displayed as she clutches her book.[44] Lawrence's physical description of Taylor matches her general appearance in the painting, which he might have seen at her residence.

Against the philistines

Having established at length the biographical context to Taylor's work, Lawrence moves into a more literary-critical analysis of her poetry and authorial identity. Taylor's romantic appearance and nostalgic poetry show her to be looking backwards to the beauty and decadence of the late nineteenth century and its fashionable mysticism and medievalism: she 'sounds the music of citherns and violes. She is medieval; she is as pagan and romantic as the old minstrels. She belongs to the company of Aucassin and Nicolette'.[45] The emphasis on musical poetry and references to the 'old minstrels' and 'Aucassin and Nicolette' again reinforce Lawrence and Taylor's links to the literary circles of Yeats and Pound, but as Helen Carr observes, the thirteenth-century love story was a 'cult book of the period, having been popularised by Pater's enthusiastic endorsement in *The Renaissance*'.[46] In December Lawrence sent Arthur McLeod a copy of Everyman's *Aucassin and Nicolette and Other Medieval Romances and Legends* translated by Eugene Mason (1910).[47] Lawrence knew that Pound gave weekly lectures in 1909 'on the minstrels'; Pound rewrote the lectures for publication in *The Spirit of Romance* (Elkin Mathews, 1910). Lawrence is probably alluding to Yeats alongside French poets such as Baudelaire, Verlaine, Rimbaud and Mallarmé when he refers to Taylor's use of 'that Celtic and French form of symbolism'.[48] Incidentally, c.28 February 1910 Lawrence composed his own 'Baudelairean prose poem', 'Malade'.[49]

Pound had courted the attention of his first British publisher Elkin Mathews because the firm had published Yeats's early work. Pound, Yeats and Mathews had a close affinity with the 'men of the Nineties', such as Lionel Johnson and Ernest Dowson, who had been members of the London-based 'Rhymer's Club' founded by Yeats and Ernest Rhys.[50] Two anthologies were published: *The Book of the Rhymers' Club* (Elkin Mathews, 1892) and *The Second Book of the Rhymers' Club* (Elkin Mathews and John Lane, 1894). Pound recalled that during these early years of his career he was 'drunk with Celticism' and his biographer states that Pound's work of the period also had a 'pervasive Pre-Raphaelite tone'.[51] As his familiarity with Yeats grew in late 1909 Pound became interested in the occult. Lawrence was attracted to, but not uncritical of, 'Celticism', the Pre-Raphaelites and the occult in the work of poets with whom he was acquainted. He recognises Taylor's similarly reflexive attitude towards literary predecessors and contemporaries, writing that she is 'an ironical romanticist'.[52]

John Worthen incisively observes that in 'Rachel Annand Taylor' Lawrence writes 'the prose of a man who has seen through a falsity and can now judge it to a hair's breadth – and yet remains nostalgic for it, and will defend it against the philistines'.[53]

The way that Lawrence emphasises Taylor's own fascination with, and interrogation of, romanticism and decadence indicates that he perceived that she was performing her authorial identity with a degree of ambivalence, too: '[t]here is a great deal of sensuous colour, but it is all abstract, impersonal in feeling'.[54] The result is a mere dream: it is 'emotionally insufficient', but 'more interesting by far to trace, than a psychological novel'.[55] For Lawrence, the chief interest of Taylor's work resides in the reworking of her life and her complex poetic representation of love and passion, so he could identify with her project, even if she struggled to articulate it subjectively. The 'Epilogue of the Dreaming Women' is, according to Lawrence, 'a very significant poem, to think over, and to think of again when one reads "Mrs Bull"'.[56] The reference to 'Mrs Bull' reveals how well-informed Lawrence was about developments in the print marketplace: the first issue of the forty-page weekly *Mrs Bull* had appeared on 29 October 1910. It was an expansion of a column entitled 'John Bull's Womenfolk' (in Horatio Bottomley's immensely popular weekly *John Bull*) which discussed 'fashion, diet and affairs of interest to the middle-class woman in her home'.[57] The allusion suggests that Lawrence positioned his Croydon audience as the type of readership that would be familiar with a publication such as *Mrs Bull*; he implies that Taylor's poetry offers women readers something far more intellectually challenging in interpreting her speakers' psychology.

Elkin Mathews

There may, however, be something more than just his identification of their similar literary tastes in Lawrence's choice of Taylor as the subject of the paper. It seems more than a mere coincidence that many of the literary figures whom we know Lawrence met during 1910 were not just those with close connections to Hueffer and the *English Review*, but those published by Elkin Mathews. Examples of these authors and their works include Dollie Radford, *A Light Load* (1897), *Poems* (1910); Yeats, *The Wind Among the Reeds* (1899), *The Tables of the Law and The Adoration of the Magi* (1904); Ernest Rhys, *The Masque of the Grail* (1908); Florence Farr, *The Music of Speech* (1909); Pound, *A Quinzaine for This Yule* (1908), *Personae* (1909), *Exultations* (1909), *Canzoni* (1911); and W. M. Rossetti, *Dante and his Convito* (1910). Pound had urged Elkin Mathews to publish Rossetti's *Dante* volume; Rossetti was

Hueffer's great uncle, whom Lawrence had met in person in July 1910. Lawrence also met the Radfords in spring 1910, probably through the Rhyses.[58] Perhaps most significantly, Mathews had published Hueffer's *Songs from London* in February 1910 and this cannot have escaped Lawrence's attention. In 1910 Lawrence was also reading volumes of poetry recently published by the imprint. In July he borrowed Grace Crawford's copy of *Ambergris: A Selection from the Poems of Aleister Crowley* (1910); Lawrence had been introduced to Crawford by Pound and visited her home on several occasions.[59] Although the upper-middle-class American Crawford (1889–1977) was not a writer herself, but a singer, actress, dancer and friend of Pound's, Lawrence writes to her in the same intimate manner that he uses to address Taylor, Hunt and Blanche Jennings.[60] In September Lawrence bought Baudelaire's *Les Fleurs du Mal*, an edition of which was published by Mathews in 1909.[61] Mathews published J. M. Synge's first book, *The Shadow of the Glen and Riders to the Sea* (1905); Lawrence was familiar with the edition in November 1909.[62] He was reading Francis Thompson in March 1910; he had copied out Thompson's 'Absence' (which had been printed in the January 1910 number of the *English Review*) for Crawford in November 1909.[63] Mathews and John Lane had published Thompson's *Poems* in 1893.

Mathews had a reputation for publishing high quality editions with small print runs, presenting his books as collector's items rather than bestsellers. Jessie remembered Lawrence in 1910 drawing her attention to 'the beautiful type and the fine old leather bindings' of the books he sent to her.[64] Mathews was 'an antiquarian at heart and a lover of Pre-Raphaelite poetry who responded in particular to verse which often amounted to little more than Celtic variations on Rossettian moods and Swinburnean dreams'; Celtic literature was 'Typified by a strange melancholy', charged emotions and 'evocation of the distant past'.[65] It was Mathews who published James Joyce's first collection of love poems, *Chamber Music*, in 1907. Priced at 1s 6d, the first edition sold just 509 copies, but Mathews sought to find the means to publish poetry at a time when there was little demand for it.[66] Lawrence's attention could have been drawn to the Elkin Mathews imprint by its reputation for publishing new poets and by his familiarity with the publisher's list. One of the members of the literary circle who was at that time being published by Mathews and attending the Rhys's poetry evenings may have suggested to Lawrence that he approach the publisher with examples of his poems.

Pound, in particular, had influence with Mathews. Another aspiring writer visiting London at this time was the American poet William Carlos Williams (1883–1963) who stayed with Pound during the first week of March 1910. Pound had recommended that Williams read 'the poetry of Yeats, Browning,

Francis Thompson, Swinburne and Rossetti to learn "something about the progress of English poetry in the last century'".[67] During his stay, Pound took Williams to Yeats's 'Monday evening' open house; they were 'ushered into a dimly lighted room where Yeats was reading Dowson's "Cynara" to a small group of Abbey actors and actresses'.[68] If the date given is accurate then it would have been 7 March, four days before Lawrence read his 'verses', possibly in the company of Pound, Yeats and Taylor, at the Rhys's on Thursday 10 March. Pound took Williams to 'a benefit lecture by W. B. Yeats, at the Adelphi Club, on the work of some of the younger Irish poets'.[69] Yeats's lectures 'to fashionable London audiences in March 1910 . . . synthesized literary commentary with autobiography'; he emphasised 'the connection between poetry and personality', which is the approach Lawrence took in 'Rachel Annand Taylor'.[70] Due to gaps in the historical record we are unable to determine whether Lawrence had been present at any of Yeats's formal lectures, but he was certainly socialising with Pound and his circle during this month. Due to illness, Lawrence had to turn down an invitation from the singer Florence Wood to attend her recital at the Bechstein Hall on 1 March, but he hoped to 'call and see you some Saturday evening'; it was Pound who had introduced them to one another.[71] Pound took Williams to dinner at the Woods's open house on Saturday 12 March; we cannot be sure whether this was also the Saturday on which Lawrence fulfilled his intention to call on Wood, but it is significant that Pound was the facilitator of the social connections of both Lawrence and Williams. Pound secured the publication by Elkin Mathews of Williams's first commercially published poetry collection *The Tempers* (1913) and he also urged Mathews to publish Robert Frost.[72] We know of Pound's later support of Lawrence (nominating him for the Polignac Prize for Poetry in December 1913) and so it is not out of the question that Pound could have suggested to Lawrence that he was able to make inroads with Mathews on his behalf.[73]

So Lawrence's choice of Taylor as the subject of his paper and his discussion of her fashionable literary influences had partly pragmatic consequences, in that it allowed him to analyse, practice, perform and promote a poetic identity that aligned with a typical 'Elkin Mathews' poet. In 1910 Lawrence was on the periphery of a network that had some bearing on his writing and his conception of the sort of literary artist he could be; he needed to fashion his poetic identity in such a way as to maintain his delicate connection with these influential circles. However, while he understood that he needed to strike a pose, he retained some ambivalence about doing so. Projecting self-confidence and setting himself apart from the 'Croydonians' was a strategy for removing himself from the confines of local society groups and provincial literary culture and seeking an entrance into professional and metropolitan publishing circles.

He reported on 18 November that he considered the paper on Taylor to have been a success: 'Croydonians seem to find the poetry highly provocative, if no more. They raved at me for bringing them this fantastic decadent stuff: but they were caught in the spell of it, and I laughed.'[74] In similar terms, he commented to Taylor that the paper was '*most* exciting. I worked my audience up to red heat.'[75] The 'Croydonians' are ultimately dismissed as risible philistines.

The paper was not a rejection of Taylor nor a mockery of her self-fashioning, but a subtle self-negotiation, in which he recognised the fashionable influences that shaped his own poetry but was restless to depart from them. In correspondence with Blanche Jennings back in January 1909, Lawrence said that he had read 'a lot of Yeats' but considered him 'vapourish, too thin'; Lawrence wanted 'to write live things, if crude and half formed, rather than beautiful dying decadent things with sad odors'.[76] In 1909 he had recognised that Pound's 'god is beauty, mine, life' and some of Taylor's poems seemed to him 'fingered by art into a grace the experience does not warrant'.[77] Lawrence perceived the need for self-fashioning and networking as a means of crafting an identity that would enable literature and authors to be marketed and sold under appropriate imprints and advertised in the all-important press. He continued to develop strategies for promoting his work and in early 1913 he was publicly affiliating himself with another contemporary poetic grouping: one that looked to the present moment rather than the past.

'That'll help perhaps to advertise me': Lawrence's 'The Georgian Renaissance' Review in *Rhythm* (1913)

At first glance, Lawrence's review of *Georgian Poetry 1911–1912* in its original site of publication in the March 1913 number of *Rhythm* magazine might seem of little consequence, particularly as it lauds the poetry of a now unfashionable group of writers. Beyond relatively brief discussions by Sandra M. Gilbert in *Acts of Attention: The Poems of D. H. Lawrence* (1972) and by Kim Herzinger in *D. H. Lawrence in His Time* (1982) the review has received little critical attention. Gilbert acknowledges that Lawrence was 'susceptible to Georgian influence' as a young poet.[78] Herzinger identifies 'some of the interconnections between Lawrence and the Georgian sensibility' and suggests that the literary group 'was expressing ideas and feelings more closely akin to [Lawrence's] own'.[79] Outside Lawrence studies, Lawrence's enthusiastic response to Georgian poetry is more often cited as evidence of his questionable status as a 'modernist', while supporters of the Georgians point to the fact that he had his work published in four out of the five *Georgian Poetry* anthologies published between 1912 and 1922.[80] When placed in context, Lawrence's association with the

'Georgian poets' was entirely contingent: it was not a considered approach on his behalf to a group with shared literary ideals, because there was no identifiable 'literary group' of Georgian poets before Edward Marsh brought seventeen contemporary poets together under the name in 1912. The other contributors to the first anthology were Lascelles Abercrombie, Gordon Bottomley, Rupert Brooke, G. K. Chesterton, W. H. Davies, Walter de la Mare, John Drinkwater, James Elroy Fletcher, Wilfrid W. Gibson, John Masefield, Harold Monro, T. Sturge Moore, Ronald Ross, Edmund Beale Sargant, James Stephens and Robert Trevelyan. Marsh (1872–1953) was Winston Churchill's private secretary as well as a classical scholar and translator. He edited each of the five anthologies, sampling the most recent work of the poets he admired. Lawrence was invited to contribute his poem 'Snap-Dragon' to the first *Georgian Poetry* anthology and he was delighted to accept Marsh's request.

The background to Lawrence's inclusion in *Georgian Poetry 1911–1912* and the publication of his review, 'The Georgian Renaissance', in John Middleton Murry and Katherine Mansfield's *Rhythm* magazine, helps us to further understand Lawrence's position-taking in approaching the literary marketplace. The recovery of texts such as Lawrence's early reviews is significant for our understanding of him as a professional writer who had to earn a living; reviews allowed him to enter into dialogue with and about others in the literary field, at a time when he was in a junior position and needed to gain experience writing for particular publications. Although he was not paid for the *Rhythm* review, it allowed him to advertise an anthology in which one of his own poems appeared and for which he was to receive substantial royalties, to publicly affiliate himself with another new poetry movement and to write himself into networks surrounding Marsh, Mansfield and Murry. Lawrence used the review and *Rhythm* as convenient platforms for asserting his identity as a young professional writer. As well as being positioned by Marsh, Lawrence took the opportunity to strategically fashion himself as one of the Georgian poets at a time when this group comprised, as Lawrence himself terms them, the 'new men' of contemporary poetry. The review also enabled him to covertly advertise his own volume of poetry, *Love Poems and Others*, which had been published in late February 1913, just before the review appeared.

On 5 October 1912, Lawrence wrote to Garnett: 'A man called E Marsh has written me from the Admiralty, and wants to put "Snapdragon" into a vol. of verse of new men he is getting up. I said yes.'[81] Lawrence replied to Marsh's request by return of post and informed him that he was soon to publish a volume of his own poetry, 'I am just correcting proofs for a volume of verse which Mr Duckworth will publish immediately . . . If there is anything else I could any time give you, some unpublished stuff, I shall be glad.'[82] Lawrence is keen to establish his credentials as a poet with a publishing agreement in place and other work that Marsh may be interested in seeing. Ten days later Lawrence once again mentioned Marsh's request to Garnett: 'Did I tell you about Marsh who is putting "Snapdragon" into a vol. of contemporary poetry that is coming out just now? That'll help perhaps to advertise me.'[83] Given that the anthology was due to be published in December 1912 (to catch the Christmas market for book sales) and his poetry volume was at proof stage, Marsh's request and the advertisement it promised was very timely for Lawrence.

Marsh's taste for poetry was 'conservative yet catholic; he did not like experiment; on the other hand, he realized that Victorian stuffiness and didacticism were out of favour'. He considered that the busy general reader 'would prefer short, self-contained, lyrical pieces' about everyday contemporary English life, leisure and the natural world.[84] Marsh's anthology was the precursor to later polemical anthologies of contemporary poetry such as Ezra Pound's *Des Imagistes* (1914), Amy Lowell's *Some Imagist Poets* (1915–17) and Edith Sitwell's *Wheels* 'cycles' (published annually from 1916–21); the anthology became, as Aaron Jaffe observes, 'one of the preferred vehicles for publicity among the modernist poets and their contemporaries' as it promised 'unheard-of exposure' and 'traded on its role as a simulation of literary society'.[85] In these respects, the anthology is not dissimilar to the little magazine. However, a writer could contribute to a variety of publications that proclaimed group identities or affiliations, since factions in the literary field were not as bounded as they appear to be if we give credence to their manifestos. Lawrence's poetry appeared in *Some Imagist Poets*, the *Egoist*, *Smart Set* and *Poetry* during the same period he was being included in the *Georgian Poetry* anthologies, showing that he was proceeding on all available fronts, even if they might in retrospect seem ideologically dissonant publications. Pound, later a severe critic of Georgian poetry, proposed a poem from his *Canzoni* (1911) for inclusion in *Georgian Poetry 1911–1912*, but Marsh considered it unsuitable (the *Canzoni* – 'songs', in Italian – were 'experiments in medieval metric forms' and imitations of the 'medieval sensibility as Pound conceived it').[86] The Imagists and the Georgians in June 1914 represented 'the two newest and most forward movements in English poetry', despite the condemnation of Georgian poetry by critics from the 1920s onward.[87]

Marsh had asked Walter de la Mare to address and post the letter to Lawrence on his behalf; De la Mare had had dealings with Lawrence during 1912 in his capacity as Heinemann's new reader. De la Mare had a particularly close relation to Lawrence's poetry: in March 1912 he had wanted 'to suggest improvements in the volume of verse' that Lawrence was originally to have published with Heinemann and he was also responsible for making the selection of poems.[88] Lawrence gave De la Mare the authority to 'Do just as you will with the poems. I should like them to appear in mags ... I'll come to London to hear your advice concerning the improvement.'[89] De la Mare sent selections of Lawrence's verses to the *Westminster Gazette* and the *English Review* and it was 'Snap-Dragon', the poem Marsh read in the June number of the *English Review*, that prompted Marsh to ask De la Mare to forward his letter to Lawrence (Marsh had written to Naomi Royde-Smith, literary editor of the *Westminster Gazette*, asking for Lawrence's address and she suggested that De la Mare 'was the best person to ask').[90] De la Mare and Austin Harrison were keen to keep Lawrence focused on the development of his career: in April 1912 Lawrence told Garnett that the two men 'want to jaw me' during his visit to London to meet them.[91] The assistance of Garnett and then the interest from Marsh meant that Lawrence was well supported by advisors in 1912, which was his first year as a full-time writer following his resignation from teaching at the end of February.

Marsh's account of the founding of the *Georgian* anthology gives the impression that he and his close friend Rupert Brooke were solely responsible for it, but Dominic Hibberd suggests that 'the initial idea' for a *Georgian Poetry* anthology, and 'even for its title had very probably come from [Harold] Monro, who had coined the phrase "Georgian poets" in 1911, the year of George V's coronation'.[92] Monro (1879–1932) had for a while been determined to revive poetry in England; along with Maurice Browne, his friend at Cambridge, Monro set up the Samurai Press, which produced thirty small books between January 1907 and spring 1909, including poetry volumes by Wilfrid Gibson, John Drinkwater and Monro himself. Several of the assistants associated with the running of the Press worked on Monro's next venture, a new sixpence monthly called *The Poetry Review*, over which Monro had full editorial and financial control. The first number appeared in January 1912 and was printed by St. Catherine's Press, which had published the first four numbers of *Rhythm*. Lascelles Abercrombie, John Gould Fletcher and Drinkwater were contributors (and often commented favourably on each other's work), as were several other poets later associated with the 'Georgians' and well-known 'Imagists' such as T. E. Hulme, Pound, Richard Aldington and F. S. Flint. Marsh was also involved: he reviewed the 'book of the month', Brooke's *Poems*, in the April 1912 number.[93]

As Hibberd notes, on 8 September 1912 Monro wrote to Browne to inform him that he was planning to open a 'poetry shop' in 'a lovely old house in Bloomsbury'; this was to be the Poetry Bookshop, which would publish the *Georgian Poetry* anthologies.[94] On 19 September, Brooke suggested to Marsh that an affordable anthology of contemporary poets might energise the reading public into buying poetry and the project was outlined. Marsh would be responsible for making the selection of contributors to the anthology; he would provide the required financial backing if Monro agreed to meet the initial expense as publisher. At a luncheon party the next day at Gray's Inn, Marsh, Brooke, Gibson, Monro, Drinkwater and the sub-editor of *The Poetry Review*, Arundel del Re, planned that an edition of 500 copies would be published before Christmas and priced at 3s 6d, with half of the royalties going to *The Poetry Review* (the Poetry Bookshop was still in its early stages) and half to Marsh, who would distribute his share among the contributors to the anthology.[95]

The project moved swiftly. By 5 November the proofs had arrived and on 9 November Brooke began writing to Marsh about his elaborate plans for 'advertisements':

> I hope you're going to get it reviewed on the Continent . . . I'm sure with a little pushing, a good hundred copies could be sold in Germany & France. I hope you're getting Gosse to do *The Times*, & Hewlett, & the others you spoke of – & getting hold of Northcliffe.

Brooke pressed his point further by using militaristic discourse to describe the extent of the promotional activity he envisaged:

> I feel sure you ought to have an immense map of England (vide *Tono Bungay*) & plan campaigns with its aid. And literary charts, each district mapped out and a fortress secured – John Buchan to fill a page of the Spectator: Filson Young in the *P[all]. M[all]. G[azette]*. (we shall be sixteen things that matter in italics): etc.[96]

On 25 November Brooke suggested that Marsh send review copies to Geoffrey Keynes, Edward Thomas, Hugh Dalton, Rose Macaulay, Garnett, Edward Shanks, Percy Lubbock and the Woolfs. Copies were sent abroad as well as to all parts of Britain; to ensure efficient distribution, a team of packers including *Rhythm* contributor Gilbert Cannan worked all night at Gray's Inn.[97] With this level of resourcefulness and boosted by the reviews of Marsh's and Brooke's contacts it is not surprising that the anthology sold well: in his 1939 memoir Marsh estimated that the first volume sold approximately 15,000 copies.[98] On receipt of a cheque for £3 as just one of his instalments of royalties on its sales, Lawrence wrote to Marsh on 12 July 1913: 'I wish you had the publishing of one's work – soon I should have a fur-lined coat.'[99]

It was not only promotional inventiveness that helped the volume to sell, but the concept of the anthology itself. Unlike Arthur Quiller-Couch's anthology, *The Oxford Book of Victorian Verse*, which was published at the same time as *Georgian Poetry*, Marsh's anthology was economically produced, slim and selective, so as to be accessible and to directly promote the freshest work of seventeen twentieth-century poets. In his October 1912 Preface, Marsh wrote that the collection was 'drawn entirely from the publications of the past two years'; in contrast to Quiller-Couch's heavyweight anthology, which surveyed the poetry published during the whole of Victoria's reign, Marsh's volume offered a selection from the poetic field at a particular moment in time. Marsh included a bibliography of each contributor's own volumes of poetry at the back of the anthology to publicise their work (although the name of Lawrence's forthcoming volume was erroneously given as 'Poems of Love'). The material artefact thereby recorded a hierarchy of literary reputations among what claimed to be the new school of Georgian poets. Lawrence appears in a junior position as the only contributor not to have published at least one volume of his own poetry by December 1912. The 'advertising' worked: Robert Bridges, to whom the anthology was dedicated, wrote to Marsh in February 1913 that he 'was glad to be introduced to Lawrence' through its pages.[100] Rather than carrying the institutional authority of a University Press like Quiller-Couch's anthology, *Georgian Poetry* was the first publication to bear the imprint of the Poetry Bookshop, which officially opened on 8 January 1913 with an inaugural speech by the poet Henry Newbolt. He wrote a complimentary review of the anthology in the opening March 1913 number of Monro's new Poetry Bookshop publication *Poetry and Drama*.[101] Reviewing both volumes in the *Manchester Guardian* that same month, Abercrombie denounced *The Oxford Book of Victorian Verse* as 'a wholesale sweeping up of Victorian remains', although as a contributor to *Georgian Poetry* he was hardly an impartial commentator.[102]

On the weekend preceding 25 September 1912, Marsh had talked over his plans for the anthology with the editors of *Rhythm*, Mansfield and Murry; Marsh had first been introduced to the couple through Brooke in spring 1912.[103] Brooke was actively involved in *Rhythm* by at least October 1912, when Marsh offered it his financial backing. From then onward an increasing number of *Georgian Poetry* contributors had their work printed in its pages and Wilfrid Gibson, who had been in dire financial straits, was appointed to the staff as assistant editor on a salary paid by Marsh. By January 1913, Brooke told a friend that *Rhythm*'s 'staff poets are me, Gibson, Davies, De la Mare and Abercrombie'.[104] Mansfield had written to Marsh on 12 October 1912 that she and Murry 'badly need the counsel of our friends' regarding the printer's debt they owed after their publisher Charles Granville (of Stephen Swift & Co) absconded with all *Rhythm*'s capital.[105] Accordingly, Marsh wrote to Filson

Young at the *Pall Mall Gazette* and asked him to write a feature on the plight of *Rhythm* in his regular column 'The Things That Matter' and to persuade his readers to send in a subscription that might help to save the magazine.[106] Young agreed and his piece was printed on 23 October; in wording the article he was probably directed by Marsh. Young wrote that *Rhythm* was committed to 'the furtherance and encouragement of English poetry', which was not exactly consistent with the publication's existing emphasis on representing all of the arts, on which it had built its reputation.[107] Its subtitle 'Art Music Literature' announced its inter-artistic intentions and it reproduced striking black and white images, including pre-Cubist drawings by Picasso and work by Cézanne, Henri Gaudier-Brzeska, J. D. Fergusson, Anne Estelle Rice and Jessica Dismorr, as well as Japanese art and decorative woodcuts.

Rhythm was the archetypal 'little magazine': it had impressive cultural and aesthetic ambitions and worked to serve a generation of new authors and artists, but it was hampered by production costs (losing approximately £30 per number) and struggled to survive for fourteen numbers between summer 1911 and March 1913.[108] Founded by the twenty-two-year-old Oxford undergraduate Murry and Michael T. H. Sadler (later Sadleir) with the aid of £50 from Sadler's father, for the first four numbers it appeared as a quarterly, before becoming a monthly publication. Murry and Mansfield first corresponded in December 1911 and Mansfield's first story, 'The Woman at the Store', was published in the spring 1912 number; she became assistant editor by July. *Rhythm* was priced at a competitive 1s per copy, though it targeted an educated readership and had internationalist aspirations. A number of articles by France correspondent Francis Carco were written in French, Murry quoted in Italian without translation and there were further 'foreign correspondents' from Poland, Russia and the USA. Yet it sold just one third of its print run, with an average readership for the first four issues at around 250 per number.[109] An avant-garde publication was not a commercially viable proposition, but *Rhythm* had cultural capital.

Perhaps Lawrence had heard about *Rhythm* from Marsh: on 17 December he wrote to Garnett 'I wonder whether *Rhythm* would take any of my stories or sketches.'[110] Sure enough he received a letter from Mansfield in January 1913 requesting a short story. Lawrence proposed to send 'The Soiled Rose' for free, but on the condition that she send 'a copy of *Rhythm*, for I've never seen your publication, only somebody said you wrote nasty things about *The Trespasser*, and second, that you let me have something interesting to review for March – German if you like'.[111] Frederick Goodyear had reviewed *The Trespasser* in the November 1912 number, calling it 'a study in morbid psychology'.[112] Lawrence eagerly read early reviews of his work, so his comment to Garnett about whether *Rhythm* might take his work and his willingness to give a story away without payment may reveal his desire to redress the attack on his novel or to claim a voice in its pages. Lawrence is specific about wanting to review a book 'for March': *Love Poems and Others* was due for publication at the end of February, so the appearance of his name as a reviewer on a German book in this cosmopolitan and increasingly 'Georgian' publication, just as his own volume hit the shelves, may have been a pragmatic strategy to raise his profile in the hope of helping along his own sales.

Reviews of *Georgian Poetry* had already supported his work: the first (unsigned) review of the anthology to appear was printed in the *Westminster Gazette* on 4 January 1913. It declared that:

> Mr D. H. Lawrence is even more deeply held by this sense of the significance of hourly life [than Wilfrid Gibson], and one of the few criticisms we have to make on the selection of poems for Georgian Poetry is that Mr Lawrence is represented only by the hyper-erotic 'Snapdragon', whereas, as readers of the 'Saturday Westminster' will remember, a group of poems by him, 'The Schoolmaster', contain very remarkable records of a phase of modern life which hitherto has found no such intimate literary expression.[113]

The reviewer suggests that Lawrence deserved more space in the anthology, albeit for a different kind of poetry to 'Snap-Dragon'. The comment about the appearance of the seven-poem sequence 'The Schoolmaster' in the *Saturday Westminster Gazette* between 11 May and 1 June 1912 (sent in by De la Mare) implies that his work is distinctive and memorable. In this comment the reviewer also claims credit for the *Gazette*'s earlier recognition of Lawrence's poetry. Three of these poems were to appear in *Love Poems and Others* under the title 'The Schoolmaster', which may have satisfied the *Gazette* reviewer of Lawrence's skill in recording the lives of a new generation of lower-middle class schoolteachers. This is another instance of Lawrence's self-fashioning (this time, as a teacher–poet), which was encouraged for marketing purposes by literary advisers such as Hueffer and De la Mare and recognised by reviewers who did much to form the tastes of the reading public.

Instead of a German book, Mansfield sent Lawrence *Georgian Poetry* to review. This might seem unusual today, but as I have indicated the volume was reviewed by several of its contributors as part of Brooke and Marsh's scheme for its extensive promotion.[114] Mansfield knew that Lawrence would provide a positive review that would flatter Marsh as patron of *Rhythm* and celebrate the work of many of her contributors. Lawrence may not have had much power to influence the literary field at this early stage of his career, but both Marsh and Mansfield had sought him out and he would have sensed that these connections with literary London might offer further openings and enable him to participate in a variety of publication networks. He was in Italy at the time, but he politely arranged a meeting with Mansfield, telling her that he would 'probably be in London at the end of March . . . and then, if your tea-kettle is still hot, I shall be glad to ask you for the cup you offered me'.[115] For Lawrence, the review offered him the opportunity to take some control over his early literary career. It was not written for payment in the short term, but advertisement of *Georgian Poetry* would help him gain royalties and his appearance in *Rhythm* could only be advantageous.

Lawrence appears to have written and sent the review to London by 5 February; by this date he expected *Love Poems* to be published in 'the first week in March'.[116] Lawrence had anticipated that the review and his first volume of poetry would appear in the same month, but in the event, Duckworth published it before 24 February.[117] The review was printed prominently on the front page of the Literary Supplement, alongside articles by Cannan on Anton Tchekoff, Murry on Baudelaire, Goodyear on 'the Canadian Kipling' and Richard Curle on Max Beerbohm. As an illustration of the way in which commerce and the ties of patronage are inevitably inseparable from aesthetic issues, the Supplement also contained advertisements for the 'third edition' of *Georgian Poetry*, providing a list of its contributors and advertising for 'Martin Secker's Series of Modern Monographs' (Secker had taken over the publishing of *Rhythm* in November 1912).[118]

Mansfield cannot have anticipated just how laudatory Lawrence's review was to be. For Lawrence, Georgian poetry is a reawakening, in which 'our lungs are full of new air' after the 'oppressive' nihilism of 'the intellectual, hopeless people – Ibsen, Flaubert, Thomas Hardy'. He makes way for new writers in the literary field by disavowing the continued authority of an older generation of European realists. The discourse of warfare near the beginning of the review might remind us of Brooke's martial campaign for the promotion of *Georgian Poetry*. Lawrence repeats 'demolition' or 'demolishing' three times: the dream of Ibsen, Flaubert, Hardy 'was a dream of demolition . . . The last years have been years of demolition . . . Art has been demolishing for us: Nietzsche the Christian religion as it stood, Hardy our faith in our own endeavor, Flaubert our belief in love.' A united formation of Georgian writers might prove a greater force to displace these reigning elders who have been damaging for readers. Lawrence writes hyperbolically of 'the terror of the night', 'a cry, fear and the pain of remembrance . . . This time Art fought the battle', but '[n]ow, for us, it is all smashed, we can see the whole again. We were in prison, peeping at the sky through loop-holes.'[119] The use of the plural first person pronoun takes possession of readers' perspectives and mobilises them into agreement with the reviewer.

He moves from a combative tone to ideas of reconstruction and growth. The impulse of the new British poets is 'romantic' and 'passionate'. He continues: 'The great liberation gives us an overwhelming sense of joy, joie d'être, joie de vivre.' The youthful Georgian poets have 'a joy of natural things, as if the poet were a child for the first time on the seashore, finding treasures'. They are 'just bursting into a thick blaze of being'. To demonstrate this burgeoning, transformative state, Lawrence enacts his own realisation of 'the joy we have in being ourselves':

> I look at my hands as I write and I know they are mine, with red blood running its way, sleuthing out Truth and pursuing it to eternity, and I am full of awe for this flesh and blood that holds this pen. Everything that ever was thought and ever will be thought, lies in this body of mine. This flesh and blood sitting here writing, the great impersonal flesh and blood, greater than me, which I am proud to belong to, contains all the future. What is it but the quick of all growth, the seed of all harvest, this body of mine. And grapes and corn and birds and rocks and visions, all are in my fingers. I am so full of wonder at my own miracle of flesh and blood that I could not contain myself, if I did not remember we are all alive, have all of us living bodies.[120]

This is a moment of live drama, written in the present tense and designed to rouse the apathetic verse-reading public into enthusiasm for the vital creativity of the new generation. Marsh and Brooke would have been delighted to read it. Lawrence emphasises the potential of the young poet, as well as his ownership of his poetic craft: 'grapes and corn and birds and rocks and visions, all are in my fingers'. His tone is triumphalist as he writes that 'we are all alive, have all of us living bodies'; 'we' are not the 'nihilists, the intellectual, hopeless people' of the previous literary generation, but 'the future'. Lawrence uses his own idiom in the review: there are recurrent Lawrentian themes such as the polarisation of the body and mind, the construction of 'flesh and blood', the affirmation of life and physicality and the choice of nature imagery (this was, of course, also an appropriate advertisement for 'Snap-Dragon'). The rhythmic, repetitive writing style that takes the reader along in the flow is uniquely his, too. Yet these themes also fit with *Rhythm*'s identity.

Murry's editorial in the first number of *Rhythm* defined the ethos of the magazine: 'to find art in the strong things of life, is the meaning of *Rhythm*'.[121]

J. D. Fergusson's image of a muscular Eve was commissioned to adorn the cover of the magazine and there are a number of images of naked women in natural settings (such as Albert Rothenstein's 'Chloe' and Derwent Lees's 'A Design') and dancing women (such as Anne Estelle Rice's 'Designs from the Russian Ballet'), all of which appear alongside Lawrence's review. Many of the magazine's images emphasise physicality, the body, fertility, virility and youthful vitality. Marsh had told De la Mare that Lawrence's 'Snap-Dragon', 'like his two novels ... seems to me to have elements of great and rather strange power and beauty'.[122] This comment uncannily echoes the terms with which Marsh opens his Prefatory note to *Georgian Poetry 1911–1912*, which announces that '[t]his volume is issued in the belief that English poetry is now once again putting on a new strength and beauty'.[123]

The little magazine, anthology and review could all provide outlets for the staging of authorial voices, identities, associations and networks; Lawrence uses each as a vehicle for exploring ways of self-fashioning and developing his public voice in order to shape his career. His exultant review is so polemical about the formation of a new 'Georgian' generation that it might be said to contribute towards the manifesto of Georgianism: he certainly stresses the 'strength and beauty' that Marsh declared representative. Lawrence was increasingly concerned about changing English readers, those 'cursed, rotten-boned, pappy hearted countrymen' who would not appreciate his work; we could, then, see the review as an earnest attempt to energise readers into sampling Georgian poetry for themselves.[124] There is, however, a deeper pragmatism at play in Lawrence's thinking. He might have considered that declaring himself to be one of the proponents of a 'Georgian Renaissance' would positively influence the reception of *Love Poems and Others*. In the review, Lawrence refers positively to the work of Michelangelo and Corot as 'triumphant', an adjective he also uses to describe Brooke's poetry. We can plausibly speculate that this is a deliberate intertextual reference to Lawrence's own poems entitled 'Michael Angelo' and 'Corot' in *Love Poems and Others*. Lawrence repeats the word 'love' nineteen times in the review. He moves from stating, 'I should say the Georgian Poets are just ripening to be love-poets', to declaring, 'Of all love-poets, we are the love-poets.'[125] In the course of the four-page review, Lawrence dramatises his assimilation into the group identity. He thereby links his own volume to the anthology, which was proving to be popular and lucrative: it had by this time entered its fourth impression.

Lawrence was particularly concerned about the reception of *Love Poems*. On 11 March 1913, he wrote to Garnett: 'I am anxious down to my vitals about the poems. I thought my friends in the field – De la Mare and so on – would review them decently for me.'[126] By aligning himself with the Georgians,

Lawrence hoped they would support his work – and they did. De la Mare's review appeared in the *Times Literary Supplement* two days later and Abercrombie reviewed the volume twice (in the *Manchester Guardian* and the *Blue Review*). Edward Thomas's *Bookman* review – significantly entitled 'More Georgian Poetry' – opened with the statement that 'The book of the moment in verse is Mr. D. H. Lawrence's.'[127] Lawrence's affiliation with the Georgians was not simply mercenary, however: for a time, friendships grew out of the connections. Gibson, R. C. Trevelyan, Abercrombie and his wife Catherine visited Lawrence and Frieda in Fiascherino on 29 November 1913; their individually signed postcard to Marsh is a fond collective greeting which pays tribute to his assembly of the group, and his patronage of their work.[128] On 10 January 1914, Lawrence wrote from Fiascherino to Arthur McLeod that he was expecting a visit from Marsh:

> I wonder if Marsh is projecting another *Georgian Poetry* issue – I must ask him. Have you ordered the Abercrombie-Gibson-Brook-Drinkwater: *New Numbers*. Gibson says he'll send it me soon. I wonder why we can't establish a real poetry number among all of us – we should do well enough if we but hang together'.[129]

New Numbers was a quarterly which only ran for four numbers; funded by Marsh, it was published in 1915 from Abercrombie's cottage in Gloucestershire. Each of the four poets selected his own poems as it had no editor; there were over 500 subscribers to the second number, but the war and Brooke's death in April stopped publication in its tracks.[130] Marsh continued to support Lawrence's work: he said 'nice things about *Sons and Lovers*' and discussed poetic technique with him at length.[131] The Lawrences were pleased to meet Brooke through Marsh in June 1914, and Drinkwater was 'anxious to do something' to help Lawrence protest against the withdrawal from sale of *The Rainbow* in November 1915.[132]

Lawrence rightly felt that allegiance to the Georgians would be beneficial for his career and he was indebted to Marsh for his inclusion in the anthology. He appreciated Brooke's and Marsh's campaign to sell new poetry to a broader readership than it had managed to attain during the early years of the twentieth century and took it as an opportunity to align himself with others in the poetic field. He took full advantage of Marsh's positioning of him as a Georgian poet and covertly promoted *Love Poems and Others*. As is demonstrated by the way he associated himself with Pound and Taylor and with Marsh's Georgian poets, the young Lawrence was more aware of the necessity to 'advertise' himself and to fashion his identity as a particular kind of writer than has been recognised. However, these two alliances did not create for Lawrence coherent poetic identities; they merely provided opportunities for him to test out ways of appearing as a member of specific publication networks. As his reputation grew, he received more approaches from editors, publishers and journalists who were keen to introduce him to their readerships in both Britain and America. As Chapter 6 will make clear, Mitchell Kennerley was the first publisher to really advocate Lawrence's work in America.

Notes

1. Collier, *Modernism on Fleet Street*, p. 202.
2. Marysa Demoor, 'Introduction' to her edited collection *Marketing the Author: Authorial Personae, Narrative Selves and Self-Fashioning, 1880–1930* (2004), pp. 1–15; p. 14.
3. *L*, I, 156. Steele suggests Lawrence met Taylor on 10 March: *STH*, xlii.
4. Rhys, *Everyman Remembers*, pp. 253–4.
5. Letter from Rachel Annand Taylor, Dundee, to Herbert J. C. Grierson, Aberdeen, January 1906, National Library of Scotland MS 9328, ff.3–6. Grierson recommended that Lawrence be awarded the James Tait Black Memorial Prize for *The Lost Girl* in 1921. See *L*, IV, 146 and fn. 2.
6. Allan Wade, *The Letters of W. B. Yeats* (1954), p. 536.
7. *L*, I, 144.
8. *Poems* III, 1429.
9. Rachel Annand Taylor, *The Hours of Fiammetta* (1910), unpaginated.
10. *L*, I, 166. Christopher Pollnitz's 'Introduction' to *Poems* III, lxxxix.
11. *L*, I, 378.
12. *L*, I, 144; 141; *English Review*, iii (October 1909): 378–9.
13. *L*, I, 187.
14. *Poems* III, pp. 1436–7; 1753.
15. *English Review*, iii (October 1909): 378.
16. *Poems* III, 1436.
17. Taylor, 'Preface', *The Hours of Fiammetta*, unpaginated.
18. Ezra Pound, *A Lume Spento* (1908), unpaginated.
19. Helen Corke, extract from 'Lawrence as I Knew Him', Corke's lecture to the Colchester Literary Society, 18 September 1950, reproduced in Nehls, I, 142.
20. *L*, I, 106.
21. *L*, I, 179–80.
22. *L*, I, 183.

23. Taylor is quoted by Aldington, *Portrait of a Genius But* . . ., p. 94.
24. *L*, I, 182; 185; 189.
25. *STH*, xliii. The manuscript of 'Rachel Annand Taylor' is Roberts E330.5 (UN). The paper is included in *STH*, pp. 145–8; quotations are taken from this edition, but I have consulted the manuscript.
26. Nehls, I, 88.
27. Nehls, I, 93.
28. Rossetti is a recurrent name in Lawrence's 1910 letters: *L*, I, 157; 159–60; see also E. T. 146.
29. David Garnett, *The Golden Echo* (1954), pp. 244–8.
30. Rhys, *Everyman Remembers*, pp. 253–4.
31. *STH*, 145.
32. Roberts E330.5.
33. Patricia Anderson, *The Printed Image and the Transformation of Popular Culture 1790–1860* (1991), p. 197.
34. Demoor, 'Introduction', p. 15.
35. Richard Salmon, 'Signs of Intimacy: The Literary Celebrity in the "Age of Interviewing"' (1997): 159.
36. McDonald, *British Literary Culture and Publishing Practice*, p. 36.
37. Demoor, 'Introduction', p. 4. See also McDonald, *British Literary Culture and Publishing Practice*, p. 8 and Raymond L. Schults, *Crusader in Babylon: W. T. Stead and the Pall Mall Gazette* (1972), pp. 61–87.
38. Matthew Rubery, *The Novelty of Newspapers: Victorian Fiction after the Invention of the News* (2009), p. 130. See also T. P. O'Connor, 'The New Journalism' (1889): 423.
39. Evelyn March Phillips, 'The New Journalism' (1895): 182–6; see also McDonald, *British Literary Culture and Publishing Practice*, p. 36.
40. Rubery, *The Novelty of Newspapers*, p. 117; Steven Stapleton, 'Society Journalism' (1905): 102. Quoted by Rubery, p. 110.
41. *STH*, 146.
42. Ibid. p. xliv.
43. Ibid. p. 145.
44. Duncan's painting of Taylor is owned by Aberdeen Art Gallery and Museums: 'Rachel Annand Taylor'.
45. *STH*, 145.
46. Helen Carr, *The Verse Revolutionaries: Ezra Pound, H. D. and the Imagists* (2009), p. 65.
47. *L*, I, 213.
48. *STH*, 147.
49. *Poems* III, lxxxix; p. 1433.

50. See James G. Nelson, *Elkin Mathews: Publisher to Yeats, Joyce, Pound* (1989) and Norman Alford, *The Rhymers' Club: Poets of the Tragic Generation* (1994). Poets associated with the group include Francis Thompson, Richard Le Gallienne, John Gray, John Davidson, Edwin J. Ellis, Victor Plarr, Selwyn Image, Lord Alfred Douglas, Arthur Cecil Hillier, John Todhunter, G. A. Greene, Arthur Symons, Ernest Radford and Thomas William Rolleston.
51. Norman, *Ezra Pound*, p. 40.
52. *STH*, 146.
53. *EY*, 233.
54. *STH*, 147.
55. Ibid. pp. 147; 148.
56. Ibid. p. 148.
57. See *STH*, 279, note 148:16.
58. Stock, *The Life of Ezra Pound*, p. 55; *L*, I, 170; 491.
59. Grace Lovat Fraser, *In the Days of my Youth* (1970), pp. 133–52.
60. Sending Crawford the manuscript of *The Widowing of Mrs Holroyd* in November 1910 Lawrence emphasises the difference in their class statuses and demarcates types of female readers: 'Here is the MSS. I shudder to think of its intruding like a muddy shaggy animal into your "den", sacred to the joss-stick and all vaporous elegantly-wreathed imaginations of literature . . . Give the thing to Miss Hunt . . . Don't let Mrs Crawford read the thing – it's too common. Mothers like things to be decently high-falutin.' *L*, I, 188.
61. *L*, I, 179.
62. *L*, I, 142.
63. *L*, I, 145. Lawrence had given Agnes Holt a copy of Thompson's *The Hound of Heaven* and inscribed it 22 March 1910 (*L*, I, 140, fn. 2).
64. *L*, I, 151.
65. Nelson, *Elkin Mathews*, p. 72.
66. Ibid., p. 118; pp. 24–5.
67. Quoted by Stock, *The Life of Ezra Pound*, p. 67.
68. Norman, *Ezra Pound*, p. 55. See also Stock, *The Life of Ezra Pound*, p. 83. Norman gives the date of Williams's arrival as April 1910 but Stock traces the date more accurately: see William Williams's account in *The Autobiography of William Carlos Williams* (1967), p. 114.
69. Williams, *Autobiography*, p. 114.
70. R. F. Foster, *W. B. Yeats: A Life, Volume I: The Apprentice Mage, 1865–1914* (1997), p. 416.
71. *L*, I, 155; Stock, *The Life of Ezra Pound*, p. 81.

72. Williams, *Autobiography*, p. 134; Paul Mariani, *William Carlos Williams, A New World Naked* (1981).
73. *L*, II, 131.
74. *L*, I, 189.
75. *L*, I, 191.
76. *L*, I, 107; 108.
77. *L*, I, 145; 187.
78. Sandra M. Gilbert, *Acts of Attention: The Poems of D. H. Lawrence* (1972), p. 33.
79. Kim A. Herzinger, *D. H. Lawrence in His Time: 1908–1915* (1982), p. 40.
80. Peter Brooker comments that we might see Lawrence's involvement with 'Marsh and the phalanx of Georgian poets' as a 'link with Murry'; Dominic Hibberd similarly dissociates Lawrence. Brooker, 'Harmony, Discord and Difference' (2009–12), p. 320 and Hibberd, 'The New Poetry, Georgians and Others' (2009–12), p. 189.
81. *L*, I, 459.
82. *L*, I, 461.
83. *L*, I, 462.
84. James Reeves, *Georgian Poetry* (1962), xiii.
85. Aaron Jaffe, *Modernism and the Culture of Celebrity* (2005), pp. 137–8.
86. Hugh Witemeyer, *The Poetry of Ezra Pound: Forms and Renewal, 1908–1920* (1969), p. 95.
87. Harold Monro, 'New Books: English Poetry' (1914): 179–80.
88. *L*, I, 371–2.
89. *L*, I, 375.
90. Christopher Hassall, *Edward Marsh: Patron of the Arts* (1959), pp. 193–4.
91. *L*, I, 384.
92. Hibberd, 'The New Poetry, Georgians and Others', p. 185.
93. *Poetry Review*, 1:4 (April 1912). See also in this issue Abercrombie's 'Appreciation' of John Drinkwater (168–70); Drinkwater's poem 'The Fires of God' (177) which was published in *Georgian Poetry 1911–1912*; Marsh's review 'The Book of the Month: Poems. By Rupert Brooke' (177).
94. Letter from Monro to Browne, quoted in Dominic Hibberd, *Harold Monro: Poet of the New Age* (2001), p. 105.
95. Hassall, *Edward Marsh*, pp. 189–90.
96. Brooke to Marsh in Geoffrey Keynes, *The Letters of Rupert Brooke* (1968), p. 406.
97. Hassall, *Edward Marsh*, pp. 200; 201.
98. Edward Marsh, *A Number of People: A Book of Reminiscences* (1939), p. 329.
99. *L*, II, 36.

100. Quoted in Hassall, *Edward Marsh*, p. 208.
101. Henry Newbolt, 'Georgian Poetry 1911–1912. Edited by E. M.' (1913): 46; 52.
102. Lascelles Abercrombie, 'Victorians and Georgians' (1913): 6. Reproduced in Timothy Rogers, *Georgian Poetry 1911–1922: The Critical Heritage* (1977), pp. 57–62; 60.
103. Hassall, *Edward Marsh*, p. 191.
104. Brooke, letter to Gwen Raverat, Sunday, [?] January 1913 in Keynes, *Letters of Rupert Brooke*, p. 419.
105. Letter from Mansfield to Marsh, 12 October 1912. Katherine Mansfield, *Collected Letters of Katherine Mansfield: Volume I: 1903–1917* (1984), p. 114. See also Faith Binckes, *Modernism, Magazines and the British Avant-Garde* (2010), pp. 24–31.
106. For an extended account of this interaction see Binckes, *Modernism, Magazines and the British Avant-Garde*, pp. 28–9.
107. Filson Young, 'The Things That Matter' (1912): 5.
108. John Middleton Murry, *Between Two Worlds: An Autobiography* (1935), p. 204.
109. This figure is based on Peter Brooker's calculation, see 'Harmony, Discord and Difference', p. 317.
110. *L*, I, 489.
111. *L*, I, 507–8. Both 'The Soiled Rose' and Lawrence's review of Thomas Mann's *Der Tod in Venedig* were printed in *Rhythm*'s short-lived successor the *Blue Review* (May–July 1913).
112. *Rhythm*, 2:10 (November 1912): 278.
113. Anon., 'Georgian Poetry of the Twentieth Century' (1913): 3.
114. De la Mare reviewed *Georgian Poetry* (he contributed to all five of the anthologies): 'An Elizabethan Poet and Modern Poetry' (1913): 377–86.
115. *L*, I, 508.
116. *L*, I, 512.
117. *L*, I, 519.
118. '"The Georgian Renaissance" by D. H. Lawrence' (March 1913): xvii–xx.
119. Ibid., xvii.
120. Ibid., xix–xx.
121. *Rhythm*, 1: 1 (Summer 1911): 36.
122. Marsh quoted by Hassall, *Edward Marsh*, pp. 193–4.
123. Edward Marsh, 'Prefatory note to the first edition', initialled 'E. M., Oct. 1912'. *Georgian Poetry 1911–1912*, unpaginated.
124. *L*, I, 422.
125. Lawrence, 'The Georgian Renaissance', xx.

126. *L*, I, 526.
127. De la Mare, *TLS* (13 March 1913). Abercrombie, *Manchester Guardian* (1 May 1913): 7; *Blue Review*, I (June 1913): 117–22. Thomas, 'More Georgian Poetry' (1913): 47.
128. *L*, II, 113.
129. *L*, II, 136.
130. See Jeff Cooper, '*New Numbers*: The Story of a Periodical' (2007): 56–66.
131. *L*, II, 61.
132. *L*, II, 186; 447.

6

Introducing Mr D. H. Lawrence, Author of *Sons and Lovers*: Transatlantic Connections

Sons and Lovers is generally considered to be Lawrence's breakthrough novel and following its publication by Duckworth on 29 May 1913 Lawrence became more widely known as a working-class writer. As we have seen, Lawrence was fully aware of the importance of fashioning an authorial identity that would allow publishers, editors, journalists and fellow writers to introduce his work to the reading public and this chapter examines two further instances in which he cooperated with such individuals in their efforts to style and promote his name. Exploring transatlantic publishing culture and assessing Lawrence's early reputation both in Britain and America, we will consider the interest that the New York publisher Mitchell Kennerley took in Lawrence's work. Kennerley's publication of four of Lawrence's early works has never been examined at length and yet he published Lawrence in his magazine *Forum* and commissioned the Swedish-American literary critic and author Edwin Björkman to write an Introduction to the first American edition of *The Widowing of Mrs Holroyd* (1914). Meanwhile, in London W. L. George wrote an article on Lawrence which was published in the February 1914 number of the *Bookman*. Lawrence supplied biographical notes to both Björkman and George, involving himself in their promotional writings. Post-*Sons and Lovers*, all these figures drew explicitly on Lawrence's background as a working-class writer to introduce him to British and American readerships.

Garnett, Mitchell Kennerley and Edwin Björkman's Introduction to *The Widowing of Mrs Holroyd*

It was Garnett who provided Lawrence with the link to Mitchell Kennerley (1878–1950). Kennerley was born into a middle-class family in Burslem, Staffordshire; Arnold Bennett (eleven years Kennerley's senior) lived close by and came to befriend him, urging him into book collecting. In 1894 the sixteen-year-old Kennerley was employed as a junior clerk by John Lane of The Bodley Head at his office on Vigo Street in the West End. Lane was impressed by Kennerley and in 1896 took him to America to establish the New York branch of the company at 140 Fifth Avenue. The Bodley Head's first New York catalogue list included several of its existing authors, including Robert Louis Stevenson, Max Beerbohm, Alice Meynell and Richard Le Gallienne. Kennerley had shown early promise, but Lane became frustrated by his increasingly shady business practices and 'had to get rid of him'. Lane wrote about his dismissal of Kennerley to Guy Eglinton on 14 December 1920: 'I took him to America too soon. He got a swelled head ... I found he had been lending money to Le Gallienne and taking money himself, all of which has not even now been repaid.'[1] Despite his dubious record, in autumn 1899 Kennerley was hired as business manager of the New York magazine *Smart Set* which was just about to be launched. Kennerley solicited material for the magazine before becoming advertising manager in 1901. In November of the following year he founded his own magazine, the *Reader*, aided by funds from his rich new wife Helen Morley. Like the *Smart Set* it was a monthly priced at 25 cents; it published much literary criticism and was generously illustrated with photographs of authors. Kennerley sold the *Reader* in 1904 and began organising his own publishing house. Kennerley's cousin Arthur Hooley (who published work under the name of Charles Vale) became reader and editor for the company and was associated with Kennerley's various ventures for the next twenty years; before he arrived in America Hooley had collaborated with Bennett on the writing of two plays.[2]

During the early years of the twentieth century in America the standard list price of novels was $1.50. Around 1907–8 Kennerley established his Little Classics Series (elegant volumes of poetry priced at 40 cents each or $2 for boxed sets of five volumes); the titles were all English imports from the small publisher Grant Richards, who provided bound copies at three pence halfpenny each (about 8 cents).[3] Richards and Kennerley did business with each other between 1906 and 1911, sharing bound books and printing plates, although Kennerley's usual order was for only 200–300 copies. Kennerley's biographer estimates that he published only twenty-one titles in 1907, but over the next two years he expanded his list and achieved more than sixty new titles by 1909, including Frank Harris's *The Man Shakespeare and His Tragic Life Story* which had struggled to find a publisher in Britain; it was endorsed by Bennett on its publication. When Kennerley read an English review of Harris's anarchist novel *The Bomb* (John Long, 1908) he wrote directly to its publisher to request a copy before arranging to publish an edition under his own imprint in 1909. Kennerley went on to publish five more of Harris's books and at the end of 1912 arranged for him to lecture in America.[4] It appears that Kennerley had no formal long-term publishing agreement with a single British publisher, but kept an eye on press reviews and relied on his judgement. Having worked in publishing on both sides of the Atlantic Kennerley had strong connections with British publishers and seems to have approached firms on an ad hoc basis to enquire about books that interested him. These titles included six of Edward Carpenter's books between 1911 and 1917, Upton Sinclair's *The Fasting Cure* and *Love's Pilgrimage* published by Heinemann in 1911, and the Irish Cuala Press limited editions of Yeats's *The Green Helmet* (1910) and *Synge and the Ireland of his Time* (1911).

During 1907 Kennerley set up his headquarters at 2 East Twenty-Ninth Street and opened a bookshop there ('The Little Book-Shop Around the Corner'), selling books that he commissioned himself as well as those under other imprints. American publishers often established offices which doubled as retail outlets and The Bodley Head had sold their own books from their premises. It was also common for publishers to issue a house journal in which they could advertise their authors and solicit contributions from potential new writers. Kennerley took over the editorship of the American monthly the *Forum* (priced at 25 cents) from 1910 to 1916. The *Forum* ran from 1886 to 1950; it incorporated the *Century* from 1930 and was then named *Forum and Century*. In its early years it was a respected journal of social and political opinion, but Kennerley substantially increased the space devoted to literature and art. Authors who appeared in its pages over these years included Frank Harris, Granville-Barker, Witter Bynner, Maurice Maeterlinck, Maurice Hewlett, Tolstoy, Pound, Le Gallienne, Jack London, Yeats, Lady Gregory, Carpenter, Robert Frost, John Drinkwater, Rabrindranath Tagore and Edna St Vincent Millay. Kennerley was interested in work that tested boundaries and dealt with social and political questions; like Garnett, he was also keen to support work by Irish authors and women writers on the suffrage movement. It was Garnett's submission to the magazine of one of Lawrence's stories that first brought his name to Kennerley's attention.

Garnett sent 'The Soiled Rose' (better known under its October 1914 title, 'The Shades of Spring') to the *Forum*. Kennerley accepted 'this most unusual story' by 8 March 1912, but it did not appear for a full year.[5] By the time the story was published Lawrence's reputation in America had grown as a result of the positive reception of *The Trespasser*. Prior to this, *The White Peacock* had been published in New York by Duffield on 19 January 1911 but it had not received a great deal of press attention. Although the prestigious *New York Times* printed a complimentary – if long delayed –

review of *The White Peacock* on 9 June, Lawrence reflected in October that '[a] good many folk have been hostile – practically all America'.[6] So Lawrence welcomed the contact with Kennerley. *The Trespasser* had been published by Duckworth in London on 23 May 1912 and it seems likely that Garnett offered the novel to Kennerley after the latter expressed interest in 'The Soiled Rose'. In a reader's report dated 27 May, Arthur Hooley called *The Trespasser* '[a] good book, though not of a popular type . . . a clever book, which suggests that the author is worth taking up'.[7] Using sheets supplied by Duckworth Kennerley published an edition of *The Trespasser* later that year; the first American reviews of the novel appeared in November 1912.[8] Kennerley was keen to include Lawrence's name on his list and Garnett facilitated the publication of three further volumes over the course of eight months between September 1913 and April 1914 (*Love Poems and Others*, *Sons and Lovers* and *The Widowing of Mrs Holroyd*). The first American edition of *Love Poems* was printed from the English sheets and reviewed in the *New York Times* on 26 October 1913. Kennerley paid Duckworth about $25 for 100 copies and commented in a letter of 7 April 1913 'this transaction will prove a loss to me, and I am only taking the books out of courtesy to the author'.[9]

By 21 June 1913 Lawrence had been approached by 'another [unidentified] American man' since by that date numerous reviews of the UK edition of *Sons and Lovers* had appeared. In addition to this new interest Pound had asked Lawrence for short stories for the *American Review*. As well as the *Forum*, publication in the *Century* was also a possibility.[10] The *Smart Set* (then under the editorship of W. H. Wright) printed the poems 'Violets', 'Kisses in the Train' and 'The Mowers' in September, October and November 1913 respectively, earning Lawrence a healthy $36.[11] In September Lawrence also submitted several of his short stories to the *Smart Set* via Pound, who was its English agent. They rejected 'Once–' for being 'too hot', so Lawrence considered sending them (or the *Forum*) 'Vin Ordinaire' and 'The Primrose Path', but it was 'The Christening' that was accepted and published in the February 1914 number.[12] Garnett, Kennerley and Pound were all pushing Lawrence's work in America at this time. Kennerley wrote to Garnett on 18 July 1913 that he had 'just finished reading *Sons and Lovers*, and think it is the biggest novel I have read in years. If Mr Lawrence can keep this up he will surpass all other modern novelists.' Garnett may have forwarded the letter to Lawrence.[13] His name was becoming known by publishers in America even before Kennerley's edition of *Sons and Lovers* was published on 17 September 1913; it was reviewed by the *New York Times* just four days later. An excerpt from the chapter 'Derelict' was printed in the *Forum* that month and Kennerley marketed the novel with enthusiasm and ingenuity. One advertisement reproduced a telegram sent to Kennerley by Jack London:

NO BOOK LIKE IT SPLENDID SAD TREMENDOUS TRUE IT SWEEPS ONE OFF HIS FEET WITH THE POWERFUL HUMAN IMPACT OF IT IN IT ARE THE HEART AND HURT OF LIFE ALL THAT IS SORDID ALL THAT IS NOBLE ALL BLENT TOGETHER IN THE FLUX OF CONTRADICTORINESS THAT IS SWEET FIRM PALPITANT HUMAN MAIL ME HIS OTHER BOOKS AND SEND BILL.[14]

Another advertisement took the form of a statement signed by 'Mitchell Kennerley'. It read: 'I do not ask you to buy it, but I do tell you that "Sons and Lovers", by D. H. Lawrence, is one of the great novels of the age.'[15]

Kennerley's endorsement was significant because at that time he was undergoing a well-publicised court case which raised the profile of his firm. In January 1913 Kennerley had published *Hagar Revelly*, a naturalistic novel about two poor sisters in New York City written by the physician (or self-styled 'social hygienist') Daniel Carson Goodman. It attracted no notable controversy on publication but on 23 September 1913 Anthony Comstock, Secretary for the Suppression of Vice and Post Office Inspector, arrived at Kennerley's office with a police officer. Both Kennerley and the bookshop clerk, William Cleary, were arrested on a magistrate's warrant for selling and distributing an immoral book.[16] All copies of *Hagar Revelly* in the shop were confiscated, along with 2,000 copies at the bindery. Kennerley defended the book in court, announcing to reporters 'we will demand that the book be read throughout from cover to cover by the jury'.[17] The trial opened on 5 February 1914 and on 9 February after five and a half hours of deliberation by the jury the verdict of 'not guilty' was returned. The *New York Evening Post* commented that Kennerley's trial was aided by his reputation as 'a publisher of radical tendencies, who has specialized in the newer, advanced literature, and in the courage of his convictions has put his name to a long list of publications of considerable merit but of little promise as bestsellers'.[18] It was under this 'radical' and 'advanced' imprint that Lawrence's early work appeared in America.

The increased attention paid to Kennerley's list by the press may have helped to promote Lawrence's work. Lawrence informed Garnett on 31 October 1913 that 'Curtis Brown wrote offering me "a considerable advance on a 20% royalty" – for America, and so for England. I told him I was due to you and Kennerley for novels: that I *might* give him a book of stories'.[19] Lawrence had been pleased enough with the terms of Duckworth's contract for

Sons and Lovers (a 15 per cent royalty on the first 2,500 copies, with 17.5 per cent on all further copies and a £100 advance payable on the date of publication; he had received £50 advance for his first two novels). The Curtis Brown literary agency could take over from Garnett all the work that Lawrence put his way and offer Lawrence's work to the two main English-speaking markets. This would have been a beneficial opportunity for Lawrence, but for the time being he remained loyal to Garnett and continued to publish with Duckworth and Kennerley, taking advantage of the more certain prospects they offered. Lawrence nevertheless made sure that Garnett knew about all the approaches he received. On 31 December Lawrence forwarded to Garnett a letter that he had been 'awfully pleased' to receive; it appears to have been an approach by an (unidentified) American publisher for a volume of Lawrence's poetry.[20] Kennerley was for a time an important ally in the launching of Lawrence's transatlantic career and following these several opportunities Lawrence must have felt fairly confident that he was breaking into the American market. A note on Lawrence as a contributor to Harriet Monroe's Chicago-based magazine *Poetry* in January 1914 states that

> Mr. D. H. Lawrence has become conspicuous of late both in England and in this country. Besides such works in prose as *The White Peacock* and *The Trespasser*, he is the author of *Love Poems and Others* (Kennerley) and of the recently published *Sons and Lovers* (Kennerley).

Lawrence had contributed eight poems to this number ('Green'; 'All of Roses'; 'Fireflies in the Corn'; 'A Woman and Her Dead Husband'; 'The Wind, the Rascal'; 'The Mother of Sons'; 'Illicit'; and 'Birthday').[21]

Again, the success of all these transatlantic publications leads back to Garnett. It was to Garnett that Kennerley initially wrote about Lawrence on 15 February 1913. Kennerley enclosed twelve pounds (approximately $60, so $10 more than he usually paid) for 'The Soiled Rose' together with reviews of *The Trespasser* 'which I think will interest you and Mr Lawrence'. A reviewer in the *New York Times Book Review* considered *The Trespasser* 'not only the frankest of serious contemporary novels; it comes near to being the best'.[22] Significantly, he noted his desire to read the manuscript of Lawrence's 'new novel' (*Sons and Lovers*): 'The reception of *The Trespasser* has been such that I should like the opportunity of copyrighting the new book.'[23] Ten days later Garnett responded to Kennerley on Lawrence's behalf, suggesting that Kennerley could also publish an American edition of *Love Poems and Others* and read the manuscript of a play. Garnett must also have written that Duckworth would sell Kennerley the advance sheets of *Sons and Lovers*. Kennerley replied to Garnett on 6 March, agreeing to 'take a small edition' of the poems 'and I look forward to reading the manuscript of the play. I might put this into my Series and print a small edition for Mr Duckworth?' Lawrence gratefully accepted Kennerley's offer and he urged Garnett to 'accept things for me without me knowing, if you think them good'.[24]

The Widowing of Mrs Holroyd and the 'Modern Drama Series'

Kennerley had practically accepted *The Widowing of Mrs Holroyd* without having read it and he already knew how he would market the play. Garnett's approach about Lawrence's play was almost certainly intentionally timely, since Kennerley had recently announced his new 'Modern Drama Series' which was to be edited by the Swedish-American writer Edwin Björkman (1866–1951). The January and February 1913 numbers of the *Forum* carried the announcement, which stated that the Series would encourage the 'play-reading habit' in America by acquainting both 'the scholar and the layman' with the 'best dramatic production of other countries'.[25] That Kennerley announces his intention to encourage the 'play-reading habit, formerly almost wholly missing' is significant, as only during the last decade of the nineteenth century did dramatic publishing gain prestige through the interest of major publishing houses; earlier in the century plays were predominantly available only in ephemeral pamphlets known as 'acting editions'. Specialist theatrical publishers printed these acting editions mainly for amateur dramatic companies, so they were aimed at the trade rather than the public and contained technical terminology that was unsuitable for general readers. The drive by publishers to provide 'reading editions' rather than acting editions was a response to the perception that there might be a new market for playtexts, which would be collected by educated middle-class consumers to build up their libraries.

At the turn of the century in Britain Duckworth became known for publishing reading editions of play-texts: an advertisement in 1900 for his series of 'Modern Plays' announced its intention to give British readers an introduction to 'the activity of the modern drama' in other countries, particularly the work of 'Continental dramatists' and Strindberg, who 'will be almost new to the British public'.[26] Many of the playwrights published in Duckworth's series were from Sweden, Russia and Belgium. Titles included Emile Verhaeren's *The Dawn* (1898), Aleksandr Ostrovski's *The Storm* (1899), Maeterlinck's *L'Intérieur* (1899) and Gerhart Hauptmann's *The Coming of Peace* (1900). The market for reading editions was still relatively new in 1913 and so to have a reading edition appear was seen as a mark of particular literary merit (for both author and publisher). Publishers relied on the author's name to sell the edition so Kennerley must have thought that Lawrence was worth the investment. These changes in the marketplace came about as a gradual response to modifications in copyright law affecting dramatic texts. The 1833 Dramatic Copyright Act attempted to understand the specific problems of the playwright (as opposed to the author of other prose and poetic work) and the difference between the publication of a literary work and its dramatic performance. Prior to this, the lack of copyright protection of public performances meant that publishers and theatre managers tended to pirate published plays and unpublished manuscripts for stage performances. The Act protected performance rights, but there was still no copyright agreement with the USA, so some dramatists held back from publication.[27] The 1891 American Copyright Act marked the turning point in making it financially worthwhile for mainstream publishers to begin to produce reading editions, since it significantly reduced instances of piracy; however, play-texts themselves could never be relied upon to make publishers or dramatists very much money.

Kennerley advertised his Modern Drama Series by discussing these issues in a piece entitled 'The Day of the Published Play' for the *New York Times*, printed on 27 December 1914. After remarking that the first book of modern plays he remembered was a volume that Arnold Bennett had given to him in 1892 (*Three Plays* by Robert Louis Stevenson and W. E. Henley), Kennerley went on to note that:

> today the serious literary artist is writing plays with a view solely to publication . . . the best plays written today are being published before they are produced, and more often than not they are not produced at all . . . There are just as many people looking today for the great American play as for the great American novel, and when it comes it will be in book form.[28]

By the time Lawrence was writing his plays, then, dramatists did not necessarily write work for the stage, but to have it published and read. Once a play was accepted for publication, the playwright would have received better copyright protection, fair opportunities in the American market and the chance of seeing the work bound in a durable, respectable reading edition. The playwright would have a far greater sense of ownership of the work and significantly more control over the reception and production of the play than dramatists had prior to 1891. Kennerley had observed that printed drama was becoming available in a quality form designed to restore literary value to the genre and aimed to capitalise on an expanded novel-reading public who might be persuaded to read plays too.[29]

Kennerley's public commendation of reading editions was partly intended to showcase his anti-commercial attitude towards publishing. The implication was that in circulating reading editions he was working in the interests of the reading public rather than his own bank balance. In a cover letter to the contract for Zoë Akins's early play *Papa: An Amorality in Three Acts* (published in the Modern Drama Series in December 1913) Kennerley explained that publication would make her play more attractive to producers. Otherwise, he urged,

> if we are both wrong, and a production is not secured, I shall lose money on the book, but I am quite prepared to put all my energies into an effort to secure an offer for you from one of the managers.

He continued: 'I can get it read by any manager in New York.'[30] Kennerley might also have advised Lawrence to pursue opportunities for getting *Widowing* produced. Given the long-term friendships and close working relationships that both Kennerley and Hooley had established with Arnold Bennett, Kennerley probably suggested to Bennett that he pull some strings in London to support a production of Lawrence's play. This would explain Bennett's timely approach to the Stage Society recommending Lawrence's work in December 1913. On 21 December Lawrence reported to Garnett:

> I had a letter from the secretary of the Stage Society today, saying that Arnold Bennett had recommended the committee to consider any work of mine I might bring out, and asking me if I cared to submit the MS. But the MS is in such a state that they could not read it – and I have no duplicate proofs – I said I would send them a copy of the play as soon as I had one. Kennerley said he would mail me them about Jan 1st.[31]

It seems as if Kennerley had already assured Lawrence that he would return the duplicate proofs and/or a copy of the play within the fortnight – perhaps to facilitate the consideration of the play by the Stage Society. On 10 January 1914 Lawrence informed Arthur McLeod of Bennett's support:

> I am awaiting the coming of my play from America: it is being published first out there. It is good, I think. The Sec. of the Stage Society wrote me and said Arnold Bennett had told them, if I ever published drama, they must get hold of it. I shall send them a copy.[32]

Lawrence twice connects the American publication of *Widowing* with Bennett and the Stage Society. If Bennett was *not* working at Kennerley's direct request, he might still have known about Kennerley's pending publication of Lawrence's play and carried out the favour for Kennerley without him knowing. We do not know how much Lawrence (or Allan Wade, the Secretary of the Stage Society) knew about the friendship between Kennerley and Bennett, so we cannot determine the extent to which Lawrence was consciously proceeding with any plans they might have outlined for him. In any case, before 5 March Lawrence had sent the proofs on to the Society.[33]

Bennett's backing of Lawrence's play was neither disingenuous nor purely pragmatic since he later proclaimed himself to be 'a tremendous admirer of Lawrence'.[34] A production by the Stage Society would not have made Kennerley or Lawrence a great deal of money. It was not a commercial theatre but a private, members-only venue specialising in the staging of new and experimental plays, often those which had been refused a licence for public performance. Any capital that accrued from a production would have been cultural rather than economic. It might, though, have generated enough interest in literary circles to sell more copies of the reading edition. Kennerley would have worried about losing money by publishing the play, especially if he could not secure a production. It was not until late February or early March 1914 that Kennerley informed Lawrence that he had offered Duckworth some sheets of the play; this would help him to recoup some of the outlay of publishing the edition. Kennerley's original print run was of 1,000 copies, half of which he sold to Duckworth.[35] In the event, the Stage Society declined *Widowing* in 1914 because they objected to its morose ending and the laying out of the dead miner's body. The Society performed *Widowing*, but not until December 1926.[36]

The conditions of the field of dramatic publication help us to understand the significance of Kennerley's project in embarking on the Series and Lawrence's position within it. Drawing on Edwin Björkman's multilingual and literary expertise, the Series would be 'chiefly made up of translations' but would 'find a place for English and American plays of a high order'. The writing and production of original drama in the British theatre had been inhibited by early Victorian legislation on international copyright, which had encouraged the adaptation of plays from foreign models (most often French, but also German) rather than new plays by British dramatists. An 1852 ruling effectively gave legal sanction for foreign adaptation, which meant that 'the London stage became an outpost of the Parisian'.[37] In a similar way, until the 1891 American Copyright Act there was a total absence of protection for British playwrights in America, so many plays intended for the London stage first appeared as American productions, which nullified copyright protection for British plays in Britain. Stage performance was considered under British law to constitute publication, so if a play was pirated in New York (for example) before it was performed in Britain, then the author lost all copyright protection in Britain.[38] Just as the British stage had so often pirated French plays via translation and adaptation, the ease of access to the plays produced on the London stage largely delayed the emergence of a native American drama: it proved far easier to steal plays from the British stage than to write new work. Therefore, Kennerley's announcement that the Series would include 'primarily ... contemporary' English and American plays showed that he hoped to promote new English-language plays, the production of which had been inhibited for a time during the previous century. The advertisement announced that each volume in Kennerley's Series would contain 'three plays by the same author, together with introduction and bibliography',[39] so the volumes were intended to be substantial (even if in the event they contained just one play). *The Widowing of Mrs Holroyd* would be the only play by an English author to appear in the Series, which ran to twelve volumes from 1913 to 1915 before it was sold to Little, Brown in 1916. The remaining playwrights were Hjalmar Bergström (Swedish), Henry Becque (French), Henrik Ibsen (Norwegian), Giuseppe Giacosa (Italian), Leonid Andreyev (Russian), Lord Dunsany (Irish), Arthur Schnitzler (Austrian) Zoë Akins, Arthur Davison Ficke, George Bronson-Howard and Edith Ellis (American). Bound within this imprint, Lawrence's play was seen to represent the 'high order' of modern plays in England, even though Lawrence was not yet known as a playwright. Following its US publication, *Widowing* received a spectacular review in the *New York Times*. Its first production and the first ever staging of a Lawrence play took place 26–31 December 1916 at the Little Theater, Los Angeles.[40]

Edwin Björkman

Björkman was a regular contributor to *Forum*. As Kennerley's series announcement highlights, Björkman was best known for translating the plays of August Strindberg into English (Strindberg's *Plays*, edited by Björkmann for Charles Scribner and Sons in 1912, was also published by Duckworth that year). He had recently published books with Kennerley, such as a critical work entitled *Is There Anything New Under the Sun?* (1911), which included essays on William James, Henri Bergson, Shaw, Galsworthy and Anatole France. When Kennerley's announcement appeared, Björkman's critical essays on modern literature were in press (*Voices of To-morrow*, 1913): the volume was dedicated to Kennerley. Alongside several other literary figures and suffragettes, Björkman was present in the courtroom to support Kennerley on 5 February 1914, during his trial.[41] As editor of the Modern Drama Series, Björkman introduced Bjørnstjerne Bjørnson and Schnitzler to an American audience.

An updated advertisement for the Series was printed in the March 1913 *Forum*, which was the number in which 'The Soiled Rose' appeared. The number also carried prominent advertisements for *Rhythm* and *Poetry and Drama*, indicating the shared periodical cultures between Britain and America: *Forum* and *Rhythm* were perhaps closely associated in Lawrence's mind, as he had considered offering 'The Soiled Rose' to *Rhythm*. The new advertisement for the Modern Drama Series introduces the playwrights Bergström, Becque and Ibsen. It offers a short blurb describing their work and stressing their significance in countries other than England and the USA. The advertisement indicates that the volumes were to be hot off the press: '[t]hese three volumes will be issued during the Spring. Others will follow as soon as the translators finish their work'. The reader is advised: '*Ask your bookseller to send you the volumes . . . as they are published.*'[42] The plays need to be sought urgently so that the reader is up to date with the latest developments in international drama; thanks to the Series, English-speaking readers need no longer fear falling behind other parts of the world in their theatrical education.

Lawrence appears in the list of contributors to this number of *Forum* because of the publication of 'The Soiled Rose'. Garnett must have sent the summary of Lawrence and his work to the magazine in early May 1912. Lawrence was asked to contribute to the writing of advertising material at this time: on 1 May he wrote to Garnett, '[h]ere is the thing you want. Isn't it hateful, this sort of business! If I haven't done it right, you alter it, will you?'[43] Boulton speculates that this comment refers to 'some publicity material for *The Trespasser*', but it could equally relate to the notice for the *Forum*. I suspect that Garnett did indeed 'alter it' on Lawrence's behalf. It reads:

> D. H. LAWRENCE was born at Eastwood, near Nottingham, in 1885, and his life in a colliery district has given him an intimate understanding of the miner's outlook and environment. A tragedy that he has written on this subject has been accepted for production in London. His first novel, *The White Peacock*, was published last year in America and in England and had considerable success. He has since written *A Game of Forfeits* and *The Trespasser*.[44]

The notice demonstrates a fashioning of Lawrence's authorial identity as a working-class writer and the sentence about his 'life in a colliery district' sounds rather more like Garnett's turn of phrase than Lawrence's. The statement about a tragedy having been 'accepted for production in London' is intriguing; we know that none of Lawrence's plays were staged in England until March 1920, when the Altrincham Garrick Society near Manchester performed an amateur production of *The Widowing of Mrs Holroyd*.⁴⁵ The London production to which the notice refers can only be the result of Lawrence's 25 April 1912 meeting and correspondence with Ben Iden Payne, to whom he had been introduced by Garnett.⁴⁶ Unless Lawrence (and/or Garnett) was getting eagerly ahead of himself, it seems that the talks with Payne were looking positive for Lawrence at this moment in time; the production of *Widowing* by Payne may briefly have seemed more definite than critics have fully realised.⁴⁷ Payne may have offered Lawrence a production, but it came at the wrong time as Lawrence was planning to leave England for Germany with Frieda on 3 May. Tellingly, the inaccurate comment in the notice that Lawrence had written a novel called *A Game of Forfeits* also dates it to April–early May 1912, when *A Game of Forfeits* was mooted by Lawrence (in a letter to Garnett) as a possible title for the work that became *The Trespasser*.⁴⁸ Since it contains this detail, the notice can only have been written by Lawrence or Garnett; again, it is more likely to have been Garnett, as by 21 May Lawrence was rather taken aback that Duckworth had decided upon the title *A Game of Forfeits* without telling him.⁴⁹ The biographical notice was probably updated close to the March 1913 publication date by a third party on the editorial staff of the *Forum*, since *The Trespasser* was added to the list of Lawrence's works, but *A Game of Forfeits* was not removed. However 'hateful' Lawrence found the business of self-marketing, as his reputation grew he found himself having to produce many more such short autobiographical notes.

Lawrence had to provide a lengthy autobiographical sketch for Björkman which would inform the editor's Introduction to *The Widowing of Mrs Holroyd*, which Kennerley published on 1 April 1914. Björkman had a close involvement with the text of the play. On Lawrence's behalf, he corrected the proofs of the revised typescript that Kennerley had made out of the heavily revised manuscript that Lawrence had sent to Kennerley in August 1913.⁵⁰ Before 18 June 1913 Kennerley asked Garnett for some biographical information about Lawrence, because Kennerley wrote again to Garnett thanking him for asking 'Mr Lawrence to send me his biography direct'.⁵¹ On 21 June Lawrence told Garnett: 'I wrote the biography, and sent it off, with what reviews of *Sons and Lovers* I had, to Mitchell Kennerley.'⁵² This 'biography' undoubtedly shaped Björkman's Introduction.

The Introduction begins by stating Lawrence's newness to the English literary field, which is appropriate for the agenda of a Series which aimed to introduce readers to the latest dramatic works in the language: 'D. H. Lawrence is one of the most significant of the new generation of writers just beginning to appear in England.' Lawrence's social status appears in the third sentence: these new, young English writers 'frequently spring from social layers which in the past had to remain largely voiceless'. Lawrence is representative of a generation and class that have something to say that readers have never heard before. Björkman then provides a brief bibliography of Lawrence's works published to date.

> Three years ago the author of 'The Widowing of Mrs Holroyd' was wholly unknown, having not yet published a single work. To-day he has to his credit three novels . . . a collection of verse . . . and the play contained in this volume.

Out of these, Björkman rates *Sons and Lovers* and *Widowing* as Lawrence's greatest achievements. Lawrence 'tell[s] the truth where even the most audacious used to falter' and yet he does so 'with a daintiness that puts offence out of the question'. Björkman does not intend to alert the censor (Kennerley had already received enough attention in this respect), so he stresses the view that Lawrence's work is progressive but not offensive. The key purposes of his Introduction are to shape the reception of the play and to advertise Lawrence's name and writing more generally.

Next, Björkman provides the biographical information that can only have come from Lawrence. Björkman's understanding of *Sons and Lovers* as an autobiographical novel leads him to emphasise the importance of reading Lawrence's background into his work:

> He was born twenty-seven years ago in a coal-miner's cottage at the little colliery town of Eastwood, on the border line between Nottingham and Derbyshire. The home was poor, yet not without certain aspirations and refinements. It was the mother who held it together, who saved it from a still more abject poverty, and who filled it with a spirit that made it possible for the boy – her youngest son – to keep alive the gifts still slumbering undiscovered within him. In 'Sons and Lovers' we get the picture of just such a home and such a mother, and it seems safe to conclude that the novel in question is in many ways autobiographical.[53]

Lawrence was twenty-seven in 1912, which provides another indication that he supplied the biographical notice before his twenty-eighth birthday on 11 September 1913. The information Lawrence supplied and which Björkman adapted is drawn upon to advertise *Sons and Lovers*, too. While Lawrence colluded in the marketing of his authorial identity as a working-class writer he cannot have had full control over Björkman's final representation of him and this is telling in the hyperbolic comment that he had a background of almost 'abject poverty', which is said to centrally inform his work. Drawing on Lawrence's biographical sketch, Björkman offers even greater detail to introduce the reader to the author:

> At the age of twelve the boy won a County Council Scholarship – and came near to giving it up because he found that the fifteen pounds a year conferred by it would barely pay the fees at the Nottingham High School and the railway fares to that city. But his mother's determination and self-sacrifice carried him safely past the seemingly impossible. At sixteen he left school to earn his living as a clerk. Illness saved him from that uncongenial fate. Instead he became a teacher, having a charge of a class of colliers' boys in one of those rough, old-fashioned British schools where all the classes used to fight alongside one another within a single large room. . . . At nineteen he found himself . . . the first on the list of the King's Scholarship examination, and from that on he was, to use his own words, 'considered clever'. But the lack of twenty pounds needed in a lump sum to pay the entrance fee at the training college for teachers made it impossible for him to make use of the gained advantage.[54]

Working with the information Lawrence provided, Björkman stresses the hardships Lawrence had faced; it is a tale which (although romanticised) is fairly accurate in its basic details. Lawrence is, however, made to seem passive in the development of his life, as if he had always been subject to the hand of fate. 'It was the mother who held it together . . . Illness saved him . . . he became a teacher . . . he found himself . . . the first on the list'. It is others who have endowed him with status: 'he was, to use his own words, "considered clever"'. The providential tone of the notice may be influenced by Lawrence's own attempt to seem self-deprecatory and indifferent to marketing his identity for commercial purposes: he was uncomfortable with these personal public notices, however shrewd he was in perceiving what kind of biographical information would be marketable.

In an accurate description of his young life, Lawrence appears in the Introduction as a sickly, double-scholarship boy who had faced adverse circumstances and who was nearly lost to literature due to insufficient funds and social opportunities. The notice moves between stressing the fateful nature of Lawrence's success and indicating his hard work (anticipating the narrative line also taken in Lawrence's late autobiographical essays, discussed in Chapter 1). He is seen as rising in social status: from his birth in a poor colliery town, to winning a scholarship to a city grammar school, to becoming a clerk, to teaching colliers' boys and finally 'matriculating at the Nottingham Day Training College'.

But by that time the creative impulse had already begun to stir within him, aided by an early love affair, and so he wrote poems and worked at his first novel when he should have been studying. At twenty-three he left the college and went to London to teach school, to study French and German, and to write.[55]

Lawrence's creative talents, 'the gifts still slumbering undiscovered within him', had 'begun to stir within him' during his time at University College Nottingham and were stimulated by 'an early love affair' (that readers would find manifested in the relationship between Paul and Miriam in *Sons and Lovers*). Lawrence then moves to the capital city as a young aspirant. The indication that he moved there 'to study French and German' is interesting, as while Lawrence extended his intensive reading of French and German works while in London it is not known that he studied the languages in any formal way. If Lawrence included this detail in the notes he supplied to Björkman then he would have done so in order to give extra credence to the 'autodidact' personality he had constructed and to stress that he had long-established cosmopolitan interests and language skills (which would be appropriate for a Series that included so many translated foreign plays). Otherwise, Björkman could have been embellishing the biographical record by drawing on his own second-hand knowledge of Lawrence's accomplishments, influenced by reading *Sons and Lovers*. Crucially, Lawrence is described as having moved to London 'to write', which indicates that his move was strategic, enabling the development of his career and subsequently the publication of his work.

Having contextualised the author, Björkman steps back from the biography to make some incisive literary-critical comments about *Sons and Lovers* and *The Widowing of Mrs Holroyd*:

What has struck me most deeply in these two works – apart from their splendid craftsmanship – is their psychological penetration, so closely paralleling the most recent conclusions of the world's leading thinkers. In the hands of this writer, barely emerged out of obscurity, sex becomes almost a new thing. Not only the relationship between man and woman, but also that of mother and child is laid bare in a new light which startles – or even shocks – but which nevertheless compels acceptance. One might think that Mr. Lawrence had carefully studied and employed the very latest theories of men such as Freud, for instance, and yet it is a pretty safe bet that most of his studies have been carried on in his own soul, within his own memories.[56]

Björkman's observation that Lawrence was trying to do 'a new thing' with the representation of sex in literature by investigating the psychology of his characters should have pleased Lawrence. The remark about his 'splendid craftsmanship' might also have bolstered Lawrence's confidence in his use of form, which had been the subject of disagreements with both Hueffer and Garnett. That Lawrence is unconsciously applying Freud's 'latest theories' to his fictional work marks him out as a prescient writer, which is even more remarkable considering that he has 'barely emerged out of obscurity'. Another discerning comment by Björkman appears towards the end of the Introduction:

> Another thing that has impressed me is the aspect in which Mr. Lawrence presents the home life of those hitherto submerged classes which are now at last reaching out for a full share in the general social and cultural inheritance. He writes of that life, not only with a knowledge obtained at first hand, but with a sympathy that scorns any apologetic phrase-mongering.[57]

It is the sympathetic and unapologetic rendering of working-class life, from an author with genuine experience of it, which marked Lawrence out in 1913. Giving voice to the 'submerged classes' was timely and enabled him to locate a position in the literary field which was far more original than the identity of the middle-class writer of tragic romance that he had appropriated when he wrote his first two novels. The market was flooded by middle-class writers writing about middle-class life, but working-class authors writing about working-class life without condescension or stock characters was a rarer proposition. It made sense to Hueffer, Garnett, Kennerley, Björkman – and now Lawrence – to draw readers' attention to his background to market the play, on the back of the publication of the 'autobiographical' *Sons and Lovers*. In July 1913 he introduced himself to his new acquaintance, the journalist and poet Henry Savage, by making proud reference to his social status: 'I am the son of a coal-miner, and very ordinary. I should probably pass as a 30/– clerk.'[58]

The publisher's contract for the play was signed on 25 November 1913 and it was published by Kennerley on 1 April 1914. The Duckworth edition, printed from Kennerley sheets, followed on 17 April. The New York edition ($1.50) was bound in red cloth, with 'THE MODERN DRAMA SERIES / EDITED BY EDWIN BJÖRKMAN' blind-stamped on the front; only the spine of the book gives the title of the play, Lawrence's name and the name of the publisher. The embodiment therefore privileges the advertisement of the Series and its editor over the name of the author. In contrast, Duckworth's edition (3s 6d) is bound in an attractive dark blue cloth with gilt lettering giving precedence to the title of the play and its author: 'THE WIDOWING of MRS. HOLROYD' / ... D. H. LAWRENCE ...'. Kennerley must have sent the proofs of Björkman's Introduction to Lawrence in late September 1913, because Lawrence commented positively on the text in a letter to Kennerley dated 5 October: 'I take unto myself all the beautiful and laudatory things he says about me in the preface: they seem to me very just. I never did read Freud, but I have heard about him since I was in Germany.'[59] As he had seen it prior to publication, Lawrence could have objected to the Introduction if he had wanted to, but this would have been unlikely given that it was positive and he was indebted to Björkman for correcting the proofs of the play; Lawrence had already effectively ceded authority over the text to Björkman and Kennerley. Lawrence's amenable and engaged response is typical of his interactions with third parties in his early career when he welcomed practical assistance from others. He hoped to continue to please Kennerley, who had just sent him a 'fearfully nice letter' together with a copy of his American edition of Sons and Lovers and the 'very laudatory' review of the novel by the New York Times.[60]

In May 1914 however, in a letter to Garnett, Lawrence vilified Björkman's Introduction when he knew that Duckworth had included it in their English edition of the play: 'I wish you hadn't included Björkman's filthy little notice on me.'[61] The description of the notice as 'filthy' (and therefore perhaps connected to Grub street gossip, or to his 'lower' class origins) may reveal Lawrence's irritation at being 'packaged' for commercial purposes. He did not indicate his anxieties in his comment to Kennerley, which focused instead on Björkman's literary criticism and his acclamatory observations on Lawrence's significance. Lawrence could promote himself through Björkman and then blame Björkman for his commercialism; the editor acted as a buffer to distance Lawrence from self-marketing activities so that he might seem indifferent to his public image. Time and again we see that despite these anxieties about his personal exposure to the public, Lawrence was keen to shape an authorial image that would help him commercially and he recognised the value of works being published simultaneously across multiple venues. He hoped that the publication of the Duckworth edition of Widowing would coincide with another piece of advertising to which he had contributed biographical information: W. L. George's article on him in the Bookman. He wrote to Garnett on 21 December 1913, '[y]ou will bring out the play in February? – that is the Bookman month. Harrison ought to be ready with the first story by then.'[62] Lawrence hoped a story – probably 'Vin Ordinaire' – would also be published in the English Review that month, but it was not published until June.

W. L. George and the *Bookman*

W. L. George (1882–1926) wrote a long letter to Lawrence in June 1913 congratulating him on the publication of *Sons and Lovers*. Shortly afterwards on 26 June Lawrence had his photograph taken in London; Boulton notes that 'the photograph was taken by W. G. Parker for the article in the *Bookman* . . . by W. L. George', which would appear in February 1914.[63] However, this is by no means certain, because it was not until 31 October 1913 that Lawrence first mentioned 'the *Bookman* article', after having received another letter from George. Lawrence told Garnett:

> I shall send him the particulars he wants. One of the photos I had in the summer has not been published – so it could be copyright if he wanted, couldn't it. It is the one with the full face – at the Cearne. Or ought I to have another done? – Is it worth much, the *Bookman* article?[64]

From this comment it seems as if Lawrence had photographs taken in June for purposes other than the *Bookman* article (perhaps for other publicity material) and Garnett had them for safekeeping. On 2 November Lawrence wrote to Garnett: 'W L George says he's fixed up the *Bookman* article with the editor for February – and with you for the photograph.'[65] In the intervening time, we know that Lawrence and George had met on at least one occasion, possibly on Tuesday 4 August, at a lunch with Frieda and 'the Murrys'.[66] Lawrence seemed pleased about making George's acquaintance and receiving his support; on 25 November he told Cynthia Asquith that

> in February I am going to be in the *Bookman* – done by W L George – and a photograph. Do you know W L George –? He is perfect on the theme of love. He wrote some books – *A Bed of Roses*, and so on. I rather like him.[67]

George was born and lived in Paris until the age of twenty-three; he learned English only three years earlier. He was a journalist for several London newspapers before his first novel *A Bed of Roses* (1911) became a popular success; it was banned by many of the circulating libraries which only served to increase its sales and secure George's notoriety. Both the title of the novel and its epigraph were taken from Shaw's *Mrs Warren's Profession*, which signalled to readers its contentious theme of prostitution. George had published several works by 1913, including *The City of Light: A Novel of Modern Paris* (1912) and a pro-suffrage tract, *Woman and To-morrow* (1913). George was also a close friend of Hunt and Hueffer.

St. John Adcock was editor of the London *Bookman* from 1908. The prominent 6d monthly journal had been founded in 1891. It combined reviews with illustrated news items about authors, publishers and booksellers, as well as essays on various literary topics. There were special features on authors in 'The Bookman Gallery', in which the lengthy piece on Lawrence appeared. Lawrence hoped that Duckworth's publication of *Widowing* might coincide with the article in the *Bookman* and the appearance of his poems 'Twilight' and 'Meeting among the Mountains' in the *English Review*. He also asked whether Garnett might 'work the *Daily Mail*, to put me a column' (Lawrence could have been requesting that Garnett arrange for an item on him in the newspaper, or suggesting that an advertisement of his play might appear in its pages).[68]

Like Lawrence had done when introducing Rachel Annand Taylor, George opens the article by stressing Lawrence's youthfulness. Matching Marsh's rhetoric in his agenda for *Georgian Poetry*, Lawrence appears as one of the forerunners of the 'new young men' now appearing in literature; George asserts that he is the youngest but 'the biggest'.[69] These new young men (who include Gilbert Cannan, J. D. Beresford and Oliver Onions) 'have no formal school', but are to be numbered among 'that small group which is rising up against the threatening State, its rules and its iron conventions'. Cannan, Beresford and Onions moved in literary circles that included George, Marsh, Mansfield, Murry – and now Lawrence. All of these writers except Onions had appeared either in *Rhythm* or the *Blue Review*.[70] Lawrence is 'very much of his time, so hot, controversial, uneasy . . . he has the sudden fury of the bird that beats against the bars of its cage'. George's notorious outspokenness made it appropriate that he should have written this article on a 'controversial' new author. Unlike the other men, however, George suggests that Lawrence 'has no plan of reform'; he does not 'sneer at society, at the family, at every institution', but instead 'claims only as a right to develop his individuality, and to see others develop theirs'. Lawrence is not considered to be a social or political activist: he is an individualist who is 'mainly passionate aspiration and passionate protest'.

As in Björkman's Introduction, Lawrence's background is deemed to be essential to a reading of his work. Lawrence, aged twenty-eight, is the '[s]on of a Nottinghamshire coal-miner, a Board-school boy'. Again, his two scholarships are mentioned: 'a county council scholarship made of him only a schoolteacher'. Here the voice is passive as it was in Björkman's piece and again Lawrence is described as having risen in social status, this time from college 'to Croydon to teach at less than £2 a week. Then the literary life.' George makes it clear that in crafting this narrative he is working from Lawrence's own notes: 'I extract from his record the delightful fact that at college they gave him a prize for history and chemistry but placed him very low in the English class.' Lawrence appears to have given George a rather more detailed and sardonic account of his background. Like Hueffer's assertion of his 'genius' and Björkman's romantic notion that Lawrence in his youth had 'gifts still slumbering undiscovered within him', George comments that 'literature grew in him and with him, and was always with him, even in the worst years of his delicate health'. Again, Lawrence's frailty is mentioned: his literary creativity is implicitly described as an organic, living process that may have helped to sustain his health. The connections between literary creativity, vitality, physicality and growth had been established by Lawrence himself in his review of *Georgian Poetry*.

George also stresses the autobiographical nature of Lawrence's work: Lawrence must have pointed out that he based the character of Cyril in *The White Peacock* and Paul Morel in *Sons and Lovers* on himself. George observes that Lawrence 'gives us unabashed autobiography – the story of his early youth, of his relation to his mother, a creature of fitful, delicate charm'. By allowing his work to be viewed as strongly autobiographical, the authorial identity that emerges from both Björkman's and George's accounts is of an observational writer from the working class writing compassionately about aspirational, regional working-class life. Paul Morel is 'delicate, passionate, artistic' like Lawrence and Lawrence's choice of the W. G. Parker photograph (reproduced on the front cover of this book) to accompany the article shows such a man. The rather modern, 'full face' portrait shows a smartly dressed but ordinary young man, unlike the exuberantly attired Miss Winifred Boggs, the author in the mounted photograph on the preceding page. The half-light of the photograph as it was reproduced in the *Bookman* casts a shadow over half of Lawrence's face; his eyes and mouth show the hint of a smile beneath a heavy moustache. He appears rather enigmatic, which is fitting for a poet who has just emerged from obscurity and the gloom of a coal-mining village. George's article presents Lawrence as suffering for his art; Lawrence 'sees too much, feels significances greater than the actual; with arms that are too short, because only human, he strives to embrace the soul of man'. He is, finally, 'a servant of literature'.

Ironically, given that it celebrates Lawrence as a writer from a less advantaged background, the article is not as sensitive to working-class aspiration as Lawrence himself is: George professes himself to 'doubt the quality of his people's culture ... I am oppressed by unbelief when I find this grouping of agriculturalists and colliers responding to the verse of Swinburne and Verlaine, to Italian, to Wagner, to Bach.' George continues, 'he may develop his illusion of culture among the vulgar until it is incredible'. It was short-sighted, perhaps unwittingly elitist, middle-class readers like George that made it important for a writer such as Lawrence to inform such readers about the culture of working-class villages like Eastwood, with its literary and political societies, libraries, theatrical activities and aspiring young writers. Björkman's Introduction was not as condescending, but any record of Lawrence's objection to aspects of George's article has not survived; on the contrary, Lawrence told several of his acquaintances about the piece. Lawrence wrote courteously to Kennerley on 7 February 1914: '[d]id W. L. George give you that article on me, which appears in this month's *Bookman*? He said he might. It isn't bad, – but it hasn't Mr Björkman's strong flavour.'[71] Lawrence's acquaintances in Fiascherino in March 1914 were 'exclaiming . . . on the truth of what [George] says. But the truth of what is said about oneself, one can never see so completely.'[72] This is a rather ambiguous comment by Lawrence, who is not usually so guarded in his responses to others' writing, but he again distances himself from the act of supplying biographical details for marketing purposes just as he had done when he reacted to Björkman's 'filthy little notice'. Inevitably, it seems, George based his critical analysis of Lawrence's work on the author's social class. We cannot know the extent of the details Lawrence supplied either in correspondence or when he met George in person; George may have gleaned further information from speaking to acquaintances from within their shared literary networks. Yet it is clear that Lawrence played a significant role in helping to shape George and Björkman's assessments of him and his work by stressing the circumstances of his upbringing and the autobiographical nature of his writing. When he provided biographical notes, he essentially collaborated with Björkman and George in marketing himself as a working-class writer. In doing so, he heeded the pragmatic advice of others who helped to shape his early career.

Overall, through the evidence presented in this book a new image emerges of Lawrence as a practical, pragmatic young author who realised the importance of addressing the needs of publishers, editors and their consumers and developed strategies for doing so. However keenly he could see through the falsities of the literary world and however much irritation he felt at having to 'package' himself for commercial sale, he knew that fashioning a marketable image and engaging with the most contemporary and influential literary cliques (even if he operated at the margins of these groups) would help him to feature in the 'right' publications, win him the attention of publishers and help his name to be made, so that he could forge and sustain the kind of professional writing career that would satisfy him: namely, a career of boundary-testing individuality and distinction.

Notes

1. John Lane Papers, University of London. Quoted by Matthew J. Bruccoli, *The Fortunes of Mitchell Kennerley, Bookman* (1986), p. 16. The biographical information on Kennerley is taken from this volume, pp. 4–6; 8; 10.
2. Bruccoli, *The Fortunes of Mitchell Kennerley*, pp. 17; 23; 25; 26.
3. Grant Richards launched the World's Classics series of cheap reprints in 1901. By 1905 Richards was declared bankrupt and the World's Classics series was sold to Oxford University Press. He started a new publishing house under 'E. Grant Richards' before publishing under 'Grant Richards' again in 1908. See Anon., 'Mr. Grant Richards: An Adventurous Publisher' (1948): 7.
4. Bruccoli, *The Fortunes of Mitchell Kennerley*, pp. 33; 37–8; 40.
5. Lawrence had written the story in late December 1911, entitling it 'The Harrassed Angel': *L*, I, 343; 372. Lawrence cites Kennerley's opinion of the story: *L*, I, 378.
6. *L*, I, 313. Heinemann imported the Duffield plates for the English edition; the Duffield edition was published a day earlier than Heinemann's edition. See Roberts A1 and *WP*, xlii.
7. Hooley's reader's report is in Box 5, Mitchell Kennerley Papers, Archives and Special Collections Library, Vassar College Libraries.
8. The date of Kennerley's publication of *The Trespasser* is unknown, but Elizabeth Mansfield (*T*, 30–1) and Roberts (10) suggest that it was as late as November.
9. Letter held at the Rare Books and Manuscripts Division, New York Public Library, quoted by Bruccoli, *The Fortunes of Mitchell Kennerley*, p. 62.
10. *L*, II, 26–7.
11. 'Violets' appeared in *Smart Set*, xli, 1 (September 1913), 'Kisses in the Train' in *Smart Set*, xli, 2 (October 1913) and 'The Mowers' in *Smart Set*, xli, 2 (November 1913).
12. *L*, II, 58; 67.
13. *L*, II, 50 fn. 4.
14. *New York Times Review of Books* (22 February 1914): 85.
15. *New York Times Review of Books* (28 September 1913): 504.
16. Anon., 'Arrest Kennerley on Comstock Writ' (1913): 6.
17. Quoted by Bruccoli, *The Fortunes of Mitchell Kennerley*, p. 70.
18. Quoted by Charles A. Madison in *Book Publishing in America* (1966), p. 311. See also Anon., '"Hagar Revelly" Not Immoral, says Jury' (1914): 515–16.
19. *L*, II, 98.

20. *L*, II, 133.
21. *Poetry*, 3:4 (January 1914): 151; pp. 115–25.
22. *New York Times Book Review* (17 November 1912), 677.
23. Kennerley's letter to Garnett is reproduced in *L*, I, 522 fn. 4.
24. *L*, I, 542. Garnett's letter to Kennerley is not extant but his communication can be inferred from Kennerley's response, which is reproduced in *L*, I, 542, fn. 2.
25. Mitchell Kennerley's 'The Modern Drama Series' announcement in the *Forum* (January 1913), unpaginated.
26. Quoted by Allardyce Nicoll, *English Drama, 1900–1930: The Beginnings of the Modern Period* (1973), p. 112.
27. On the complex modifications in copyright law affecting theatre and dramatic publishing, see John Russell Stephens, *The Profession of the Playwright: British Theatre 1800–1900* (1992).
28. Mitchell Kennerley, 'The Day of the Published Play' (1914): 3.
29. Stephens, *Profession of the Playwright*, p. 132.
30. Letter from Kennerley to Akins, 2 July 1913. Held at the Huntington Library, San Marino, California, quoted by Bruccoli, *The Fortunes of Mitchell Kennerley*, p. 63. See also Alan Kreizenbeck, *Zoe Akins: Broadway Playwright* (2004), p. 80. Kennerley sent *Papa* to Lawrence, who criticised it in his reply dated 7 February 1914 (*L*, II, 145).
31. *L*, II, 127.
32. *L*, II, 136.
33. *L*, II, 152.
34. Arnold Bennett, 'A Tribute of Admiration' (1930): 9.
35. *L*, II, 152; *Plays*, xlii.
36. Moran, *The Theatre of D. H. Lawrence*, p. 42; *L*, II, 127 fn. 5.
37. Stephens, *Profession of the Playwright*, p. 103.
38. Ibid., p. 104.
39. Kennerley, 'The Modern Drama Series'.
40. Moran, *Theatre of D. H. Lawrence*, p. 69.
41. Bruccoli, *The Fortunes of Mitchell Kennerley*, p. 72.
42. Further announcement for Kennerley's 'Modern Drama Series', *Forum*, Vol. XLIX (March 1913), unpaginated.
43. *L*, I, 389.
44. 'Contributors to the March *Forum*', *Forum*, Vol. XLIX (March 1913), unpaginated.
45. *Plays*, lvi.
46. See *L*, I, 384 (17 April, 'It is huge to think of Iden Payne acting me on the stage'); 386 (23 April, 'I had a letter from Iden Payne appointing me a

meeting at the Managers Club on Thursday . . . I should think it wouldn't matter, would it, if I weren't in London when the little play was performed? . . . I want to go to Germany [with Frieda] more'); 389 (1 May, 'Have just got the drama from Payne . . . He was going to show me what he wanted altering').

47. 'Lawrence and Iden Payne then chatted together, but the meeting hardly proved a success. Payne failed to offer a proposal of a production, but merely suggested changes to one of Lawrence's existing scripts.' Moran, *Theatre of D. H. Lawrence*, p. 57.
48. *L*, I, 378.
49. *L*, I, 408.
50. *L*, II, 80; see *Plays*, xl–xli for details of the revision process.
51. *L*, II, 26, fn. 3. Boulton's third footnote is likely misleading in noting that 'Kennerley apparently wanted some biographical information to publicise the American edition of *Sons and Lovers*'; it is likely that the biography Lawrence sent was primarily to help Björkman write his Introduction.
52. *L*, II, 26.
53. Björkman, 'Introduction' (1914): vi.
54. Ibid., viii–ix.
55. Ibid., ix.
56. Ibid., ix–x.
57. Ibid., x.
58. *L*, II, 35.
59. *L*, II, 80.
60. *L*, II, 82.
61. *L*, II, 174.
62. *L*, II, 127.
63. *L*, II, 26; 28 fn. 2.
64. *L*, II, 98.
65. *L*, II, 100.
66. *L*, II, 51.
67. *L*, II, 108.
68. *L*, II, 135.
69. W. L. George, 'The Bookman Gallery: D. H. Lawrence' (1914): 244–6.
70. George and Cannan (1884–1955) both had work published alongside 'The Soiled Rose' in the *Blue Review*, I: I (May 1913). Onions (1873–1961) is mentioned in an article on 'Fiction' by Hugh Walpole in this number (p. 47). Beresford (1873–1947) is published alongside Marsh in the June 1913 number.
71. *L*, II, 144.
72. *L*, II, 152.

Coda

Seven years after Lawrence's death Hueffer recalled their first meeting in September 1909 at Hueffer's home in Kensington, which served as the offices of the *English Review*. Hueffer described his reaction on first seeing Lawrence:

> [He was] leaning, as if panting, beside the door post . . . I had had only the impression of the fox-coloured hair and moustache and the deep, wary, sardonic glance . . . as if he might be going to devour me – or something that I possessed.
> And that was really his attitude of mind. He had come, like the fox, with his overflood of energy – his abounding vitality of passionate determination that seemed always too big for his frail body – to get something – the hypnotic two thousand a year; from somewhere. . . . And he remarked in a curiously deep, rather musical chest-voice:
> 'This isn't my idea, Sir, of an editor's office.'[1]

Hueffer's depiction of Lawrence as '[a] fox going to make a raid on the hen-roost before him' stresses Lawrence's 'passionate determination' to come away from the meeting with an agreement that Hueffer might be of assistance to him and enlighten him about metropolitan publication opportunities.[2] The description of Lawrence's 'deep, wary, sardonic glance' seems plausible, in light of Hueffer's position of authority and Lawrence's characteristically defensive and guarded attitude towards his own writing. Hueffer's recollection of being put on edge by Lawrence's mischievous comment about the journal's offices indicates that their relationship was, from the beginning, tense and challenging. Hueffer admitted to feeling unsettled by Lawrence: 'I cannot say that I liked Lawrence much . . . He remained too disturbing even when I got to know him well.' Offering a fascinating final insight, he continued: '[h]e had so much need of moral support to take the place of his mother's influence that he kept one – everyone who at all came into contact with him – in a constant state of solicitude'.[3]

As this book has shown, Lawrence did indeed require a great deal of emotional and practical support for his writing from friends (such as Jessie Chambers, Louie Burrows and Blanche Jennings), new acquaintances who became 'mentor' figures (most notably Hueffer, Violet Hunt, Edward Garnett and Edward Marsh) and supporters (such as Ezra Pound and – albeit to a lesser extent – the 'Georgian poets', Walter de la Mare, Austin Harrison, Arnold Bennett and W. L. George). His early experiences of discussing literature with Jessie, writing and revising short stories with Louie and gaining feedback on his work from Blanche, were formative; from the very beginning Lawrence understood that literary value is constructed collaboratively and he wrote with a specific readership in mind. Hueffer described Lawrence as a 'super-vitalized creature from a world outside my own' and it was the differences between them in terms of background, character and literary taste that led to Hueffer being supplanted as Lawrence's mentor by Garnett when he came on the scene in August 1911.[4] While Lawrence recognised that Hueffer's early support was crucial, Garnett's sympathetic appreciation of Lawrence's working-class upbringing was more congenial to Lawrence than Hueffer's notion of him as the self-taught 'genius'. On 30 December 1913 Lawrence commented to Garnett that '[t]he Hueffer-Pound faction seems inclined to lead me round a little as one of their show-dogs'.[5] Lawrence and Garnett swiftly established a close friendship that greatly benefited Lawrence's career; Garnett recommended that Duckworth publish *The Trespasser, Love Poems and Others, Sons and Lovers, The Widowing of Mrs Holroyd* and *The Prussian Officer and Other Stories* and his connections and reputation in London literary circles also helped to get Lawrence's books published in America by Mitchell Kennerley.

The young D. H. Lawrence, then, was deeply pragmatic, ambitious, precociously determined and adaptable; he became adept at understanding the requirements of the literary marketplace even if at times he contravened notions of conventional respectability. Placing his writing in context allows us to see that he was certainly not alone in testing the boundaries of acceptability. A previous generation of authors had set the precedent, not least Hardy and George Moore; New Woman writers followed by Edwardian 'sex novelists' and dramatists such as George Bernard Shaw were also pressing against traditional perceptions of gender relations. Lawrence's expressions of disinterest in – and disdain for – literary business belie his constant attention to professional matters. In January 1911 he wanted 'a little individual name in the literary world . . . I want a measure of success.'[6] These are the words of the aspirational young man with a 'small ginger moustache' who Richard Aldington described as 'looking rather like a competent private soldier in evening dress' as he entered a private suite at the Berkeley Hotel for dinner in 1914; such an appearance is markedly different from the bearded devilish outsider figure Aldington found Lawrence to be in his later years, who responded to social snobbery by 'plung[ing] into stories of his childhood as a miner's son and drop[ping] into Derbyshire dialect'.[7]

I have described how in 1905 Lawrence fashioned himself as a romantic poet and in 1908 as an aesthete and autodidact with socialist concerns. He sought to offer a challenge to readers, provoking them to question their preconceptions and to probe their understandings of society and private experience. His interest in journalism in 1908 demonstrates his determination to establish a writing career by working through the usual channels, as his cousin Alfred Inwood and his friend Willie Hopkin had done; G. K. Chesterton, Shaw and A. R. Orage were high profile models of how this could be achieved. By learning about preparing copy and writing in a range of genres Lawrence ensured that, given the opportunity, he could supply work to different areas of the marketplace to increase his chances of success.

An unsigned review of *Sons and Lovers* printed in the *Saturday Review* on 21 June 1913 opened with the comment: '[w]hen were there written three novels so strange as these of Mr. Lawrence?'[8] The reviewer went on to state that 'we know of no active English novelist – today – who has Mr. Lawrence's power to put in words the rise and fall of passion'. It was Lawrence's 'strangeness' and 'power' that had first struck Hueffer and Hunt and by 1913 these qualities were beginning to distinguish him in the competitive literary marketplace. However, Lawrence's position in that marketplace was provisional, fraught and shaped by a range of internal and external factors. As Peter D. McDonald notes, examining the literary field 'means looking beyond the sanitized and simplified version of events embodied in the canon, and rescuing the fractured, mobile figure of the author in the process of making a career'.[9] By concentrating on these early years and on hitherto neglected aspects of Lawrence's *oeuvre*, I have endeavoured to understand how Lawrence achieved a degree of distinction within a relatively short period of time and before he received professional assistance from J. B. Pinker, his first literary agent. Lawrence was a skilful, yet measured, self-publicist: even if he disliked packaging his authorial identity for marketing purposes, he understood the necessity of doing so and worked with publishers, editors and journalists in their advertisement of him. Figures such as Hueffer and Hunt, Garnett, Edward Marsh, Mansfield and Murry, Edwin Björkman, Kennerley and W. L. George variously spoke of Lawrence as a romance writer, an erotic writer, a Georgian poet, a working-class realist, an accomplished writer for the stage representative of contemporary English drama and as a leading figure among a new generation of male writers who were, to use George's adjectives, hot, controversial, uneasy.

This book has examined how Lawrence gained a foothold in the pre-war literary marketplace by taking account of the conditions under which authors worked during this time. It has redressed simplified accounts of Lawrence's early career (which he himself shaped in his late autobiographical writings), stressing his practical negotiation of the literary field and the challenges he overcame in becoming a professional writer. Inevitably, there is much else to say on this topic and the story of Lawrence's career only begins here. Lawrence's desire for social transformation and the outspoken nature of his work left him open to the threat of alienation from the marketplace and financial ruin. The onset of the Great War placed the literary marketplace under severe financial and practical pressures and the heat of censorship increased even further; Lawrence's career received a damaging setback when *The Rainbow* (Methuen, 1915) was suppressed and withdrawn a month after its publication. That year, in typical modernist fashion, he attempted to create a counter-realm to the wider public sphere by setting up his anti-war journal *The Signature* with John Middleton Murry and Katherine Mansfield and circulating fliers for an unrealised 'Rainbow Books and Music' private publishing scheme. Lawrence would continue to seek out and respond to the comments of women – most frequently and intimately his wife Frieda, but in the years to come he would also engage with women who could act as financial patrons of his work (such as Lady Ottoline Morrell and Mabel Dodge Luhan). Retaining his chameleon-like sociability and reaching out to others while remaining independent of cliques, Lawrence found ways of keeping his career afloat while trying to operate within the constraints of the constantly evolving literary marketplace. He maintained his integrity as a principled author who believed in shifting the parameters of acceptability, but it also helped, of course, that across all forms he was capable of outstandingly perceptive writing. Lawrence was never 'destined' to succeed, but how much brighter English Literature is for his vivid contribution.

Notes

1. Ford, *Portraits from Life*, p. 77.
2. Ibid., p. 76.
3. Ibid., p. 85.
4. Ibid., p. 78.
5. L, II, 132–3.
6. L, I, 223.
7. Aldington, *D. H. Lawrence: An Indiscretion*, pp. 15; 16.
8. Draper, 65.
9. McDonald, *British Literary Culture and Publishing Practice*, p. 117.

Bibliography

This bibliography does not reproduce the works listed in the 'Cue titles'.

Lawrence Studies

Allott, Kenneth and Miriam Allott. 'D. H. Lawrence and Blanche Jennings'. *A Review of English Literature* I (1960): 57–76.

Atkins, A. R. 'A Bibliographical Analysis of the Manuscript of D. H. Lawrence's The White Peacock'. *Studies in Bibliography* 44 (1991): 345–64.

Baron, Helen. 'Some Theoretical Issues Raised by Editing *Sons and Lovers*' in Charles L. Ross and Dennis Jackson (eds), *Editing D. H. Lawrence: New Versions of a Modern Author*. Ann Arbor: University of Michigan Press, 1995, pp. 59–77.

Bell, Michael. *D. H. Lawrence: Language and Being*. Cambridge: Cambridge University Press, 1992.

Black, Michael H. *D. H. Lawrence: The Early Fiction*. Basingstoke: Macmillan, 1986.

— 'A Bit of Both: George Eliot and D.H. Lawrence', *Critical Review* 29 (1989): 89–109.

Booth, Howard J. (ed.). *New D. H. Lawrence*. Manchester: Manchester University Press, 2009.

— '*The Rainbow*, British Marxist Criticism of the 1930s and Colonialism' in Howard J. Booth (ed.), *New D. H. Lawrence*. Manchester: Manchester University Press, 2009, pp. 34–58.

— 'Same-Sex Desire, Cross-Gender Identification and Asexuality in D. H. Lawrence's Early Short Fiction', *Études Lawrenciennes* 42 (2011): 37–57.

Brown, Keith (ed.). *Rethinking Lawrence*. Buckingham: Open University Press, 1990.

Cushman, Keith. *D. H. Lawrence at Work: The Emergence of the* Prussian Officer *Stories*. Charlottesville: University Press of Virginia, 1978.

Daleski, H. M. *The Forked Flame: A Study of D. H. Lawrence*. Wisconsin: University of Wisconsin Press, 1987.
Daly, Macdonald. 'D. H. Lawrence and Labour in the Great War'. *The Modern Language Review* 89:1 (January 1994): 19–38.
Delavenay, Emile. *D. H. Lawrence and Edward Carpenter: A Study in Edwardian Transition*. London: Heinemann, 1971.
Eggert, Paul. 'D. H. Lawrence and Literary Collaboration'. *Études Lawrenciennes* 3. (Nanterre: Université Paris X, May 1988): 153–62.
— 'The Cambridge Edition' in Andrew Harrison (ed.), *D. H. Lawrence in Context*. Cambridge: Cambridge University Press, 2018, pp. 304–14.
Ellis, David. *D. H. Lawrence: Dying Game, 1922-1930*. Cambridge: Cambridge University Press, 1998.
— *Love and Sex in D. H. Lawrence*. Clemson: Clemson University Press, 2015.
Fernihough, Anne. *D. H. Lawrence: Aesthetics and Ideology*. Oxford: Clarendon, 1992.
— *Freewomen and Supermen: Edwardian Radicals and Literary Modernism*. Oxford: Oxford University Press, 2013.
Game, David. *D. H. Lawrence's Australia: Anxiety at the Edge of Empire*. Farnham: Ashgate, 2015.
Gilbert, Sandra M. *Acts of Attention: The Poems of D. H. Lawrence*. Ithaca: Cornell University Press, 1972.
Grice, Annalise. 'Journals, Magazines, Newspapers' in Andrew Harrison (ed.), *D. H. Lawrence in Context*. Cambridge: Cambridge University Press, 2018.
Harrison, Andrew. 'Dust-Jackets, Blurbs and Forewords: The Marketing of *Sons and Lovers*' in Howard J. Booth (ed.), *New D. H. Lawrence*. Manchester: Manchester University Press, 2009.
— '*The White Peacock* and "The School of Lorna Doone"'. *DHLR* 38:1 (2013): 45–56.
— *The Life of D. H. Lawrence: A Critical Biography*. Oxford: Wiley Blackwell, 2016.
— 'Private Publication' in Andrew Harrison (ed.). *D. H. Lawrence in Context*. Cambridge: Cambridge University Press, 2018.
— (ed.). *D. H. Lawrence in Context*. Cambridge: Cambridge University Press, 2018.
Harrison, Andrew and John Worthen (eds). *Sons and Lovers: A Casebook*. Oxford: Oxford University Press, 2005.
Herzinger, Kim A. *D. H. Lawrence in His Time: 1908–1915*. London and Toronto: Bucknell University Press, 1982.
Hough, Graham. *The Dark Sun: A Study of D. H. Lawrence*. London: Duckworth, 1956.

Huxley, Aldous (ed.). *The Letters of D. H. Lawrence*. London: Heinemann, 1932.

Hyde, G. M. *D. H. Lawrence*. Basingstoke: Macmillan, 1990.

Kinkead-Weekes, Mark. 'The Marble and the Statue: The Exploratory Imagination of D. H. Lawrence' in Maynard Mack and Ian Gregor (eds), *Imagined Worlds: Essays on some English Novels and Novelists in Honour of John Butt*. London: Methuen, 1968, pp. 371–418.

Lawrence, Ada and G. Stuart Gelder. *Early Life of D. H. Lawrence*. London: Martin Secker, 1932.

Leavis, F. R. *D. H. Lawrence: Novelist*. Harmondsworth: Penguin [1955] 1994.

Mack, Maynard and Ian Gregor (eds). *Imagined Worlds: Essays on Some English Novels and Novelists in Honour of John Butt*. London: Methuen, 1968.

Meyers, Jeffrey (ed.). *D. H. Lawrence and Tradition*. Amherst: University of Massachusetts Press, 1985.

Moore, Harry T. *The Life and Works of D. H. Lawrence*. London: Allen and Unwin, 1951.

— *The Intelligent Heart: The Story of D. H. Lawrence*. London: Heinemann, 1955.

— (ed.). *The Collected Letters of D. H. Lawrence*. New York: Viking, 1962.

— *The Priest of Love: A Life of D. H. Lawrence*. New York: Farrar, Straus and Giroux, 1975.

Moran, James. *The Theatre of D. H. Lawrence*. London: Bloomsbury, 2015.

Page, Norman (ed.). *D. H. Lawrence: Interviews and Recollections, Vol. II*. London: Macmillan, 1981.

Partlow, Robert J. and Harry T. Moore (eds). *D. H. Lawrence: the man who lived: Papers Delivered at the D. H. Lawrence Conference at Southern Illinois University, Carbondale, April 1979*. Carbondale and Edwardsville: Southern Illinois University Press, 1978.

Pinkney, Tony. *D. H. Lawrence and Modernism*. Iowa City: University of Iowa Press, 1990.

Poplawski, Paul. *The Works of D. H. Lawrence: A Chronological Checklist*. Nottingham: D. H. Lawrence Society, 1995.

Reid, Susan. *D. H. Lawrence, Music and Modernism*. Basingstoke: Palgrave Macmillan, 2019.

Roberts, Neil. *D. H. Lawrence, Travel and Cultural Difference*. Basingstoke: Palgrave Macmillan, 2004.

Ross, Charles L. and Dennis Jackson (eds). *Editing D. H. Lawrence: New Versions of a Modern Author*. Ann Arbor: University of Michigan Press, 1995.

Ruderman, Judith. *Race and Identity in D. H. Lawrence*. Basingstoke: Palgrave Macmillan, 2014.

Stanford, Raney. 'Thomas Hardy and Lawrence's *The White Peacock*'. *Modern Fiction Studies* 5:1 (1959): 19–28.

Turner, John. *D. H. Lawrence and Psychoanalysis*. New York and Abingdon: Routledge, 2020.

Wallace, Jeff. *D. H. Lawrence, Science and the Posthuman*. Basingstoke: Palgrave Macmillan, 2005.

Wexler, Joyce Piell. *Who Paid for Modernism? Art, Money, and the Fiction of Conrad, Joyce, and Lawrence*. Fayetteville: University of Arkansas Press, 1997.

— 'Book Publishers' in Andrew Harrison (ed.), *D. H. Lawrence in Context*. Cambridge: Cambridge University Press, 2018.

Worthen, John. *D. H. Lawrence: A Literary Life*. London: Macmillan, 1989.

— 'D. H. Lawrence and the Society for the Study of Social Questions'. *Notes and Queries* 41 (September 1994): 364–6.

— *D. H. Lawrence: The Life of an Outsider*. London: Allen Lane, 2005.

— *Experiments: Lectures on Lawrence*. Nottingham: Critical, Cultural and Communications Press, 2012.

Worthen, John and Andrew Harrison (eds). 'Further Letters of D. H. Lawrence'. *JDHLS* 2:3 (2011): 7–11.

Zytaruk, George (ed.). 'The Collected Letters of Jessie Chambers'. *DHLR*. 12: i–ii. (Spring and Summer 1979).

General Secondary Criticism

Adams, Amanda. *Performing Authorship in the Nineteenth-Century Transatlantic Lecture Tour*. Surrey: Ashgate, 2014.

Alexander, Neal and James Moran (eds). *Regional Modernisms*. Edinburgh: Edinburgh University Press, 2013.

Alford, Norman. *The Rhymers' Club: Poets of the Tragic Generation*. Houndmills: Palgrave Macmillan, 1994.

Anderson, Patricia. *The Printed Image and the Transformation of Popular Culture 1790–1860*. Oxford: Clarendon, 1991.

Anesko, Michael. *Friction with the Market*. Oxford: Oxford University Press, 1986.

Ardis, Ann L. *Modernism and Cultural Conflict, 1880–1922*. Cambridge: Cambridge University Press, 2002.

— 'Democracy and Modernism: *The New Age* under A. R. Orage (1907–22)' in Peter Brooker and Andrew Thacker (eds), *The Oxford Critical and Cultural History of Modernist Magazines, Volume I, Britain and Ireland 1880-1955*. Oxford: Oxford University Press, 2009–2012, pp. 205–25.

Bassett, Troy J. 'T. Fisher Unwin's Pseudonym Library: Literary Marketing and Authorial Identity'. *English Literature in Transition, 1880–1920* 47:2 (2004): 143–60.

Belford, Barbara. *Violet: The Story of the Irrepressible Violet Hunt and Her Circle of Lovers and Friends – Ford Madox Ford, H. G. Wells, Somerset Maugham, and Henry James.* New York: Simon and Schuster, 1990.

Binckes, Faith. *Modernism, Magazines and the British Avant-garde: Reading Rhythm, 1910–1914.* Oxford: Oxford University Press, 2010.

Bloch, Maurice. *Anthropology and the Cognitive Challenge.* Cambridge: Cambridge University Press, 2012.

Bornstein, George. *Material Modernism: The Politics of the Page.* Cambridge: Cambridge University Press, 2001.

Bourdieu, Pierre. *Distinction: A Social Critique of the Judgement of Taste.* Trans. Richard Nice. Cambridge, MA: Harvard University Press [1979] 1984.

— *The Field of Cultural Production: Essays on Art and Literature.* Ed. Randal Johnson. Cambridge: Polity, 1993.

Bradshaw, David and Rachel Potter (eds). *Prudes on the Prowl: Fiction and Obscenity in England, 1850 to the Present Day.* Oxford: Oxford University Press, 2013.

Brooker, Peter. 'Harmony, Discord and Difference' in Peter Brooker and Andrew Thacker (eds), *The Oxford Critical and Cultural History of Modernist Magazines, Volume I: Britain and Ireland 1880–1955.* Oxford: Oxford University Press, 2009–12.

Brooker, Peter and Andrew Thacker (eds). *The Oxford Critical and Cultural History of Modernist Magazines.* Oxford: Oxford University Press, 2009–12.

Brown, Tony (ed.). *Edward Carpenter and Late Victorian Radicalism.* London: Frank Cass, 1990.

Bruccoli, Matthew J. *The Fortunes of Mitchell Kennerley, Bookman.* London and New York: Harcourt Brace Jovanovich, 1986.

Carey, John. *The Intellectuals and the Masses.* London: Faber and Faber, 1992.

Carr, Helen. *The Verse Revolutionaries: Ezra Pound, H. D. and the Imagists.* London: Jonathan Cape, 2009.

Collier, Patrick. *Modernism on Fleet Street.* Aldershot: Ashgate, 2006.

Cooper, Jeff. '*New Numbers*: The Story of a Periodical'. *Dymock Poets and Friends: Journal of the Friends of the Dymock Poets* 6 (2007): 56–66.

Coustillas, Pierre. *The Heroic Life of George Gissing, Part II: 1888–1897.* London: Pickering & Chatto, 2012.

Cranfield, Jonathan. *Twentieth-Century Victorian: Arthur Conan Doyle and the Strand Magazine, 1891-1930.* Edinburgh: Edinburgh University Press, 2016.

Cummins, Anthony. 'Émile Zola's Cheap English Dress: The Vizetelly Translations, Late-Victorian Print Culture, and the Crisis of Literary Value'. *Review of English Studies* 60 (2009): 108–32.

Delany, Paul. *Literature, Money and the Market: from Trollope to Amis*. Basingstoke: Palgrave, 2002.

Demoor, Marysa (ed.). *Marketing the Author: Authorial Personae, Narrative Selves and Self-Fashioning, 1880–1930*. Houndmills: Palgrave Macmillan, 2004.

Dettmar, Kevin J. H. and Stephen Watt (eds). *Marketing Modernisms: Self-Promotion, Canonization, and Rereading*. Ann Arbor: University of Michigan Press, 1996.

Dibb, Geoff. *Oscar Wilde: A Vagabond with a Mission. The Story of Oscar Wilde's Lecture Tours of Britain and Ireland*. London: Oscar Wilde Society, 2013.

Dickson, B. 'Taylor, Rachel Annand (1876–1960)'. *Oxford Dictionary of National Biography*. Oxford: Oxford University Press, 2004.

Dickson, Lovat. *H. G. Wells: His Turbulent Life and Times*. London: Macmillan, 1971.

Dilks, Stephen. *Samuel Beckett in the Literary Marketplace*. Syracuse: Syracuse University Press, 2011.

Dooley, Allan C. *Author and Printer in Victorian England*. Charlottesville and London: University Press of Virginia, 1992.

Dubino, Jeanne (ed.). *Virginia Woolf and the Literary Marketplace*. New York: Palgrave, 2010.

Dunn, Waldo Hilary. *R. D. Blackmore: A Biography*. London: Robert Hale, 1956.

Eliot, T. S. *After Strange Gods: A Primer of Modern Heresy*. London: Faber and Faber, 1934.

Flint, Kate. *The Woman Reader 1837–1914*. Oxford: Oxford University Press, 1993.

Foster, R. F. *W. B. Yeats: A Life, Volume I: The Apprentice Mage, 1865–1914*. Oxford: Oxford University Press, 1997.

Frazier, Adrian. *George Moore, 1852–1933*. New Haven and London: Yale University Press, 2000.

Freedman, Jonathan L. *Professions of Taste: Henry James, British Aestheticism and Commodity Culture*. Stanford: Stanford University Press, 1990.

Garnett, Richard (ed.). *The International Library of Famous Literature*. 20 vols. London: Edward Lloyd, 1899.

Garnett, Richard. *Constance Garnett: A Heroic Life*. London: Sinclair-Stevenson, 1991.

Genette, Gérard. *Paratexts: Thresholds of Interpretation*. Trans. Jane E. Lewin. Cambridge: Cambridge University Press, 1997. [Published in French as *Seuils*, 1987.]

Greenblatt, Stephen. *Renaissance Self-Fashioning: From More to Shakespeare*. Chicago: University of Chicago Press, 1980.

Griest, Guinevere L. *Mudie's Circulating Library and the Victorian Novel*. Bloomington: Indiana University Press, 1970.

Guy, Josephine M. and Ian Small. *Oscar Wilde's Profession: Writing and the Culture Industry in the Late Nineteenth Century*. Oxford: Oxford University Press, 2000.

Hagen, June Steffenson. *Tennyson and His Publishers*. London: Pennsylvania State University Press, 1979.

Halperin, John. *Gissing: A Life in Books*. Oxford: Oxford University Press, 1982.

Hand, Richard J. *The Theatre of Joseph Conrad*. London: Palgrave Macmillan, 2005.

Heilbrun, Carolyn G. *The Garnett Family: The History of a Literary Family*. London: George Allen and Unwin, 1961.

Hepburn, James. *The Author's Empty Purse and the Rise of the Literary Agent*. London: Oxford University Press, 1968.

Heyck, T. W. *The Transformation of Intellectual Life in Victorian England*. New York: St Martin's Press, 1982.

Hibberd, Dominic. *Harold Monro: Poet of the New Age*. Basingstoke: Palgrave, 2001.

— 'The New Poetry, Georgians and Others' in Peter Brooker and Andrew Thacker (eds), *The Oxford Critical and Cultural History of Modernist Magazines, Volume I: Britain and Ireland 1880–1955*. Oxford: Oxford University Press, 2009–12.

Hipsky, Martin. *Modernism and the Women's Popular Romance in Britain, 1885–1925*. Athens: Ohio University Press, 2011.

Holroyd, Michael. *Bernard Shaw, Vol. I: 1856–98: The Search for Love*. London: Chatto & Windus, 1988.

Houghton, Walter E. (ed.). *The Wellesley Index to Victorian Periodicals, 1824–1900*. Vol. II. Toronto: University of Toronto Press and London: Routledge & Kegan Paul, 1972.

Huyssen, Andreas. *After the Great Divide: Modernism, Mass Culture, Postmodernism*. Bloomington and Indianapolis: Indiana University Press, 1986.

Jaffe, Aaron. *Modernism and the Culture of Celebrity*. Cambridge: Cambridge University Press, 2005.

Jefferson, George. *Edward Garnett: A Life in Literature*. London: Jonathan Cape, 1982.

Keating, Peter. *The Haunted Study: A Social History of the English Novel 1875–1914*. London: Secker and Warburg, 1989.

Kemp, Sandra, Charlotte Mitchell and David Trotter (eds). *The Oxford Companion to Edwardian Fiction*. Oxford: Oxford University Press, 1997.

Kendrick, Walter. *The Secret Museum: Pornography in Modern Culture*. New York: Viking, 1987.

Ker, Ian. *G. K. Chesterton: A Biography*. Oxford: Oxford University Press, 2011.

Kiberd, Declan. *Synge and the Irish Language*. London: Macmillan, 1979.

Kingsford, R. J. L. *The Publishers Association, 1896–1946*. Cambridge: Cambridge University Press, 1970.

Kreizenbeck, Alan. *Zoe Akins: Broadway Playwright*. Westport: Praeger, 2004.

Macdonald, Kate and Nathan Waddell (eds). *John Buchan and the Idea of Modernity*. London: Pickering & Chatto, 2013.

McDonald, Peter D. *British Literary Culture and Publishing Practice, 1880–1914*. Cambridge: Cambridge University Press, 1997.

McDonnell, Jenny. *Katherine Mansfield and the Modernist Marketplace: At the Mercy of the Public*. Basingstoke: Macmillan, 2010.

McGann, Jerome J. *The Textual Condition*. Princeton: Princeton University Press, 1991.

McKenzie, D. F. *Bibliography and the Sociology of Texts*. Cambridge: Cambridge University Press, 1994. [Published as The Panizzi Lectures by the British Library in 1986.]

Madison, Charles A. *Book Publishing in America*. New York: McGraw-Hill Book Co., 1966.

Mariani, Paul. *William Carlos Williams: A New World Naked*. New York, McGraw-Hill, 1981.

Marshik, Celia. *British Modernism and Censorship*. Cambridge: Cambridge University Press, 2009.

Martin, Wallace. *'The New Age' Under Orage: Chapters in English Cultural History*. Manchester: Manchester University Press, 1967.

Mauriello, Christopher E. 'The Strange Death of the Public Intellectual: Liberal Intellectual Identity and the "Field of Cultural Production" in England, 1880–1920'. *Journal of Victorian Culture* 6:1 (2001): 1–26.

Milton, John and Paul Fadio Bandia (eds). *Agents of Translation*. Amsterdam: John Benjamins, 2009.

Moody, A. David. *Ezra Pound: Poet, A Portrait of the Man and his Work, I: The Young Genius 1885–1920*. Oxford: Oxford University Press, 2007.

Morgan, Ted. *Somerset Maugham*. London: Jonathan Cape, 1980.

Morrisson, Mark S. *The Public Face of Modernism: Little Magazines, Audiences, and Reception, 1905–1920*. Madison: University of Wisconsin Press, 2001.

— 'The Myth of the Whole and Ford's *English Review*' in *The Public Face of Modernism: Little Magazines, Audiences, and Reception, 1905–1920*. Madison: University of Wisconsin Press, 2001, pp. 17–53

Mourant, Chris. *Katherine Mansfield and Periodical Culture*. Edinburgh: Edinburgh University Press, 2019.

Mullin, Katherine. 'Pernicious Literature: Vigilance in the Age of Zola (1886–1899)' in David Bradshaw and Rachel Potter (eds), *Prudes on the Prowl: Fiction and Obscenity in England, 1850 to the Present Day*. Oxford: Oxford University Press, 2013, pp. 30–51.

Mursia, Ugo. *Scritti Conradiani*. Milano: Mursia, 1983.

Nelson, James G. *The Early Nineties: A View from the Bodley Head*. Cambridge, MA: Harvard University Press, 1971.

— *Elkin Mathews: Publisher to Yeats, Joyce, Pound*. Wisconsin: University of Wisconsin Press, 1989.

— *Publisher to the Decadents: Leonard Smithers in the Careers of Beardsley, Wilde, Dowson*. University Park: Pennsylvania State University Press, 2000.

Nicholson, Steve. *The Censorship of British Drama 1900–1968. Vol. I: 1900–1932*. Exeter: University of Exeter Press, 2003.

Nicoll, Allardyce. *English Drama, 1900–1930: The Beginnings of the Modern Period*. Cambridge: Cambridge University Press, 1973.

Norman, Charles. *Ezra Pound*. London: Macdonald, 1969.

Osteen, Mark. *The Economy of 'Ulysses': Making Both Ends Meet*. Syracuse: Syracuse University Press, 1995.

Pease, Allison. *Modernism, Mass Culture, and the Aesthetics of Obscenity*. Cambridge: Cambridge University Press, 2000.

Rainey, Lawrence S. *Institutions of Modernism: Literary Elites and Public Culture*. New Haven: Yale University Press, 1998.

Reeves, James. *Georgian Poetry*. Middlesex: Penguin, 1962.

Rogers, Timothy (ed.). *Georgian Poetry 1911–1922: The Critical Heritage*. London: Routledge and Kegan Paul, 1977.

Rose, Jonathan. *The Intellectual Life of the British Working Classes*, 2nd edn. New Haven: Yale University Press [2001] 2010.

Ross, Robert H. *The Georgian Revolt: Rise and Fall of a Poetic Ideal, 1910–22*. London: Faber and Faber, 1967.

Rowbotham, Sheila. *Edward Carpenter: A Life of Liberty and Love*. London: Verso, 2008.

Rubery, Matthew. *The Novelty of Newspapers: Victorian Fiction after the Invention of the News*. Oxford: Oxford University Press, 2009.

Russell, Percy. *The Literary Manual; or, a Complete Guide to Authorship*. London: London Literary Society, 1886.

Salmon, Richard. 'Signs of Intimacy: The Literary Celebrity in the "Age of Interviewing"'. *Victorian Literature and Culture* 25:1 (1997): 159–77.
— *The Formation of the Victorian Literary Profession*. Cambridge: Cambridge University Press, 2013.
Samuel, Raphael. 'British Marxist Historians, 1880–1980: Part I'. *New Left Review* 120 (March–April 1980): 21–96.
Saunders, Frederic. *The Author's Printing and Publishing Assistant*, 2nd edn. London: Saunders & Otley, 1839.
Saunders, Max. *Ford Madox Ford: A Dual Life*, vol. I. Cambridge: Cambridge University Press, 1996.
Scholes, Robert and Clifford Wulfman. *Modernism in the Magazines: An Introduction*. New Haven: Yale University Press, 2010.
Schults, Raymond L. *Crusader in Babylon: W. T. Stead and the* Pall Mall Gazette. Lincoln: University of Nebraska Press, 1972.
Secor, Marie. 'Violet Hunt, Novelist: A Reintroduction'. *English Literature in Transition, 1880–1920* 19:1 (1976): 25–34.
Skinner, Paul (ed.). *International Ford Madox Ford Studies, Vol. 6: Ford Madox Ford's Literary Contacts*. Amsterdam: Rodopi, 2007.
Small, Ian and Marcus Walsh (eds). *The Theory and Practice of Text-Editing: Essays in Honour of James T. Boulton*. Cambridge: Cambridge University Press, 1991.
Smith, Helen. 'Opposing Orbits: Ford, Edward Garnett, and the Battle for Conrad' in Paul Skinner (ed.), *International Ford Madox Ford Studies, Vol. 6: Ford Madox Ford's Literary Contacts*. Amsterdam: Rodopi, 2007.
Steele, T. *Alfred Orage and the Leeds Arts Club, 1893–1923*. Aldershot: Scolar Press, 1990.
Stephens, John Russell. *The Profession of the Playwright: British Theatre 1800–1900*. Cambridge: Cambridge University Press, 1992.
Stevenson, Iain. *Bookmakers: British Publishing in the Twentieth Century*. London: The British Library, 2010.
St John, John. *William Heinemann: A Century of Publishing 1890–1990*. London: Heinemann, 1990.
Stirling, A. M. W. *William de Morgan and his Wife*. London: Thornton Butterworth, 1922.
Stock, Noel. *The Life of Ezra Pound*. London: Routledge and Kegan Paul, 1970.
Sullivan, Alvin (ed.). *British Literary Magazines*. Vol. III. Westport: Greenwood Press, 1983.
Sutherland, John. *Mrs Humphry Ward: Eminent Victorian, Pre-eminent Edwardian*. Oxford: Clarendon, 1990.

Thacker, Andrew. '"that trouble": Regional Modernism and "little magazines"', in Neal Alexander and James Moran (eds), *Regional Modernisms*. Edinburgh: Edinburgh University Press, 2013, pp. 22–43.

Towheed, Shafquat (ed.). *The Correspondence of Edith Wharton and Macmillan, 1901–1930*. Basingstoke: Palgrave Macmillan, 2007.

Vogeler, Martha S. *Austin Harrison and the* English Review. Colombia: University of Missouri Press, 2008.

Watts, Cedric. *Joseph Conrad: A Literary Life*. Basingstoke: Macmillan, 1989.

Weedon, Alexis. *Victorian Publishing: The Economics of Book Production for a Mass Market, 1836–1916*. Aldershot: Ashgate, 2003.

Whittier-Ferguson, John. *Framing Pieces: Designs of the Gloss in Joyce, Woolf, and Pound*. New York: Oxford University Press, 1996.

Wilson, Nicola. 'Circulating Morals (1900–1915)' in David Bradshaw and Rachel Potter (eds), *Prudes on the Prowl: Fiction and Obscenity in England, 1850 to the Present Day*. Oxford: Oxford University Press, 2013, pp. 52–70.

Willison, Ian, Warwick Gould and Warren Chernaik (eds). *Modernist Writers and the Marketplace*. Basingstoke: Macmillan, 1996.

Wilson, Jean Moorcroft. *Edward Thomas: From Adlestrop to Arras. A Biography*. London: Bloomsbury, 2015.

Witemeyer, Hugh. *The Poetry of Ezra Pound: Forms and Renewal, 1908–1920*. Berkeley and Los Angeles: University of California Press, 1969.

Worthen, John. 'D. H. Lawrence and the "Expensive Edition Business"' in Ian Willison, Warwick Gould and Warren Chernaik (eds), *Modernist Writers and the Marketplace*. Basingstoke: Macmillan, 1996.

Wright, Martin. 'Robert Blatchford, the Clarion Movement and the Crucial Years of British Socialism, 1891–1900' in Tony Brown (ed.), *Edward Carpenter and Late Victorian Radicalism*. London: Frank Cass, 1990, pp. 74–99.

The Literary Field – Memoirs/Lawrence's Contemporaries

Abercrombie, Lascelles. 'Victorians and Georgians'. *Manchester Guardian*, 6 January 1913.

— Review of D. H. Lawrence, *Love Poems and Others*. *Blue Review* I (June 1913): 117–22.

Aldington, Richard. *D. H. Lawrence: An Indiscretion*. Seattle: University of Washington Chapbooks, 1927.

— *Portrait of a Genius But* . . . London: Heinemann, 1950.

Anon. 'London Publishers: Mr T. Fisher Unwin'. *Bookman*, May 1893.

— 'George Moore, Esther Waters'. *Pall Mall Gazette*, 13 April 1894.

— 'The Future of THE NEW AGE'. *New Age*, i, 2 May 1907.

— 'The University College Difference'. *Nottingham Evening Post*, Thursday 28 November 1907.
— 'SUFFRAGISTS HOWLED DOWN'. *Nottingham Evening Post*, Tuesday 3 December 1907.
— 'Fifty Years of Modern Painting: Corot to Sargent'. *New Age* iii, 8 August 1908.
— 'Circulating Libraries Association: The Question of Improper Books'. *The Times*, 2 December 1909.
— 'Censorship of Books'. *Library Association Record*, 15 January 1910.
— 'What to Read'. *Madame*, 26 August 1911.
— '*The Trespasser* by D. H. Lawrence'. *Outlook*, 29 June 1912.
— '"Marriage" and Another'. *Nation*, 19 October 1912.
— 'Georgian Poetry of the Twentieth Century'. *Westminster Gazette*, 4 January 1913.
— Review of *Sons and Lovers*, London *Standard*, 30 May 1913.
— 'Arrest Kennerley on Comstock Writ'. *New York Times*, 24 September 1913.
— '"Hagar Revelly" Not Immoral, Says Jury'. *Publisher's Weekly* 85, 14 February 1914.
— 'Mr Sydney Pawling'. *The Times*, 4 January 1923.
— *Fifty Years 1898–1948*. London: Duckworth, 1948.
— 'Mr. Grant Richards: An Adventurous Publisher'. *The Times*, 25 February 1948.
— 'Mr Alfred Inwood'. *The Times*, 5 January 1951.
Beardsley, Aubrey. *The Letters of Aubrey Beardsley*. Eds Henry Maas, John Duncan and W. G. Good. Rutherford: Fairleigh Dickinson University Press, 1970.
Bennett, Arnold. 'Why I Am a Socialist'. *New Age* ii (30 November 1907): 90.
— 'A Tribute of Admiration'. *Evening Standard*, 10 April 1930.
Björkman, Edwin. 'Introduction' to D. H. Lawrence, *The Widowing of Mrs Holroyd*. New York: Kennerley, 1914.
Blackmore, R. D. *Lorna Doone*. Ware: Wordsworth Classics, 2004.
Carswell, Catherine. *The Savage Pilgrimage*. London: Secker, 1932.
Carswell, John. *Lives and Letters: A. R. Orage, Beatrice Hastings, Katherine Mansfield, John Middleton Murry, S. S. Koteliansky, 1906–1957*. London: Faber, 1978.
Chesterton, G. K. 'Why I Am Not a Socialist'. *New Age* ii (4 January 1908): 189–90.
— 'A. R. Orage: An Obituary', *Chesterton Review* 20:1 (February 1994): 16.
Conrad, Joseph and Ford Madox Hueffer. *The Inheritors*. London: Heinemann, 1901.

— *Romance* [1903]. Edinburgh and London: John Grant, 1925.
Corke, Helen. *Neutral Ground*. London: Arthur Barker, 1933.
— *D. H. Lawrence: The Croydon Years*. Austin: University of Texas Press, 1965.
— *In Our Infancy: An Autobiography*. Cambridge: Cambridge University Press, 1975.
Crichton, Kyle S. '"An Interview with Lawrence" Kyle S. Crichton' in Norman Page (ed.), *D. H. Lawrence: Interviews and Recollections*. London and Basingstoke: Palgrave Macmillan, 1981, pp. 215–21.
Davies, W. H. *The Autobiography of a Supertramp*. London: A. C. Fifield, 1908.
De la Mare, Walter. 'An Elizabethan Poet and Modern Poetry'. *Edinburgh Review*, April 1913.
Douglas, James. 'He, She and It: A Weekly Causerie'. *Throne and Country*, 15 April 1911.
Ford, Ford Madox. 'The Reader'. *transatlantic review* ii (November 1924): 503–4.
— *Return to Yesterday*. London: Gollancz, 1931.
— *Portraits from Life: Reminiscences on Henry James, Stephen Crane, W. H. Hudson, Joseph Conrad, Thomas Hardy, H. G. Wells, John Galsworthy, D. H. Lawrence, Ivan Turgenev, Theodore Dreiser, and Algernon Charles Swinburne*. Boston and New York: Houghton Mifflin, 1937.
— *Mightier Than the Sword*. London: George Allen and Unwin, 1938.
— *Letters of Ford Madox Ford*. Ed. Richard M. Ludwig. Princeton: Princeton University Press, 1965.
Fraser, Grace Lovat. *In the Days of My Youth*. London: Cassell, 1970.
Garnett, David. *The Golden Echo*. New York: Harcourt Brace & Co., 1954.
— *Great Friends: Portraits of Seventeen Writers*. London: Macmillan, 1979.
Garnett, Edward. 'The Novel of the Week'. *Nation*, 22 June 1907.
— 'The Censorship of Public Opinion'. *Fortnightly Review*, July 1909.
— 'The "Sex Novel"'. Preface to Maud Churton Braby, *Downward: 'A Slice of Life'*. London: T. Werner Laurie, 1910.
— *Friday Nights: Literary Criticisms and Appreciations*. First series. London: Jonathan Cape, 1922.
— (ed.). *Letters from W. H. Hudson to Edward Garnett*. London: Dent, 1925.
— (ed.). *Letters from Conrad, 1895 to 1924*. London: Nonesuch Press, 1928.
— 'D. H. Lawrence: His Posthumous Papers'. *London Mercury* Vol. XXXV (1936): 152–60.
George, Ewart. 'The Day D. H. Lawrence Came for Advice'. *The Times*, 22 March 1963.
George, W. L. 'The Bookman Gallery: D. H. Lawrence'. *Bookman*, xlv (February 1914): 244–6.

Gerber, Helmut E. (ed.). *George Moore in Transition: Letters to T. Fisher Unwin and Lena Milman, 1894–1910*. Detroit: Wayne State University Press, 1968.
— (ed.). *George Moore on Parnassus: Letters (1900–1933) to Secretaries, Publishers, Printers, Agents, Literati, Friends and Acquaintances*. London and Toronto: Associated Literary Presses, 1988.
Goldring, Douglas. *Reputations: Essays in Criticism*. London: Chapman & Hall, 1920.
— *South Lodge; Reminiscences of Violet Hunt, Ford Madox Ford and the English Review Circle*. London: Constable, 1943.
— *The Last Pre-Raphaelite: A Record of the Life and Writings of Ford Madox Ford*. London: Macdonald, 1948.
— *Life Interests*. London: MacDonald, 1948.
Goodyear, Frederick. 'The Trespasser by D. H. Lawrence'. *Rhythm* 2:10 (November 1912): 278.
Hankin, St John. 'The Censorship of Plays Again'. *Academy*, 19 October 1907.
Harris, Frank. 'Thoughts on Morals'. *English Review* (June 1911): 434–43.
Harrison, Austin. 'The Spectator: A Reply'. *English Review* (July 1911): 666–70.
Hassall, Christopher. *Edward Marsh: Patron of the Arts*. London: Longmans, 1959.
Hilton, Enid Hopkin. *A Nottinghamshire Childhood with D. H. Lawrence*. Stroud: Alan Sutton, 1993.
Hooley, Arthur. [reader's report, 'The Trespasser']. Box 5, Mitchell Kennerley Papers, Archives and Special Collections Library, Vassar College Libraries.
Hueffer, Ford Madox. *Fifth Queen* trilogy. London: Alston Rivers, 1906–8.
— 'The Functions of the Arts in the Republic: I. Literature'. *English Review* i (December 1908): 159.
— 'The Political and Diplomatic'. *English Review* i (December 1908): 162–3.
— 'The Critical Attitude: The Two Shilling Novel'. *English Review* iii (September 1909): 317–23.
— *Ancient Lights and Certain New Reflections*. London: Chapman and Hall, 1911.
— *When Blood Is Their Argument: An Analysis of Prussian Culture*. London: Hodder and Stoughton, 1915.
— *Collected Poems of Ford Madox Hueffer*. London: Martin Secker, 1916.
Hunt, Violet. 'The Coach'. *English Review* i (March 1909): 665–80.
— *The Flurried Years*. London: Hurst & Blackett, 1926.
— *I Have This to Say: The Story of my Flurried Years*. New York: Boni and Liveright, 1926.
Jackson, Holbrook. *George Bernard Shaw*. London: Grant Richards, 1907.

Karl, Frederick R. and Laurence Davies (eds). *The Collected Letters of Joseph Conrad: Volume 3, 1903–1907*. Cambridge: Cambridge University Press, 1988.

Kennerley, Mitchell. 'The Modern Drama Series' [advertisement], *Forum*, Vol. XLIX, January 1913.

— *New York Times Review of Books*, 28 September 1913.

— 'The Day of the Published Play'. *New York Times*, 27 December 1914.

Keynes, Geoffrey (ed.). *The Letters of Rupert Brooke*. London: Faber and Faber, 1968.

Lawrence, Ada and G. Stuart Gelder. *Young Lorenzo: Early Life of D. H. Lawrence*. Florence: G. Orioli, 1932.

Lawrence, D. H. '"The Georgian Renaissance" by D. H. Lawrence', *Rhythm*, 2:14 (March 1913): xvii–xx.

Lazarus, John. 'Saturday Love Song'. *English Review* iii (September 1909): 194.

— 'Ferrer's Funeral Hymn'. *New Age* v (28 October 1909): 473.

— 'Three Poems'. *English Review* iii (November 1909): 566–8.

Long, John to G. Herbert Thring. Letter, 7 June 1911. BL, Society of Authors. MS Add 56978.

Mansfield, Katherine. *Letters of Katherine Mansfield*. 2 vols. Ed. John Middleton Murry. London: Constable, 1928.

— *Collected Letters of Katherine Mansfield: Volume I: 1903–1917*. Eds. V. O'Sullivan and M. Scott. Oxford: Oxford University Press, 1984.

Marsh, Edward (ed.). *Georgian Poetry 1911–1912*. London: Poetry Bookshop, 1912.

— 'The Book of the Month: Poems by Rupert Brooke'. *Poetry Review* 1:4 (April 1912): 177.

— *A Number of People: A Book of Reminiscences*. London: Heinemann, 1939.

Monro, Harold. 'New Books: English Poetry'. *Poetry and Drama* 2:2 (June 1914): 179–80.

Moore, George. 'A New Censorship of Literature'. *Pall Mall Gazette*, 10 December 1884.

— *Literature at Nurse, or, Circulating Morals*. London, 1885.

— 'A Reaction'. *Speaker* 12:289 (13 July 1895): 42–3.

— *Esther Waters*. Introduction by David Skilton. Oxford: Oxford University Press [1894] 1983, pp. vii–xxii.

Morris, William. 'Art and Socialism: A Lecture Delivered before the Secular Society of Leicester'. London: E.E.M. and W.L.S., 1884.

Morrison, Arthur. *Tales of Mean Streets*. Boston: Roberts Brothers, 1895.

Mumby, Frank A. 'Mainly About Books'. *The Throne*. 15 August 1912.

Murry, John Middleton. *D. H. Lawrence: Son of Woman*. London: Jonathan Cape, 1931.

— *Between Two Worlds: An Autobiography*. London: Jonathan Cape, 1935.
Neville, G. H. *A Memoir of D. H. Lawrence: The Betrayal*. Ed. Carl Baron. Cambridge: Cambridge University Press, 1981.
Newbolt, Henry. 'Georgian Poetry 1911–1912. Edited by E. M.'. *Poetry and Drama* 1:1 (March 1913): 46.
London, Jack. [telegram]. *New York Times Review of Books*, 22 February 1914.
O'Connor, T. P. 'The New Journalism'. *New Review* i (1889): 423.
Penty, A. J. 'The Restoration of Beauty to Life'. *New Age* i (May 1907): 5.
Phillips, Evelyn March. 'The New Journalism'. *New Review* (August 1895): 182–6.
Pinker, James B. Letter to Violet Hunt. 28 February 1908. Cornell University Kroch Library, Ford Madox Ford Collection.
Pound, Ezra. *A Lume Spento*. Venice: A. Antonini, 1908.
— *The Spirit of Romance*. London: J. M. Dent, 1910.
— *Canzoni*. London: Elkin Mathews, 1911.
— 'Love Poems and Others by D. H. Lawrence' [review]. *Poetry* ii (July 1913): 49–51.
— *The Letters of Ezra Pound 1907–1941*. Ed. D. D. Paige. London: Faber and Faber, 1951.
Powell, Anthony. *To Keep the Ball Rolling: The Memoirs of Anthony Powell. II.* London: Heinemann, 1978.
Purdy, Richard L. and Michael Millgate (eds). *The Collected Letters of Thomas Hardy: Volume I, 1840–1892*. Oxford: Oxford University Press, 1978.
Reynolds, Stephen. *A Poor Man's House*. London: John Lane, 1908.
Rhys, Ernest. *Everyman Remembers*. London: J. M. Dent, 1931.
Scott-James, R. A. 'Edward Garnett'. *Spectator*. 26 February 1937.
Shaw, George Bernard. *Plays Pleasant and Unpleasant*. London: Grant Richards, 1898.
— 'The Author's Apology'. *Mrs Warren's Profession*. London: Grant Richards, 1902.
— 'Belloc and Chesterton'. *New Age* ii (15 February 1908): 309–11.
Stapleton, Steven. 'Society Journalism'. *The Monthly Review* 21 (1905): 102.
Strachey, John St Loe. 'A Poisonous Book'. *Spectator*, 20 November 1909.
— 'The Great Adult Review'. *Spectator*, 10 June 1911.
Strong, S. H. 'The Breaking Point'. *The Musical Standard*, 11 April 1908.
Swinnerton, Frank. *The Georgian Literary Scene: A Panorama*. London: Heinemann, 1935.
— *Georgian Literary Scene*. London: J. M. Dent, 1938.
— *Background with Chorus: A Footnote to Changes in English Literary Fashion between 1901 and 1917*. London: Hutchinson, 1956.

Taylor, Rachel Annand. Letter to Herbert J. C. Grierson. January 1906. National Library of Scotland. MS 9328, ff.3–6.
— 'Modern Poetry'. *English Review* iii (October 1909): 378–9.
— *The Hours of Fiammetta*. London: Elkin Mathews, 1910.
Thomas, Edward. 'More Georgian Poetry'. *Bookman* xliv (April 1913): 47.
Tolstoy, Leo. *What is Art?* Trans. Richard Pevear and Larissa Volokhonsky. London: Penguin, 1995.
Unwin, Philip. *The Publishing Unwins*. London: Heinemann, 1972.
Unwin, Stanley. *The Truth about Publishing*. London: George Allen & Unwin, 1926.
— *The Truth about a Publisher*. London: George Allen & Unwin, 1960.
Wade, Allan (ed.). *The Letters of W. B. Yeats*. London: Rupert Hart-Davis, 1954.
Wells, H. G. *Mankind in the Making*. London: Chapman and Hall, 1903.
— 'About Chesterton and Belloc'. *New Age* ii (11 January 1908): 209–10.
— *Ann Veronica: A Modern Love Story*. London: T. Fisher Unwin, 1909.
Whyte, Frederic. *William Heinemann: A Memoir*. London: Jonathan Cape, 1928.
Williams, William Carlos. *The Autobiography of William Carlos Williams*. New York: New Directions, 1967.
Young, Filson. 'On Shaw, Wells, Chesterton and Belloc'. *New Age* ii (7 March 1908): 370.
— 'The Things That Matter'. *Pall Mall Gazette*, 23 October 1912.
Yoxall, Henry. 'Books and Pictures'. *Schoolmaster*, 25 December 1909.

Journals/Magazines/Newspapers

BLAST
The *Century*
The *Daily Mail*
The *Daily News*
Eastwood and Kimberley Advertiser
The *English Review*
The *Forum*
The *Gong*
Nation
Madame
The *New Age*
The *New Statesman*
New York Times/New York Times Book Review
Nottingham Evening Post

Nottinghamshire Guardian
Poetry
Poetry and Drama
Rhythm
Smart Set
The Throne
The *Tramp*
The *Westminster Gazette/Saturday Westminster Gazette*

Archives

Allen and Unwin Archive, University of Reading.
The Bancroft Library, University of California, Berkeley.
The Berg Collection; Rare Books and Manuscripts Division. New York Public Library.
The British Library.
D. H. Lawrence Collection. Manuscripts and Special Collections. University of Nottingham.
George Lazarus Collection, Manuscripts and Special Collections, University of Nottingham.
The Harry Ransom Center. University of Texas at Austin.
University of Liverpool, Special Collections and Archives.
Mitchell Kennerley Papers, Archives and Special Collections Library, Vassar College Libraries.
The National Library of Scotland.

Web sources

Bolton, Paul. 'Education: Historical Statistics'. Library of the House of Commons (27 November 2012) <http://researchbriefings.files.parliament.uk/documents/SN04252/SN04252.pdf> (last accessed 13 November 2019).
Codell, Julie F. 'Unwin, Thomas Fisher (1848–1935)', *Oxford Dictionary of National Biography*, May 2015 online edn <http://www.oxforddnb.com/view/article/47454> (last accessed 27 October 2019).
Duncan, John McKirdy. 'Rachel Annand Taylor'. Aberdeen Art Gallery and Museums <http://www.aagm.co.uk/theCollections/objects/object/Portrait-of-Rachel-Annand-Taylor> (last accessed 27 April 2020).
Modernist Journals Project <http://modjourn.org> (last accessed 19 June 2019).
Nottingham Mechanics Institute <http://www.nottinghammechanics.com/before-the-fire-of-1867.htm> (last accessed 23 February 2019).

Index

Note: Publishing houses are listed under the names that are most familiarly known, e.g. John Lane under 'J' (John Lane), but William Heinemann under 'H' (Heinemann, William)

Abercrombie, Lascelles, 167, 169, 171, 177
Academy, 122
Adams, Amanda, 61
Adcock, St. John, 99, 203
advertising, 33, 107, 110, 159–60, 171, 174, 185, 195, 201
Akins, Zoë, 192, 194
Alcott, Louisa May, 26
Aldington, Richard, 169, 210–11
Alston Rivers (publisher), 41
American Copyright Act, 191, 193
American Review, 187
anthology, 63, 84, 152, 167–77
Arnold, Matthew, 61
Asquith, Lady Cynthia, 64, 202
Athenaeum, 69, 111
Atkinson, Frederick, 1, 8, 96, 115, 126–7, 129–30, 132, 133
authorship, 4, 6, 10, 21–2, 23, 33, 37, 61, 108, 140, 159
Author's Printing and Publishing Assistant, 33

Bacon, Francis, 26
Baker, John E., 59

Balzac, Honoré de, 26, 27, 48, 96
    Eugénie Grandet, 48
    'La Messe de l'athée' ('Atheist's Mass'), 48
    La Peau de chagrin ('The Asses Skin'), 48
    Le Père Goriot ('Old Goriot'), 48
Barrie, J. M., 33
Baudelaire, Charles, 113, 162, 164, 174
Beardsley, Aubrey, 110
Becque, Henry, 194, 195
Beerbohm, Max, 32, 174, 185
Belgian Poetry, 48
Bell, Neil, 25
Belloc, Hillaire, 69, 91, 125
Bennett, Arnold, 8, 24, 31, 39, 69, 82, 184, 185, 191, 192, 193, 210
Benson, E. F., 93
Benson, Father Hugh, 91
Beresford, J. D., 203
Bergson, Henri, 194
Bergström, Hjalmar, 194, 195
Bernhardt, Sarah, 99
Besier, Rudolf, 42
bestseller, 8, 26, 91, 104, 115, 164, 188
Binns, Henry Bryan, 69

232 INDEX

Björkman, Edwin, 12, 184, 190, 193, 194, 196–205, 211
Bjørnson, Bjørnstjerne, 194
Black and White, 92
Blackmore, R. D.
  Lorna Doone, 90
Blake, William, 10, 45
BLAST, 80
Blatchford, Robert, 55, 68
Blue Review, 177, 203
Board School, 22, 25, 30
Bodley Head, The, 114, 153, 185, 186,
Bondfield, Margaret, 61
Bookman, 12, 177, 184, 201, 202, 203–5
booksellers, 46, 92, 97, 108, 121, 195, 203
bookshop, 64, 96, 169, 170, 171, 186, 188
Booth, Howard J., 55, 113
Boots Circulating Library (Boots Booklovers'), 94, 120
Boulton, James T., 195, 202
Bourdieu, Pierre, 6–9, 21, 84
Braby, Maud Churton, 119, 134
Bridges, Robert, 171
Brontës, The, 26
  Brontë, Charlotte, *Jane Eyre*, 48
Brooke, Rupert, 167, 169, 170, 171, 174, 175, 176, 177
Brown, Ford Madox, 107
Buchan, John, 108, 170
Burns, Robert, 26, 60, 67, 139
Burrows, Louie, 1, 23, 28, 34, 36–40, 41, 42, 45, 46, 48, 49, 57, 62, 98, 114, 124, 125, 126, 128, 134, 140, 153, 210
  'Cupid and the Puppy', 37, 39
  'The Chimney Sweeper', 37
Butt, Clara, 158
Byles, Réné, 41, 99
Bynner, Witter, 186

Caine, Hall, 33
Cambridge Edition, 3, 59
Cannan, Gilbert, 25, 170, 174, 203
Cape, Jonathan (publisher), 108, 118
Carlyle, Thomas, 24, 26, 67

Carpenter, Edward, 61, 64, 111, 186
  Love's Coming of Age, 111
  Towards Democracy, 111
Cearne, the, 111, 126, 139, 140, 202
Celtic literature, 161, 162, 164
censorship, 11, 12, 105, 112, 113, 119, 120, 121, 122, 123, 133, 138, 141, 151, 212
census (1861), 23
Century Company, 124
  The Century Illustrated Monthly Magazine, 124, 125, 186, 187
Chace Act (1891), 23, 114
Chamberlain, Lord, 122
Chambers, Alan, 28, 39, 43, 66
Chambers, Jessie, 19, 20, 23, 24, 27, 28, 29, 31, 34, 36, 37, 38, 39, 40, 41, 43, 44, 45, 46, 48, 49, 55, 58, 60, 64, 65, 66, 70, 77, 78, 79, 83, 85, 86, 87, 90, 91, 127, 153, 164, 210
  'The Rathe Primrose', 85
Chambers (Holbrook), May, 28
Chapman's, 92
Chesson, W. H., 107, 109, 110
Chesterton, Frances, 29
Chesterton, G. K., 29–30, 32, 34, 38, 50, 58, 69, 70, 85, 107, 167, 211
Cholmondeley, Mary, 41
Church, Richard, 25
Churchill, Winston, 167
Circulating Libraries Association, 120, 121
Clarion, 55
colonial editions, 108
Collings, Ernest, 20
Compton, C. G., 93
Comstock, Anthony, 123, 188
Conan Doyle, Arthur, 8
Conrad, Joseph, 8, 24, 80, 81, 82, 91, 105, 108, 111, 114, 116, 124, 125, 132, 133
  Almayer's Folly, 111
Contemporary, 81
Cooper, James Fenimore, 26

Cooper sisters (Frankie and Grit), 28
copyright, 23, 107, 114, 191, 193, 194, 202
Corelli, Marie, 62, 91
Corke, Helen, 37, 43, 44, 45, 78, 111, 113, 127, 128, 130, 131, 135, 153, 154, 155
   Neutral Ground, 43
   'The Cornwall Writing', 43
   'The Freshwater Diary', 37, 127
Cosmopolis: An International Review, 111, 113
Country Life, 39
Cowper, William, 26
Crawford, F. Marion, 115
Crawford, Grace, 41, 92, 135, 164
Crichton, Kyle, 77
Crockett, S. R., 91, 112
Cross, Victoria, 121, 134
Croydon, 23, 77, 78, 79, 93, 98, 111, 153, 203
   English Association, 12, 152, 155, 159, 163, 165, 166
   Davidson Road Elementary School, 5, 30, 80
   Grand Theatre, 42, 128
Cuala Press, 186
Cunninghame Graham, R. B., 79, 119
Curtis Brown literary agency, 188, 189

Daily Chronicle, 92
Daily Mail, 31, 90, 91, 203
Daily News, 29, 30, 31, 70, 126
Daniel, Arnaut, 63
D'Arcy, Ella, 79
Darwin, Charles, 55, 65
Dante, Alighieri, 67, 163
Daudet, Alphonse, 27
Davies, W. H., 125, 167, 171
Dax, Alice, 43, 44, 47, 49, 58, 64, 66, 67, 153
de la Mare, Walter, 5, 84, 115, 134, 167, 168, 169, 171, 173, 176, 177, 210
Delavenay, Emile, 58, 61

Dell, Ethel M., 112
del Re, Arundel, 170
de Maupassant, Guy, 27, 48, 66, 90, 119
   Tales, 48
de Morgan, William, 90, 91
Dent, J. M. (publisher), 25, 63, 114, 118
De Quincey, Thomas, 26
Despard, Charlotte, 61
Dickens, Charles, 30, 62
   David Copperfield, 84
Donald, Robert, 92
Douglas, Lord Alfred, 156
Dramatic Copyright Act (1833), 191
Drinkwater, John, 167, 169, 170, 177, 186
Duckworth, Gerald (publisher), 5, 12, 104, 105, 106, 114, 115, 118, 122, 125, 127, 131–4, 137, 138, 139, 167, 174, 184, 187–90, 193, 194, 196, 200, 201, 203, 210
   'Greenback Library' series, 118
   'Modern Plays' series, 119, 190
Duffield (publisher), 186
Duncan, John McKirdy, 161

Eastwood, 22, 42, 50, 195, 60, 77, 80, 94, 139, 195, 197, 205
   British School, 27, 28
   Congregational Chapel, 60
   Debating Society, 34, 57, 60, 61, 65, 67, 69
   Literary Society, 60, 61
Eastwood and Kimberley Advertiser, 30
Edinburgh Review, 80
Education Act (1870), 25
Edward Arnold (publisher), 114
Eggert, Paul, 37
Egoist, 168
Elkin Mathews (publisher), 5, 28, 153, 162, 163, 164, 165
Eliot, George, 26
Eliot, T. S., 2, 151, 152
Emerson, Ralph Waldo, 26
English Illustrated Magazine, 109

English Review, 4, 5, 11, 19, 20, 24, 25, 37, 39, 40, 41, 45, 60, 63, 77–85, 87, 90, 91, 92, 93, 94, 95, 105, 119, 133, 154, 159, 163, 164, 169, 201, 203, 209
eroticism, 5, 12, 99, 106, 112, 113, 129, 130, 131, 132, 133, 135, 153, 155, 157, 161, 173, 211
Everyman's Library (J. M. Dent), 25, 162
Examiner of Plays, 122

Faber and Faber
    'Criterion Miscellany' series, 151
Fabian Arts Group, 64
Farr, Florence, 12, 70, 153, 163
Fergusson, J. D., 172, 176
Fiascherino, 177, 205
Flaubert, Gustave, 87, 90, 128, 129, 174
Fleet Street, 30
Fletcher, James Elroy, 167
Fletcher, John Gould, 169
Flint, F. S., 69, 84, 169
Flint, Kate, 47
Ford, Ford Madox *see* Hueffer, Ford Madox
Forster, E. M., 25
Fortnightly Review, 81, 123
Forum, 5, 12, 105, 184, 186, 187, 190, 194, 195, 196
Forum and Century, 186
Freedman, Jonathan, 22
Freud, Sigmund, 199, 200, 201
Frost, Robert, 165, 186

Galsworthy, John, 79, 93, 108, 109, 118, 119, 124, 125, 194
    Strife, 42
Gardiner, A. G., 31, 32
Garnett, Constance, 105, 109, 111, 117, 118, 130
Garnett, David ('Bunny'), 87, 140, 158
Garnett, Edward, 5, 6, 11, 12, 19, 20, 37, 70, 99, 104–41, 167, 168, 169, 170, 172, 173, 176, 184, 186, 187, 188, 189, 190, 192, 195, 196, 200, 201, 202, 203, 210, 211
    The Breaking Point, 121, 122, 124
Gautier, Théophile, 27
Genette, Gérard, 9, 10
George, Ewart, 30
George, W. L., 12, 184, 201, 202–5, 210, 211
Georgian Poetry anthologies, 84, 152, 166–77, 203, 204
German literature, 117, 128, 172, 173, 193, 199
Germany, 63, 65, 170, 196, 201
Gibson, Wilfrid W., 167, 169, 170, 171, 173, 177
Gissing, George, 32, 33, 105, 109, 110, 116
Gladstone, Herbert, 123
Goldring, Douglas, 39, 85, 114, 130
Gong, The, 34, 36, 38
Goodman, Daniel Carson
    Hagar Revelley, 188
Goodyear, Frederick, 172, 174
Gosse, Edmund, 115, 170
Grant Richards (publisher), 114, 123, 185
Granville, Charles, 171
Granville-Barker, Harley, 186, 122
    Waste, 121, 123
Grierson, H. J. C., 153
Guardian, The, 37

Haeckel, Ernst, 55
Hall, Beatrice, 27
Haggs Farm, 39, 79
Hardy, Thomas, 26, 80, 81, 82, 84, 90, 91, 122, 174, 210
    'A Sunday Morning Tragedy', 81
    Jude the Obscure, 122
Harmsworth, Alfred, 31, 90; *see also* Lord Northcliffe
Harris, Frank, 81, 185, 186
Harrison, Andrew, 3, 6
Harrison, Austin, 80, 81, 87, 133, 140, 159, 169, 201, 210
Harrison, Frederic, 91

Harry Ransom Humanities Research
    Centre, 59
Hauptmann, Gerhart, 128, 190
Heinemann, William (publisher), 1,
    5, 11, 20, 29, 41, 77, 85, 86,
    87, 89, 91–8, 106, 107, 108,
    111, 112, 114, 115–18, 126,
    127, 128, 129, 131–8, 156,
    168, 186
  'International Library', 115
Henley, W. E., 160, 191
Herbart, Johan Friedrich, 65, 68
Herbertson, Jessie Leckie, 93
Hewart, Tom, 34, 35
Hewlett, Maurice, 80, 115, 170, 186
  The Forest Lovers, 115
'Hicklin Ruling' (1868), 112
Hooley, Arthur ('Charles Vale'), 185,
    187, 192
Holt, Agnes, 41, 45, 78, 85, 153
Hope, Anthony, 26
Hopkin, Sallie, 34, 57, 58, 59, 64, 66
Hopkin, Willie, 30, 31, 34, 43, 57, 58,
    59, 60, 61, 64, 66, 211
Hough, Graham, 3
Howells, W. D., 91
Hudson, W. H., 118, 119
Hueffer, Ford Madox, 5, 7, 8, 11, 19, 20,
    21, 23, 24, 25, 29, 31, 34, 38,
    39, 40, 41, 42, 44, 45, 60, 63,
    70, 77–99, 106, 107, 108, 114,
    116, 119, 125, 126, 128, 129,
    130, 131, 132, 133, 135, 137,
    138, 139, 140, 141, 153, 154,
    163, 164, 173, 200, 202, 204,
    209, 210, 211
  Collected Poems, 84
  Portraits from Life, 86
  Songs from London, 164
  The Inheritors, 8, 116
  The Fifth Queen trilogy, 41
Hüffer, Franz, 128
Hulme, T. E., 169
Hunt, Alfred W., 97–8
Hunt, Margaret Raine, 41

Hunt, Violet, 5, 7, 11, 24, 39, 41, 42, 44,
    63, 77–99, 129, 135, 156, 164,
    202, 210, 211
  I Have This to Say, 85, 95
  Tales of the Uneasy, 81, 93
  The Flurried Years, 78, 85
  The Governess, 92
  The Wife of Altamont, 93
  White Rose of Weary Leaf, 93, 94, 97
  Zeppelin Nights, 92
Hunt, William Holman, 22
Hutchinson (publisher), 114, 126, 133
Huxley, T. H., 55

Ibsen, Henrik, 119, 174, 194, 195
Independent Review, 111
Inwood, Alfred, 30, 31, 211
Isle of Wight, 38, 127

Jackson, Holbrook, 64, 65
Jacobs, W. W., 37, 91
James, Henry, 115, 118, 122, 159
Jennings, Blanche, 11, 26, 28, 30, 32, 43,
    44, 46, 47, 48, 49, 57, 58, 59,
    60, 64, 164, 166, 210
  'Victorine Cow', 49
John Bull, 163
John Lane (publisher), 80, 114, 162,
    164, 185
John Long (publisher), 114, 121, 134, 185
John Murray (publisher), 114
Jones, John, 23
journalism, 4, 8, 11, 20, 30, 31, 33, 57,
    58, 69, 151, 159, 160, 211
Joyce, James, 121, 151, 152, 164
Joynson-Hicks, Sir William ('Jix'), 151

Keating, Peter, 107
Keats, John, 26
Kennerley, Mitchell (publisher), 5, 12, 105,
    111, 178, 184–205, 210, 211
  'Little Classics' series, 185
  'Modern Drama Series', 190–2,
    194–5, 200
  'The Little Book-Shop Around
    the Corner', 186

Kipling, Rudyard, 33, 115, 174
Kinkead-Weekes, Mark, 3, 104
Krenkow, Fritz, 63

Labour Press, The, 111
Lamb, Charles, 25
Lawrence, Ada, 27, 59, 60, 161
Lawrence, D. H.
   aesthete, 24, 49, 211
   autodidact, 24, 45, 199, 211
   co-authorship/collaboration, 37, 38
   composition methods, 21, 27, 34, 37, 43, 59, 154
   genius, 2, 19, 20, 25, 86, 128, 131, 204, 210
   'Lektorship', 63
   literary values, 6, 26, 43, 49, 90, 135, 140, 191, 210
   performativity/personae/mimicry, 19, 46, 156, 158
   'Rainbow Books and Music' publishing scheme, 212
   readership, 1, 4, 7, 9, 20, 26, 31, 38, 43, 49, 50, 63, 67, 68, 77, 99, 125, 156, 161, 163, 177, 178, 184, 210
   reception of, 43, 138, 176, 186, 189, 197
   religion, 57, 174
   reviews of, 1, 129, 138, 170, 172, 173, 187, 189, 196, 201, 203, 211
   sociability, 43, 212
  Works: Non-fiction
   'Art and the Individual', 11, 34, 49, 50, 57–60, 64, 65, 68, 70
   Cavalleria Rusticana, 108
   'Getting On', 19
   'Myself Revealed', 20
   'Pornography and Obscenity', 151
   'Rachel Annand Taylor', 152, 155, 158, 161, 163, 165
   'The Bad Side of Books', 111
   'The Crown', 63
   'The Georgian Renaissance', 152, 166, 167, 175, 176
   'Which Class I Belong To', 20
  Works: Novels
   Lady Chatterley's Lover, 3, 25, 140
   'Scargill Street', 140
   Sons and Lovers, 1, 5, 12, 19, 85, 86, 105, 106, 111, 121, 177, 184, 187, 188, 189, 196, 197, 199, 200, 201, 202, 204, 210, 211
   'Paul Morel', 37, 127, 129, 131, 134, 138, 139, 204
   The Rainbow, 5, 6, 22, 121, 177, 212
   'The Sisters', 123
   The Trespasser, 1, 8, 11, 12, 37, 99, 105, 106, 111, 113, 128, 132, 134, 135, 137, 138, 140, 172, 186, 187, 189, 195, 196, 210
   'The Saga of Siegmund', 11, 37, 127, 128, 129, 130, 131, 132, 134, 135, 152, 154
   The White Peacock, 1, 11, 19, 20, 21, 26, 27, 43, 45, 46, 77, 85, 92, 93, 94, 95, 96, 98, 112, 125, 128, 129, 135, 138, 156, 186, 187, 189, 195, 204
   'Laetitia', 11, 26, 27, 30, 31, 32, 33, 34, 40, 41, 43, 46, 47, 48, 49
   'Nethermere', 11, 41, 43, 45, 77, 85, 87, 89, 90, 91, 94, 96, 127
  Works: Plays
   A Collier's Friday Night, 40, 42, 80, 92, 126, 127
   The Daughter-In-Law, 124
   The Fight for Barbara, 124
   The Married Man, 124
   The Merry-Go-Round, 126
   The Widowing of Mrs Holroyd, 1, 12, 92, 126, 184, 187, 190, 192, 193, 194, 196, 197, 199, 201, 203, 210
  Works: Poems
   'Ah, Muriel!', 159

'A Life History in Harmonies and
    Discords', 153
'All of Roses', 189
'Amour', 153
'A Still Afternoon' sequence, 20, 79
'A Woman and Her Dead
    Husband', 189
'Baby-Movements' ('Running
    Barefoot'; 'Trailing Clouds'), 79
'Birthday', 189
'Campions', 27
'Corot', 176
'Discipline', 79, 83
'Dream', 153
'Dreams Old and Nascent', 79,
    83, 90
'Fireflies in the Corn', 189
Foreword to *Collected Poems*, 27
'Green', 189
'Guelder Roses', 27
'Illicit', 189
'Kisses in the Train', 187
'Liaison' ('The Yew Tree on the
    Downs'), 154, 155
'Lightning', 105
Love Poems and Others, 84, 152, 167,
    173, 176, 177, 187, 189, 210
'Malade', 162
'Meeting among the Mountains',
    203
'Michael Angelo', 176
'Sigh No More', 159
'Snap-Dragon', 84, 152, 167, 168,
    169, 173, 175, 176
'Song', 41
'Study', 26, 34, 38
'The Collier's Wife', 139
'The Drained Cup', 139
'The Mother of Sons', 189
'The Mowers', 187
'The Schoolmaster' sequence, 173
'The Wind, the Rascal', 189
'Twilight', 203
'Tired of the Boat', 159
'Violets', 105, 187

'Whether or Not', 139
**Works: Short stories and
    sketches**
'A Lesson on a Tortoise', 41, 80
'A Miner at Home', 105
'A Modern Lover' ('The Virtuous'),
    41, 46, 113, 152
'A Prelude', 26, 31, 34, 36, 38
'Daughters of the Vicar' ('Two
    Marriages'), 125
'Delilah and Mr Bircumshaw', 140
'Goose Fair', 34, 37, 38, 41, 42,
    45, 87
'Lessford's Rabbits', 41, 80
'New Eve and Old Adam', 140
'Odour of Chrysanthemums', 41,
    42, 45, 80, 86, 87, 133
'Once –', 140, 187
'Ruby-Glass', 34, 36, 38
'The Christening', 187
'The Primrose Path', 187
*The Prussian Officer and Other
    Stories*, 104, 105, 121, 210
'The Shades of Spring' ('The Soiled
    Rose'; 'The Harassed Angel'),
    105, 172, 186, 187, 189, 195
'The Vicar's Garden', 34
'The White Stocking', 31, 34, 36
'The Witch à la Mode' ('Intimacy'),
    47, 125
'Two Schools', 41
'Vin Ordinaire', 187, 201
Lawrence, Emily, 27, 55, 57
Lawrence, Ernest, 22
Lawrence, Frieda, 5, 37, 106, 177, 196,
    202, 212
Lawrence, Lydia, 27, 43, 45, 157, 197,
    198, 204, 209
Lazarus, George, 56
Lazarus, John, 82, 83
Le Gallienne, Richard, 185, 186
Lee, Vernon, 80, 108
Leeds Art Club, 64
Leeds Platonists, 64
Lewes, G. H., 81

Lessing, Gotthold Ephraim, 25
Lewis, Wyndham, 80, 82, 152
Libraries
    circulating libraries, 11, 23, 92, 97, 113, 119, 120, 121, 138, 202
        Boots Booklovers' Library, 94, 120
        Cawthorn and Hutt, 120
        Day's Library, 120
        Mudie's Select Library, 26, 96, 97, 98, 112, 120
        The Times Book Club, 120
        W. H. Smith and Son, 113, 120, 134
    public libraries, 121
literary agent, 6, 23, 33, 81, 87, 108, 128, 211
'Littlejohns' cartoonist, 121
'little magazine', 32, 168, 172, 176
London, 1, 12, 19, 22, 23, 31, 32, 38, 39, 42, 44, 62, 63, 64, 66, 77, 79, 82, 83, 85, 86, 91, 94, 107, 114, 118, 130, 134, 162, 164, 165, 169, 174, 192, 193, 194, 195, 196, 199, 202, 210
    Adelphi Club, 165
    Bloomsbury, 64, 169
    Hampstead, 41, 152
    Holland Park Avenue, 41, 82
    Kensington, 41, 209
    Mont Blanc restaurant, Soho, 125
    National Gallery, 41
    'O. P. Club' ('The Savile'), 92
    Pall Mall, 86
    Reform Club, Adelphi Terrace, 41, 92
    South Lodge, 82, 94
    see also Theatre
London and Provincial Press Agency, 34, 35, 36
London, Jack, 186, 188
London Opinion, 25
Longfellow, Henry Wadsworth, 26, 60
Longman, Charles (publisher), 114
Lowell, Amy, 168

Lowndes, Mrs Belloc, 93
Luhan, Mabel Dodge, 212

Macartney, Herbert, 37, 127
Macaulay, Rose, 151, 170
MacDonald, Ramsay, 61
McDonald, Peter D., 8, 24, 123, 211
McCarthy, Justin, 42
McGann, Jerome, 9, 10
MacKenzie, Compton, 25
McKenzie, D. F., 9, 10
McLeod, Arthur, 43, 44, 63, 78, 162, 177, 192
Macmillan, Frederick (publisher), 114, 115, 121
Madame, 5, 11, 98, 99
Maeterlinck, Maurice, 186, 190
Manchester Guardian, 171, 177
Mansfield, Katherine, 12, 61, 152, 167, 171, 172, 173, 174, 203, 211, 212
Marks, A. D., 107, 113
Marsh, Edward, 5, 12, 84, 152, 167, 168, 169, 170, 171, 172, 173, 174, 175, 176, 177, 203, 210, 211
Martindale, Elizabeth ('Elsie'), 41, 119, 156
Marwood, Arthur, 81, 82
Masefield, John, 167
Mason, Agnes, 44, 45, 78, 85, 127
Massingham, H. W., 32
Maugham, William Somerset, 97, 108, 124
Mechanics' Institution, 60, 61, 62, 68
melodrama, 11, 49, 91
Mercure de France, 80
Meredith, George, 82, 84
Methuen (publisher), 6, 114, 212
Millais, John Everett, 22
modernism/modernist, 2, 4, 80, 82, 151, 152, 166, 168, 212
Modernist Journals Project, 2
Mond, Alfred, 80
Monro, Harold, 167, 169, 170, 171

Monroe, Harriet, 189
Moore, George, 82, 108, 112, 113, 115, 121, 134, 210
   A Modern Lover, 112, 113
   A Mummer's Wife, 112, 113
   Esther Waters, 113, 121
   Evelyn Innes, 113, 127
   Literature at Nurse, or, Circulating Morals, 113
Moore, Harry T., 2, 96
Moore, Thomas Sturge, 119, 167
Morrell, Lady Ottoline, 63, 212
Morris, William, 58, 64, 68
Morrisson, Mark, 80, 81
Mrs Bull, 163
Murray, Gilbert, 159, 160
Murry, John Middleton, 2, 12, 61, 167, 171, 172, 174, 175, 202, 203, 211, 212

Nation, 66, 84, 105, 138
National Vigilance Association, 112
Nehls, Edward, 2
Neville, George, 27, 28, 31, 43, 113
Nevinson, H. W., 66
New Age, 5, 11, 34, 50, 58, 64, 65, 67–70, 121
Newbolt, Henry, 171
New Journalism, 159, 160
New Numbers, 177
Newspaper Press Directory, 32
New Statesman, 84
New Woman, 94, 110, 121, 210
New York, 115, 123, 124, 184, 185, 186, 188, 192, 193
New York Evening Post, 188
New York Times, 186, 187, 191, 194, 201
New York Times Book Review, 1, 189,
Nietzsche, Friedrich, 64, 68, 174
Nineteenth Century, 81
Northcliffe, Lord, 31, 170; *see also* Harmsworth, Alfred
Nottingham, 49, 55, 61, 62, 139, 195, 197, 198, 203

Nottingham High School, 22, 198
   University College, 22, 30, 32, 61, 63, 199
Nottinghamshire Guardian, 36, 38, 43, 62

Obscene Publications Act (1857), 5, 112
obscenity, 112, 134, 151
O'Connor, T. P., 32, 160
Oliphant, Margaret, 115
Onions, Oliver, 203
Open Court, The (publisher), 115
Orage, A. R., 11, 58, 64, 65, 68, 69, 70, 211
Oxford, 70, 159, 160, 172

Palgrave, F. T., 26
Pall Mall Gazette, 61, 92, 113, 160, 172
Pankhurst, Sylvia, 61
Parker, W. G., 202, 204
Pater, Walter, 22, 58, 64, 162
Patterson, J. E., 93
Pawling, Sydney, 94–8, 116, 117, 126, 128, 129
Payne, Ben Iden, 124, 196
Peacock, Thomas Love, 25
Penty, A. J., 67
Phythian, J. E., 68
Pinker, J. B., 6, 81, 97, 211
Playgoers Club, 123
playwright, 190, 191, 193, 194, 195
Poetry, 168, 189
Poetry and Drama, 171, 195
Poetry Bookshop, 169, 170, 171
Poetry Review, 169, 170
Poets' Club, 63
Polignac Prize, 165
Pollinger, Laurence, 140
Pound, Ezra, 5, 10, 12, 28, 41, 42, 62, 63, 64, 82, 84, 90, 92, 98, 130, 152, 153, 155, 158, 162, 163, 164, 165, 166, 168, 169, 177, 186, 187, 210
   A Lume Spento, 62, 155
   'Ballad of the Goodly Fere', 63, 130
   Canzoni, 63, 163, 168

Pound, Ezra (*cont.*)
  Exultations, 28, 163
  lectures at Regent Street
    Polytechnic, 62
  The Spirit of Romance, 63, 162
Pre-Raphaelite, 22, 97, 119, 155, 156, 159, 161, 162, 164
Prévost, Antoine François
  Manon Lescaut, 48
printers, 6, 10, 46, 121, 171
provincial press, 20
Public Morality Council, 112
Publisher's Association, 114
publisher's reader, 11, 12, 46, 105, 106, 116, 119, 120, 122, 139

Quarterly Review, 80
Quiller-Couch, Arthur, 170, 171

Radford, Dollie, 163, 164
Ransome, Arthur, 39
Reade, Charles, 26
Reader, The, 185
Redford, George, 122
Redway (publisher), 29
Reid, Reverend Robert, 55, 60, 68
Renan, Ernest, 55
Remington and Company (publisher), 33
reviewers, 1, 9, 32, 46, 82, 98, 110, 120, 138, 173, 175, 189, 211
Revue des deux Mondes, 81
Reynolds, Stephen, 125
Rhymers' Club, 130, 162
Rhys, Ernest, 12, 25, 41, 42, 63, 90, 130, 152, 153, 155, 158, 162, 163, 164, 165
Rhys, Grace, 12, 41, 42, 90, 130, 152, 153, 155, 164, 165
Rhythm, 5, 12, 80, 152, 166, 167, 169, 170–5, 195, 203
Rice, Anne Estelle, 172, 176
Robertson, J. M., 55
Robertson, Stewart A., 158, 161
Rolland, Romain, 94

romance, 5, 32, 49, 77, 84, 93, 211
  American romance, 118
  historical romance, 26, 36
  medieval romance, 115, 157, 158, 162
  tragic romance, 26, 127, 135, 138, 200
Rose, Jonathan, 25, 30
Rossetti, D. G., 27
Rossetti, W. M., 163
Rossetti circle/'Rossettian', 98, 119, 158, 161, 163, 164, 165
royalty system, 28, 94, 97, 107, 115, 188, 189
Royde-Smith, Naomi, 169
Ruskin, John, 24, 25, 58, 64
Russell, Bertrand, 63, 64
Rutter, Dolcie, 57, 114

Sadler, Michael T. H. ('Sadleir'), 172
St. Catherine's Press (publisher), 169
Salmon, Richard, 21, 159–60
Samurai Press, 169
Saturday Review, 111, 211
Savage, Henry, 200
Savoy, The, 110
Schoolmaster, 82
Schopenhauer, Arthur, 25
Schreiner, Olive, 108, 110
Scott, C. P., 32
Scott, Walter, 26; *see also* Walter Scott, publisher
Scott-James, R. A., 125, 126
Scribner, Charles and Sons (publisher), 194
Scrutiny, 2
Secker, Martin (publisher), 114–15, 133, 161, 174
sentimentalism, 11, 26, 36, 37, 42, 49, 83, 90, 155
serialisation, 8, 31, 32, 90, 91, 93, 99, 108, 125
sex novel, 119, 120, 121, 134, 135, 210
Shakespear, Dorothy, 62
Shakespeare, William, 26, 185

Shaw, George Bernard, 24, 32, 57, 64, 65,
    66, 69, 70, 91, 121, 122, 123,
    134, 194, 202, 210, 211
  Immaturity, 32
  journalist, 32
  Mrs Warren's Profession, 121, 123, 202
  Plays Pleasant and Unpleasant, 123
  The Shewing-Up of Blanco Posnet,
    121–2
Shelley, Percy Bysshe, 26
short stories/fiction, 4, 11, 20, 26, 30,
    32, 33, 34, 37, 38, 39, 40, 41,
    48, 49, 80, 81, 92, 96, 104, 105,
    108, 124, 133, 172, 187, 210
Shorter, Clement, 109
Signature, 61, 63, 64, 65, 212
Silberrad, Una, 39
Sinclair, Upton, 121, 186
  Love's Pilgrimage, 134
Slater, Nellie, 57
Smart Set, 168, 185, 187
Smith, Ernest Alfred ('Botany'), 57
Smith, Philip F.T., 44, 157
Smithers, Leonard, 110
socialism, 11, 32, 34, 47, 49, 50, 55–70,
    211
Social Progress Society, 65
Society for the Study of Social
    Questions, 32, 56, 114
Society for the Suppression of Vice, 112
Society of Authors, 23, 111, 114, 134
Speaker, The, 30
Spectator, 69, 170
Spencer, Herbert, 55, 58, 65
Spender, J. A., 32
Standard, 129
Stage Society, 124, 192, 193
Stead, W. T., 160
Steele, Bruce, 59, 67
Stephen Swift & Co (publisher), 171
Stevenson, Robert Louis, 26, 185, 191
Strand, 37, 80
Strindberg, August, 118, 190, 194
suffragism, 11, 47, 49, 58, 79, 80, 98, 120,
    123, 134, 186, 194, 202

Sutro, Alfred, 41
Swinburne, Algernon, 22, 27, 91, 164,
    165, 204
Swinnerton, Frank, 104
syndication, 20, 32
Synge, J. M., 164, 186

Taylor, Rachel Annand, 12, 135, 152–66,
    177, 203
  Poems, 153, 157
  Rose and Vine, 153, 156, 157
  The Hours of Fiammetta, 154,
    155, 156
Tennyson, Alfred Lord, 26, 45, 60
Terriss, Ellaline, 41
Theatre, 41, 42, 61, 62, 112, 122, 124,
    128, 191, 193
  Altrincham Garrick Society, 195
  Garrick Theatre, 41
  Grand Theatre, Croydon, 42, 128
  Haymarket Theatre, 42, 122
  Little Theater, Los Angeles, 194
  Lyceum Theatre, 42
  Manchester Gaiety Theatre, 124
  Royalty Theatre, Soho, 112
Thomas, Edward, 39, 104, 125, 170, 177
Thompson, Francis, 164, 165
Thoreau, Henry, 26
three-decker novel, 23, 97, 108, 109
Thring, G. Herbert, 134
Throne, The, 99
Thurlby, Mabel, 44
Times, The, 120, 121, 123, 128, 134, 170
Times Literary Supplement, 177
Tit-Bits, 80
Tolstoy, Leo, 66, 186
Tramp: an Open Air Magazine, 39
translation, 41, 48, 55, 66, 92, 108,
    111, 112, 115, 117, 119,
    128, 162, 167, 172, 193,
    194, 195, 199
Trevelyan, Robert, 167, 177
Trollope, Anthony, 81
Turgenev, Ivan, 128, 129
Twain, Mark, 91

Underwood, 19, 39
University of Nottingham archives
    Manuscripts and Special
        Collections, 35, 56, 87, 88, 93
Unwin, Stanley, 132
Unwin, T. Fisher (publisher), 5, 29,
        106–17, 121, 124, 132, 133
    'Autonym Library' series, 109, 110
    'Cameo' series, 109
    'Pseudonym Library' series, 108,
        109, 111
    'Reformer's Bookshelf' series, 111

Vallette, Alfred, 80
Verhaeren, Emile, 190
Vivian, Charles E.
    Passion Fruit, 134
Vivian, Philip, 55
Vizetelly, Henry, 112, 113

Wade, Allan, 193
Wagner, Richard, 42, 62, 113, 128, 204
    Tannhäuser, 62, 113
    Tristan and Isolde, 42
Wallace, Lewis ('M. B. Oxon'), 64
Walter Scott (publisher), 48, 113, 114
Walpole, Hugh, 25
Ward, Mrs Humphry, 33, 115
Watt, A. P., 33
Weekley, Ernest, 63
Wells, H. G., 24, 32, 33, 41, 69, 70, 81,
        82, 86, 91, 107, 121, 134, 138
    Ann Veronica, 121, 134
    Marriage, 138
Werner Laurie, T. (publisher), 107, 119
West, Rebecca, 151

Westminster Gazette, 84, 138, 169, 173
Wexler, Joyce, 6
Wharton, Edith, 115
W. H. Smith and Son, 113, 120, 121, 134
Whistler, James Abbott McNeill, 22
Whitman, Walt, 82, 83
Wilde, Oscar, 22, 24, 58, 61, 62, 64, 65,
        111, 156
Williams, William Carlos, 164, 165
Wordsworth, William, 26
Woman, 31
woman reader, 11, 26, 31, 32, 43, 46–7,
        48, 49, 94, 97, 98, 99, 110, 113,
        135, 160, 163, 212
Women's Co-operative Guild, 60
Wood, Florence, 165
Woolf, Virginia, 151, 170
working class, 1, 5, 12, 19, 20, 24,
        25, 42, 68, 78, 79, 80, 81, 86,
        91, 133, 139, 140, 184, 195,
        197, 198, 200, 204, 205,
        210, 211
Worthen, John, 1, 2, 3, 5, 25, 28, 29, 31,
        43, 44, 48, 57, 96, 104, 163
Wright, W. H., 187

Yeats, W. B., 12, 41, 82, 84, 109, 113, 124,
        130, 152–3, 155, 158, 162, 163,
        164–5, 166, 186
yellowback volumes, 108
Yellow Book, The, 80, 110
Young, Filson, 70, 170, 171–2
Yoxall, Henry, 82

Zangwill, Israel, 91
Zola, Emile, 66, 96, 112, 113

EU representative:
Easy Access System Europe
Mustamäe tee 50, 10621 Tallinn, Estonia
Gpsr.requests@easproject.com

www.ingramcontent.com/pod-product-compliance
Lightning Source LLC
Chambersburg PA
CBHW070325240426
43671CB00013BA/2367